NEW LABOUR TRIUMPHS

New Labour Triumphs

Britain at the Polls

ANTHONY KING

DAVID DENVER

IAIN McLEAN

PIPPA NORRIS

PHILIP NORTON

DAVID SANDERS

PATRICK SEYD

Chatham House Publishers, Inc.
Chatham, New Jersey

New Labour Triumphs: Britain at the Polls

Chatham House Publishers, Inc.
Post Office Box One / Chatham, New Jersey 07928

Publisher: Edward Artinian
Production editor: Katharine Miller
Cover design: Lawrence Ratzkin
Composition: Bang, Motley, Olufsen
Printing and binding: R.R. Donnelley and Sons Company

LIBRARY OF CONGRESS CATALOGING-IN-PUBLICATION DATA

New labour triumphs : Britain at the polls / Anthony King
  ... [et al.].
    p. cm.
  Includes bibliographical references and index.
  ISBN 1-56643-057-7
    1. Great Britain. Parliament—Elections, 1997. 2. Elections—
Great Britain. 3. Great Britain—Politics and government—1997–
4. Labour Party (Great Britain) I. King, Anthony Stephen.
JN956.N46   1998
324.941'0859—dc21   97-33818
                                                      CIP

Manufactured in the United States of America
10 9 8 7 6 5 4 3 2 1

Contents

Tables

Figures

Preface

The 1997 British general election will be subjected to closer scrutiny than any previous election in British history. Part of the explanation relates to the results. Within hours of the first results being declared, it was clear that the scale of Labour's victory was going to be without precedent in the party's history. Tony Blair's majority was going to be larger than that of Clement Attlee in 1945, larger than that of Harold Wilson in 1966. The outcome exceeded Labour's wildest hopes, was far worse than the worst the Conservatives had feared. Such a phenomenon cries out for analysis and explanation.

But the 1997 election will also be more closely scrutinised because the number of scrutineers is unusually large. David Butler, the Oxford political scientist who is by now virtually part of the British constitution, will co-author another volume in the Nuffield College election series, which has been appearing since 1945 (under David Butler's aegis since 1951). A special issue of the journal *Parliamentary Affairs* will be devoted to the subject. Not least, the ongoing British Election Study will in due course yield a wealth of quantitative data based on an unprecedentedly wide range and variety of sample surveys.

This book differs from the others in two principal respects. The first is simply that the audience is meant to be a wider one: general readers as well as academic political scientists and people outside Britain, especially in North America, as well as the British themselves. The second is that this book's approach is meant to be "macro" rather than "micro"—that is, to describe and explain the large political forces that shaped the 1997 outcome rather than to explore in detail either the specific events of the campaign or the constituency-by-constituency results. For example, tactical voting—the phenomenon of voters backing their second-preference candidate when they think their first-preference candidate has no chance of winning—had a considerable effect on the 1997 outcome and is referred to in chapter 7; but a detailed analysis of who voted tactically and why, and what the effects were in individual constituencies, is left to more specialised treatments.

Unlike previous volumes in the "Britain at the Polls" series, this one devotes a separate chapter to Scotland. In many ways politics in Scotland resembles politics south of the border; the Conservative, Labour, and Liberal Democrat parties contest every constituency (and, in 1997, Labour won much more often than not). But in other ways the Scottish people march politically to the beat of their own pipes and drums. Not only does the Scottish National Party exist north of the border and obtain a substantial proportion of the vote there, but the political balance between the Conservative and Labour parties is strikingly different in Scotland (indeed, after 1997, "balance" is hardly the right word). Accordingly, a whole chapter is devoted to Scotland, a chapter made more essential by Labour and the Liberal Democrats' joint commitment to a devolved Scottish parliament.

With the election now over, two tantalising questions remain. How will New Labour under Tony Blair actually govern? And what lessons will the Conservatives, now led by the unknown and untested William Hague, learn from their defeat and especially from the magnitude of their defeat? It goes without saying that the outcome of the first British election of the next millennium will largely depend on the answers to those questions.

Acknowledgement

The editor would like to thank Jack Kneeshaw of the University of Essex for his invaluable assistance in the preparation of this volume, including the editor's own chapters.

ANTHONY KING

1

The Night Itself

Anthony King

No one in Britain who is remotely interested in politics will ever forget the night of 1 May 1997. The Labour Party—dubbed "New Labour" by Tony Blair—was swept into power. Paddy Ashdown's Liberal Democrats more than doubled their parliamentary representation. Sinn Fein elected two MPs in Northern Ireland constituencies. But, above all else, the Conservative Party, for more than a century one of the most powerful political forces in any democratic country, was devastated, losing power after eighteen continuous years in office. One television pundit insisted that "landslide" was far too weak a word for what happened in Britain on 1 May: "It's more like an asteroid hitting the planet and destroying practically all life on earth."[1]

Millions stayed up to watch the election results on television. At ten o'clock, when the polls closed, the viewing audience numbered 10.9 million (with many more listening on radio). By eleven o'clock the total had risen to 11.7 million. At midnight it was still 9.2 million. At three o'clock in the morning no fewer than 3.2 million people were still glued to their sets.[2] The peak viewing audience constituted nearly a third of the entire adult population. In the United States a television audience of comparable size would have numbered at least 60 million.

As the polls closed, both of the main television channels, the BBC and ITN, announced the results of their exit polls. Both showed Labour winning by a landslide. At once, huge cheers went up in the packed Labour Club in Tony Blair's home constituency of Sedgefield. For the rest of the night, television became an integral part of the world it was reporting. Blair's supporters in Sedgefield would have cheered anyway, but they cheered with even greater gusto knowing that they could see and hear themselves on television as well as being seen and heard across the country.

But the exit polls might be wrong. Five years before they had given a highly misleading impression. No one could be entirely confident—or could entirely abandon hope—until the first real results came in.

The very first, from Sunderland South in the northeast of England, came within the hour. Labour had easily held the seat—that was no surprise—but the swing from the Conservatives to Labour was fully 10.5 percent, far more than Labour would need nationally to win an outright majority. The next result, from Hamilton South in Scotland, also showed a pro-Labour swing.

But it was the result from Birmingham Edgbaston that did it. Edgbaston is one of the most prosperous parts of a mainly prosperous city, Britain's second largest. The seat had been Conservative since 1922. Labour had never won it. Moreover, the local Labour candidate was German-born and some local Conservatives had campaigned against her on the grounds that she was a German and that, when she married, she had adopted her husband's name, which was Stuart, in order, it was alleged, to conceal her national origin from voters. As it turned out, the local voters did not seem desperately interested one way or the other. Gisela Stuart gained Edgbaston with a swing to Labour of 10.0 percent. Her delighted smile as she greeted her supporters told the story of the whole night. Labour was in.

The only questions remaining—but they were big questions—concerned precisely how large Labour's majority would be and which individual Conservative MPs would fall victim to the Labour onslaught. The stately manner in which British ballots are counted only added to the drama. There is no electronic or mechanical voting in the United Kingdom. Voters mark their crosses on paper ballots, and the ballots at the end of the day are transported to a central location before being counted by hand. The process is protracted. It can take hours in a large constituency. All the while, the tension for the candidates, their families, and their supporters is mounting inexorably.

The first famous Tory to fall was Nicholas Budgen, a free spirit and one of the most articulate of the Conservatives' "Eurosceptic" rebels, in Wolverhampton South West, a constituency, like Birmingham Edgbaston, in the industrial West Midlands. The seat had once been held by an even more famous Conservative rebel, Enoch Powell. The swing against Budgen was 9.9 percent. Moments later, Labour claimed its first ministerial victim: John Bowis, a junior minister at the Department of Transport, defeated in Battersea, in London south of the Thames, on a pro-Labour swing of 10.2 percent. He was soon followed by the former national heritage secretary, David Mellor, who lost Putney, also south of the Thames in London, on a swing of 11.2 percent. One of the other Putney candidates was a tycoon, Sir James Goldsmith, who had founded his own Referendum Party to oppose further European integration. His supporters chanted "Out, out, out" as Mellor went down. Goldsmith himself, however, had not done well (attracting only 1,518 votes), and an angry Mellor, alluding to the fact that Goldsmith owned a mansion in Mexico as well as large houses in London and Paris, summed up Putney's verdict on the Referendum Party: "Up your hacienda, Jimmy."

At his count at Sedgefield in County Durham, Tony Blair, aware that he would become Britain's youngest-ever prime minister in only a few hours' time and appearing somewhat shaken as well as tired, thanked his family and local supporters for their help: "It is an honour to serve you, and I feel this evening a deep sense of honour, a deep sense of responsibility and a deep sense of humility. You have put your trust in me, and I intend to repay that trust. I will not let you down."

David Mellor was the first cabinet minister or ex-cabinet minister to lose his seat, but he was not the last. Moments after the declaration of the Putney result, it became clear that Michael Forsyth, the Scottish secretary, had lost his seat in Stirling on the southern edge of the Scottish Highlands. The swing against him was 7.7 percent. That night and the next day he was followed by Malcolm Rifkind, foreign secretary, who lost Edinburgh Pentlands to Labour on a swing of 9.8 percent; Ian Lang, president of the Board of Trade, who lost Galloway and Upper Nithsdale to the Scottish National Party on a swing of 9.5 percent; William Waldegrave, chief secretary to the Treasury, who lost Bristol West to Labour on a swing of 12.1 percent; Tony Newton, leader of the House of Commons, who lost Braintree in Essex, also to Labour, on a swing of 12.9 percent; and Roger Freeman, chancellor of the Duchy of Lancaster, who went down in Kettering in Northamptonshire, yet again to Labour, on a swing of 10.6 percent.

As the dreadful results for the Tories began to accumulate, the television cameras located—at his count at Wokingham in Surrey—John Redwood, the man who only two years before had challenged John Major for the Conservative leadership and prime ministership. The former Welsh secretary easily held his own seat, but his thoughts were clearly far from Wokingham. He could be seen conferring with his aides and allies on his mobile phone, frantically scribbling notes on scraps of paper. The night was still young, but the contest for the Tory leadership was already under way.

But the undoubted sensation of the night was the defeat of Michael Portillo, the defence secretary, in Enfield Southgate, a prosperous suburban constituency on London's northern outskirts. Portillo, a man of unquestioned ability, was thought by almost nobody to be at risk; rumour had it that he had urged his local supporters to canvass in neighbouring, more marginal constituencies. He was also thought to be one of the people most likely to succeed John Major as party leader. But when the

Southgate result was declared, Portillo, too, was out—on a swing of 17.4 percent. His Labour opponent, a young (and gay) Fabian Society official named Stephen Twigg, looked ever so slightly embarrassed, as though he had just unexpectedly won a school prize.

After the count Portillo was gracious in his speech conceding defeat, but on television a few minutes later he revealed the extent of his hurt. Interviewed on the BBC by an affable but blunt-spoken Jeremy Paxman, Portillo pleaded with his party to eschew the public displays of disunity that had marred the Conservatives' last few years in office. But Paxman responded: "How can the party unite around the present policy on the single currency?"

Portillo: Well, I'm now a man outside the House of Commons so I don't
          have to bother with questions like that.
Paxman: Is the present policy the right policy?
Portillo: Oh Jeremy, do stop this nonsense.
Paxman: Well, I think we'll have to stop the interview unless you've got
          anything else you particularly want to tell us this evening.
Portillo: It was you that wanted the interview.

One of the most striking features of the night was Labour's success in parts of the country from which it had effectively been driven during the 1980s. Between 1979, when the Conservatives under Margaret Thatcher first came to power, and 1992, when they won their fourth successive election victory, the Labour Party won almost no seats in southern England outside London. Great swathes of the country were painted blue. In 1983, to take the extreme case, Labour won only 3 of the 186 seats in the whole of England outside London south of the Severn and the Wash.[3] The Labour Party looked like becoming a party merely of the innercities and the old industrial North.

The 1997 election changed all that. Labour not only swept most of urban England, Scotland, and Wales, but it reestablished itself—indeed, in some cases, established itself for the first time—across large tracts of rural and suburban England, chiefly, but not only, in the prosperous South. One feature of the 1980s had been the Conservatives' success in a crescent of rural and suburban constituencies to the north and east of London in the two counties of Hertfordshire and Essex, a crescent that extended south of the Thames into a third county, Kent. This, it was said, was the home of Essex Man, "Maggie's Mauler"—male (but often female), upper-working-class or lower-middle-class, family centered, property conscious, conservative with a small "c," hard-nosed, ambitious, and intensely patriotic.[4]

In 1987, for example, the Tories won every one of the 10 seats in Hertfordshire, every one of the 16 seats in Essex, and every one of the 16 seats in Kent—a total for Labour in the three counties of zero. However well the Labour Party continued to do in the great cities of the North, such as Glasgow, Liverpool, Manchester, Newcastle and Leeds, it scarcely existed any longer in this deep-blue southern crescent. Until, that is, 1 May 1997. That night Labour scored its greatest successes in precisely those parts of the country where it had previously done worst. When all the votes had been counted, Tony Blair's Labour Party had won 5 of the 11 seats in Hertfordshire, 6 of the 17 in Essex, and 8 of the 17 in Kent—a total of 19. It was now the Tories' turn to be a party with an extremely narrow geographical base. After the event, someone calculated that one could drive from Land's End at one end of the country to John O' Groats at the other without passing through more than one Conservative-held constituency.

Some of the seats that fell to Labour that night bear names that, until 1 May 1997, were so redolent of Tory England that it was almost impossible to imagine their ever being won by a Labour candidate, names that conjure up images of shady oaks, mock Tudor villas, well-watered lawns, and a Jaguar (or at least one of the larger Fords) in every drive: Broxtowe, Crosby, Eastwood (then the safest Tory seat in Scotland), Finchley and Golders Green (Margaret Thatcher's old constituency), Harrow West (home of the famous school), Hove, St. Albans, and Sittingbourne and Sheppey (described in one of the standard reference books as "a marginal only in the opposition's wildest dreams").[5] Labour in its moment of triumph took them all.

But perhaps the most remarkable single result of the night came in Tatton in Cheshire. At the time of the election, Tatton, based on the comfortable country towns of Knutsford, Wilmslow, and Alderley Edge ("one of the most desirable and Conservative communities in the North of England") was, at least according to the numbers, the Conservative Party's fifth-safest seat in the whole of Great Britain (safer even than the prime minister's seat of Huntingdon).[6] Tatton's Conservative member of Parliament, Neil Hamilton, had been the member since 1983; he was sitting on a majority of more than 22,000. It would take an explosion to oust him.

The explosion duly occurred. Hamilton insisted on fighting the election, even though he had been plausibly accused of accepting illicit payments (in brown envelopes) from a wealthy businessman, failing to declare relevant financial interests in the House of Commons Register of Members' Interests, and lying to, among others, the deputy prime minister. However, both the Labour and Liberal Democrat candidates in the constituency stood aside in favour of an independent "anti-sleaze" candidate, a former BBC war correspondent named Martin Bell. There were gasps of astonishment when the results in Tatton were read out. Hamilton, five years before, had won 62.2 percent of the vote. Now Bell, a man with no political party, no previous political experience, and until the very start of the campaign, no local contacts or organisation, won 60.2 percent. Standing at the microphone in the crumpled white suit that had become his trademark as a television reporter in Bosnia, Bell was visibly moved:

> What you have accomplished here has been to me some kind of political miracle.... I am deeply grateful to all of you. And may I just repeat, for the last time, a couple of lines from G.K. Chesterton that I used during the campaign:
>
>> Smile at us, pay us, pass us; but do not quite forget
>> That we are the people of England and we have not spoken yet.[7]

Now in Tatton, and not only in Tatton, they had spoken.

The night was Labour's; but the Liberal Democrats, benefiting from widespread tactical voting against the Conservatives, also did well. They lost four seats—Rochdale; Inverness East, Nairn, and Lochaber; Oldham East and Saddleworth; and Christchurch (the last two won in by-elections)—and at Rochdale the defeated member, Liz Lynne, could be seen comforting weeping local supporters; but their gains far outweighed their losses, and the Liberal Democrats' steady if unspectacular advances, in almost every part of the country, were one of the major subtexts of the night. In 1992 the Liberal Democrats had been bitterly disappointed to win only 20 seats. In 1997 they were rightly elated to win 46. All their gains were from the Conservatives. Their most famous victim, fighting Harrogate and Knaresborough in Yorkshire, was Norman Lamont, a former chancellor of the exchequer. Lamont's name will recur frequently in these pages.

John Major, the prime minister, gracious and remarkably calm in defeat, conceded in the early hours. "I telephoned Mr. Blair a little over an hour ago to congratulate him on his success," he told the waiting television cameras, "and to wish him every good fortune in the great responsibilities that he will have in the years that lie ahead." As he spoke, Blair was flying south from Sedgefield to London to join Labour supporters at a victory celebration at the Royal Festival Hall on London's South Bank. "The size of our likely majority," he told them as dawn broke, "imposes a special sort of responsibility upon us. We have been elected as New Labour and we will govern as New Labour."

The transfer of power in Britain—far more than in the United States and many other democracies—is a brisk, even brutal affair. The victor drives to Buckingham Palace to "kiss hands" as prime minister; the vanquished packs his bags (if he has not already packed them). There is no transition, no period of reflection, no elaborate handing-over ceremony. The business is done and done quickly.

Tony Blair arrived in Downing Street at one o'clock on the afternoon of 2 May, greeted by hundreds of almost delirious supporters waving Union Jacks. His overnight tiredness shed, his wife and three children at his side, he worked the crowd as though he still had many votes to win. Then, suddenly businesslike, he approached a small lectern positioned in front of the door of Number 10 and said simply: "Enough of talking. It's time now to do." Meanwhile, at the back of the building, in Horseguards Parade, a large van from Michael Gerson Overseas Moving waited to remove John and Norma Major's possessions. They themselves had already departed. "When the curtain falls," the former prime minister told the cameras, "it's time to get off the stage and that is what I propose to do." He would not be continuing as Conservative Party leader. "I hope," he added, "that Norma and I will be able—with the children—to get to the Oval in time for lunch and for some cricket this afternoon." He left as he had arrived, true to himself—and they *were* in time for lunch. The whole business, all of it, was over within hours.

The 1997 general election established a number of records. Merely to list them is to gain a sense of the immensity of what happened in British politics on that May Day.

- The Labour Party won a total of 419 seats, the largest number the Labour Party had ever won and the largest number that any party had won since the National Government's overwhelming victory of 1935 (almost two decades before Tony Blair was born).[8]
- Labour's majority in the new House of Commons, 179 seats, was the Labour Party's largest ever (the majority in 1945 was only 146) and the largest secured by any party since 1935.
- Labour gained a total of 145 seats compared with 1992, the largest gain made by any party since Labour's own landslide victory—its previous best performance—in 1945.
- The swing from the Conservatives to Labour was 10.0 percent, a postwar record. It was roughly double the two-party swing that brought Margaret Thatcher to power in 1979 (5.2 percent) and very nearly as large as the swing to Labour in 1945 (12.2 percent).

• Labour's share of the popular vote was less impressive, a relatively modest 43.2 percent. Even so, it was Labour's largest vote share since 1966 (i.e., for more than 30 years).

• The Conservatives suffered a total catastrophe. Their share of the popular vote, 30.7 percent, was not only 11.2 points lower than their share in 1992; it was the lowest proportion of the popular vote cast for the Conservative Party since immediately after the passage of the Great Reform Act in 1832, when the party was led by the Duke of Wellington, the man who had vanquished Napoleon at Waterloo. The figure then was 29.4 percent. (At the time of the 1832 election in Great Britain, the American president was Andrew Jackson.)

• The Conservatives won only 165 seats in the House of Commons, their lowest total since their landslide defeat at the hands of the Liberals in 1906, when they won only 156. Even in 1945 they managed to hold on to 213.

• The Conservatives lost 177 seats compared with 1992, their largest number of losses since 1945, when they contrived to lose 190.

• The seven cabinet ministers who lost their seats on 1 May constituted the highest total in history. The previous record, five, had been set, also by the Conservatives, in 1945.

• The Conservatives were totally wiped out in Scotland, losing all 11 of the seats they had won at the 1992 election. The Conservatives had never before been without parliamentary representation north of the border.

• The Conservatives also lost all of their remaining 6 seats in Wales—the first time they had been wiped out in the Principality since 1906. As a result of what happened in Wales and Scotland, the Conservatives became, at least in the House of Commons, an exclusively English political organisation.

• The Conservatives also disappeared from virtually the whole of urban Britain. The Parliament elected in 1997 contained 172 seats in either Greater London or the country's other major conurbations. Of the 172, the Conservatives won only 17. Not only had the Tories become an exclusively English party; they had become, at least in the House of Commons, an almost exclusively rural and suburban one.[9]

• The Liberal Democrats' share of the popular vote, 16.8 percent, by no means set a record and was actually lower than their vote share in the two 1974 elections, 1983, 1987, and 1992; but because their support was more efficiently concentrated in their best areas, they won a total of 46 seats, more than any party other than the Conservatives and Labour had won since 1929 (when the old Liberal Party won 59).

• The 2 seats Sinn Fein won in Northern Ireland—Belfast West and

Mid Ulster—were more than that party had won since 1955.

• Martin Bell, the white-suited victor of Tatton, was the first genuine independent, totally free of any party connection, to win a seat at a general election in Britain since 1945.

• Thanks largely to Labour's positive discrimination in favour of women, a record number of women were elected: 119 (101 of them Labour) compared with only half that number, 60, in 1992. After the 1997 election, women constituted nearly one-fifth, 18.1 percent, of the House of Commons. One of those elected, Ruth Kelly, gave birth to her first child shortly after polling day.

• Because until very recently homosexual men and women did not feel free to reveal their sexual orientation, no one will ever know whether the number of gay men in the House of Commons after 1997 was a record; but certainly there had been no previous election that resulted in the election of 3 MPs who were openly gay: Chris Smith, a member of Labour's shadow cabinet (shortly to become national heritage secretary); Stephen Twigg, the shy victor of Southgate; and Ben Bradshaw, who gained Exeter. Bradshaw, a London-based BBC journalist, made no secret of his sexual proclivities, and the election in Exeter took the form of a head-on conflict between him and Dr. Adrian Rogers, a local general practitioner and founder of the Conservative Family Campaign, who, had he been an American, would have been active on the Christian Right. Rogers invited the voters of Exeter to reject Bradshaw on the ground (among others) that he was gay; Bradshaw invited them to back him because he was the local Labour candidate. As in the case of Birmingham Edgbaston, the voters of Exeter seemed unbothered one way or the other. They elected Bradshaw on a swing to Labour of 11.9 percent, one of the largest swings in the South West.

• The number of MPs from ethnic minorities elected in 1997 was also the highest ever (though still lower than their proportion of the population might be thought to warrant). Oona King, one of Labour's 101 women, joined Diane Abbott, Paul Boateng, and Bernie Grant to become the fourth black member of the House. The number of Asian members doubled from 3 to 6. Of the total of 10 black and Asian MPs, all but one sat on the Labour benches. Jonathan Sayeed, the member for Mid Bedfordshire, was the sole Conservative.

• The turnout of voters in 1997, 71.4 percent, was the lowest since 1935, when it was 71.1 percent. For the time being, no one knows quite why the turnout was so low. During the campaign there was much talk of voter disaffection, especially among the young. It was said that many potential voters were switched off the whole political process and could see little or nothing to choose between the parties. Many undoubtedly did feel that way, but the low turnout could also be explained by a lack of interest in an election the outcome of which, according to all the polls, was virtually predetermined. Some disillusioned former Conservatives may also have stayed at home, no longer willing to vote for their own party but unable to bring themselves to vote for any other.

The sheer scale of the changes that took place between 1992 and 1997 and that brought Labour to power on 1 May are suggested by table 1.1, based on the Gallup Organisation's postelection survey, conducted on 2 and 3 May with 1,849 respondents who had earlier responded to Gallup's immediate preelection survey. The postelection survey largely corroborates the findings of Gallup's much larger "rolling" poll conducted throughout the whole campaign and based on a total of 13,991 interviews. Both surveys somewhat overstated Labour's strength and somewhat understated that of the Conservatives and Liberal Democrats. Nevertheless, there is no reason to suppose that these relatively minor errors seriously distort the pattern of findings set out in the table.

The first point to note about the table is that both sexes, all age groups, all occupational groups, and all parts of the country swung heavily to the Labour Party. The swing in any one of the subgroups shown in the table would have been enough, on its own, to carry Labour to victory. To be sure, the swings to Labour were somewhat smaller in those groups where the party was already most deeply entrenched—notably among unskilled manual workers and Scottish and Welsh voters —but, even among them, the swings recorded were on an almost unprecedented scale. There is not a hint of polarization in the table. The change in the country's political mood showed itself everywhere and in all sections of society.

In 1992 there had been some signs that a gender gap might be opening up between women and men, with women more inclined to support the Conservatives and men more inclined to support Labour or one of the other Opposition parties. Whatever the causes of this phenomenon in 1992, they must have been evanescent because five years later they (or at least their effects) had totally disappeared. As the table shows, women and men on 1 May voted Labour and Conservative in virtually identical proportions, and the other differences between the two sexes are well within the range of normal sampling error. During the 1997 campaign the Conservatives made much of women's alleged suspicion of Blair (on the grounds that he was insincere and "smarmy"), but there was no trace of any such suspicion in the final results.

The Labour Party similarly had a clear advantage in every age group, though its support was markedly greater among the young and

TABLE 1.1
THE VOTE BY SOCIAL GROUPS
(IN PERCENTAGES)

% of 1997 vote		1992 Con.	1992 Lab.	1992 Lib. Dem.	1997 Con.	1997 Lab.	1997 Lib. Dem.	Swing to Lab.
	Gender							
46	Men	40	37	20	30	49	14	11
54	Women	46	34	17	30	49	16	16
	Age							
8	18–24	38	34	22	22	57	13	20
23	25–34	38	39	18	26	51	17	12
21	35–44	39	38	21	27	55	13	15
29	45–64	45	35	18	29	44	18	13
19	65 and over	52	32	14	37	45	12	14
	Occupation							
	Professional, managerial,							
27	and executive (AB)	59	16	21	36	36	21	22
20	Routine white-collar (C1)	50	27	20	31	46	18	19
20	Skilled manual (C2)	38	41	18	28	58	9	14
33	Unskilled manual (DE)	30	50	15	24	58	12	7
	Region							
72	England	46	34	19	34	44	18	11
20	South East	55	21	24	41	32	21	13
9	South West	48	19	31	37	26	31	9
11	London	45	37	15	31	50	15	14
8	East Midlands	45	39	15	35	48	14	10
9	West Midlands	47	37	15	34	48	14	12
4	East Anglia	51	28	20	39	38	18	11
11	North West	38	45	16	27	54	14	10
8	Yorkshire	38	44	16	28	52	16	9
5	Northern	33	51	16	22	61	13	11
9	Scotland	26	39	13	18	46	13	8
5	Wales	29	50	12	20	55	12	7

SOURCES: For the breakdowns by gender, age, and occupation, the Gallup poll (see text). For the 1992 regional breakdowns, David Butler and Dennis Kavanagh, *The British General Election of 1992* (London: Macmillan, 1992), 286. For the 1997 regional breakdowns, the BBC's Political Research Unit.

relatively young than among the middle-aged and elderly. The 18- to 24-year-olds in the electorate were sometimes known as "Thatcher's children" because they had been born and largely brought up during the Thatcher years. Either their parenting had been seriously defective or they were in a state of advanced rebellion because they gave Labour its largest absolute majority and swung most sharply to Labour. (A more prosaic explanation would be the tendency of young voters at almost every election to swing whichever way the whole country is swinging —only more so.)

The figures in the table relating to the four broad occupational categories give the lie to any idea that Britain's is a deeply class-ridden—and class-riven—society. As usual, Labour fared best among its traditional supporters: skilled and unskilled manual workers. But, as the table shows, much the biggest swings were among the middle classes, with the biggest of all among the professional, business, and executive classes. Never before had so many "toffs" turned their backs on the Tories; never before had so many voted Labour. Following the 1997 election, there is hardly more than a one-in-three chance that someone meeting a lawyer, bank manager, or health service administrator is in the presence of a Conservative supporter. David Sanders explores the implications of this "class dealignment" in more detail in chapter 8.

The regional swings between 1992 and 1997 were also broadly uniform, with, as we noted earlier, Labour gaining most where it had most to gain, principally in London and the rest of southern England outside London. On 1 May, a total of 54 constituencies swung to Labour by 15 percent or more. Of the 54, no fewer than 26 were in Greater London, and a further 14 were in the so-called Home Counties around London. After nearly two decades of semi-isolation, Labour had become a genuinely national party again.

The Labour Party's victory was thus comprehensive in scope. The Conservatives' defeat was even more so. The rest of this book is devoted to explaining what happened on 1 May and to exploring the implications of that day's events. We begin with an account of the Conservatives' last five years in office, one of the strangest five years in recent political history. In 1992 it seemed possible that the Labour Party had more or less expired as a serious contender for power. By 1997 it seemed that there was nothing that could stop it. Something had clearly happened in between. What was it?

Notes

1. Unless otherwise indicated, all of the direct quotations in this chapter are taken from BBC Worldwide's edited video highlights of the BBC's own election night coverage, *Election 97*, presented by David Dimbleby and edited by Peter Horrocks.
2. Figures provided by the BBC's Political Research Unit.
3. David Butler and Dennis Kavanagh, *The British General Election of 1983* (London: Macmillan, 1984), 290.
4. Essex Man, one of the great verbal icons of the early 1990s, was the inspiration of Simon Heffer. See "Maggie's Mauler," *Sunday Telegraph,* 7 October 1990.
5. Robert Waller and Byron Criddle, *The Almanac of British Politics,* 5th ed. (London: Routledge, 1996), 744.
6. The quotation is from ibid., 816.
7. Actually Bell got the quotation slightly wrong (though the meaning is the same). Chesterton's second line reads: "For we are the people of England, that never have spoken yet." See *The Oxford Dictionary of Quotations,* 2d ed. (London: Oxford University Press, 1953), 141.
8. The historical data in this part of the chapter are largely drawn from David Butler and Gareth Butler, *British Political Facts,* 1900–1994, 7th ed. (London: Macmillan, 1994), 216–19.
9. For these purposes a "major conurbation" is defined as a city with five or more parliamentary constituencies, that is, a city with a population of roughly half a million or more. The list comprises Bristol, Edinburgh, Glasgow, Leeds, Liverpool, Greater London, Greater Manchester, West Midlands, and Sheffield.

2

The Government That Could Do No Right

David Denver

Between 1992 and 1997 the Prince and Princess of Wales separated and then divorced; all four nations of the UK failed to qualify for the football World Cup finals in the United States; two eleven-year-old boys were found guilty of abducting and murdering two-year-old James Bulger in Liverpool; women were ordained as priests in the Church of England; the Channel Tunnel opened for business; a national lottery was instituted; and a gunman massacred sixteen schoolchildren in Dunblane, a quiet, small Scottish town. These are some examples of events that caught the attention of the nation during the interelection period, and they were probably more important to the mass of ordinary people than more obviously political developments. But, although some may have signalled or reflected significant changes in British society and all commanded massive media coverage, these events had little or no bearing on the outcome of the 1997 election and are not discussed in this survey of the period.

The same applies to a wide variety of events and issues that were undoubtedly political but that (in some cases because they were routine or technical) did not favour one party rather than another. Issues such as divorce law reform, the implementation of European Union directives on weights and measures, and the progress of the Northern Ireland "peace process" are of little interest here, even though they may have important consequences for British society in the long term. Similarly, the institution of the national lottery in November 1994 may have been a major success for the government, because millions take part in it. But, although a few voices were raised against the whole idea and there was some controversy over the division of the spoils, the lottery was never a matter of party division and had no effect on party popularity. Instead, this chapter focuses on incidents, policies, personalities, and developments that appeared to influence the cycle of party popularity following the 1992 general election and the eventual result in 1997. Between the two elections John Major and the Conservatives plumbed depths of un-popularity never before experienced by a modern government. Why did this happen?

The Conservative victory in April 1992 had been unexpected. Most pundits and pollsters predicted a win for Labour, or at least a very close race, but the Conservatives returned with sixty-five more seats than Labour and an overall majority of twenty-one. John Major's dogged performance during the campaign impressed his party, and he was credited with rescuing the Conservatives from a losing position. Still flushed with their success in the general election, the Conservatives reversed a long series of local election losses in May, making significant gains and easily leading the other parties in terms of vote share (see table 2.1).

Even in the first few months of the Parliament there were harbingers of problems to come, however. In May 1992, twenty-two Conservative MPs voted against the government, and four abstained on the second reading of the bill to ratify the Maastricht treaty, which involved increasing the pace of progress towards closer European integration. This was the first in a series of battles over Europe that would eventually split the Conservative Party from top to bottom. In July, national heritage secretary David Mellor offered to resign when details of his affair with an ex-

TABLE 2.1

TRENDS IN PARTY SUPPORT:
"NATIONAL EQUIVALENT" SHARE OF VOTE AND GAINS/LOSSES
OF SEATS IN LOCAL ELECTIONS, 1992–96

	1992	1993	1994	1995	1996
Percentage of vote					
Conservative	47	31	28	25	28
Labour	32	41	40	47	44
Liberal Democrat	19	24	27	23	23
Net gain/loss of seats					
Conservative	+305	−478	−440	−2,018	−683
Labour	−374	+94	+115	+1,807	+512
Liberal Democrat	+68	+392	+386	+487	+173

SOURCE: Colin Rallings and Michael Thrasher, *Local Elections Handbook* series, 1992–96, University of Plymouth.

NOTE: Local election results are not strictly comparable from year to year because different types of authority have different election cycles and it is never the case that there are elections covering the whole country. The "national equivalent" vote share is an estimate of the shares that the three parties would have obtained had elections been held throughout Great Britain.

otically named actress, Antonia De Sancha (including the fact that he wore a football shirt when engaged in sexual activity), became public. Initially the prime minister refused his offer of resignation and Mellor himself was unrepentant, saying that an adulterous affair "was not a reason in this day and age for a Cabinet minister to resign."[1] But the tabloids kept up relentless pressure, and Mellor finally resigned in September following the further revelation that the daughter of a Palestine Liberation Organisation official, Mona Bauwens, had paid for holidays for him and his family. Again, this was only the first of a series of sexual and financial scandals that rocked the government. But the most important development of the summer of 1992 was the fact that the pound came under severe pressure on the foreign exchange markets, resulting in the government's withdrawal from the European Exchange Rate Mechanism (ERM) in September.

Fall from Grace: The ERM Fiasco, September 1992

The weakness of the pound sterling against other currencies has been a recurring problem of British economic management since 1945. "Sterling Crisis" and "Run on the Pound" have been all too familiar newspaper headlines. In 1949 and again in 1967 Labour governments were forced into formal devaluations of the pound, and these were portrayed as national humiliations by the Conservatives and their supporters in the national press. In September 1992, however, it was the Conservative government of John Major that suffered a similar humiliation.

From the early 1980s, successive chancellors and foreign secretaries had pressed Margaret Thatcher to abandon the policy of allowing the pound to "float" against other currencies and to take Britain into the ERM. But Thatcher vetoed any such move, largely because she believed that the ERM was a step on the road to European economic and monetary union (EMU), to which she was adamantly opposed. Although Nigel Lawson as chancellor of the exchequer attempted to "shadow" the German mark from 1987 to 1988 (apparently, at first, without the prime minister's knowledge), exchange rate policy was largely ad hoc and, according to Helen Thomson, "the government was left to manage a series of sterling crises and maintain a real interest rate premium over most of the ERM states."[2]

In June 1989, however, at the Madrid meeting of the European Council, Thatcher reluctantly agreed that Britain would join the ERM when a number of conditions were met, including lower inflation in Britain, the abolition of exchange controls in the Community, and significant progress being made towards the Single European Market. Finally, in October 1990, just seven weeks before he replaced her as prime minister, John Major, who had succeeded Lawson as chancellor, persuaded Thatcher that the Britain should join the ERM. The announcement and the decision about the rate at which the pound would be set (£1 = DM2.95) were made unilaterally, without discussion or agreement with the other members of the EU, in particular the German Bundesbank. Helen Thomson argues that the decision contained the seeds of future disaster, as little serious thought had been given to the question of how British membership of the ERM was supposed to work: the country was in recession and there was a large balance-of-payments deficit. Once Britain was in the ERM, scope for cutting interest rates to deal with the recession was limited, since the trend in German rates was upwards. Moreover, Britain's balance-of-payments deficit suggested that the pound was overvalued and, in particular, that the fixed exchange rate with the mark was too high.[3]

Chickens duly came home to roost during the summer of 1992. On 2 June Danish voters narrowly rejected the Maastricht treaty in a referendum, and this development, together with the fact that the French also intended to have a referendum on the treaty, created uncertainty in the foreign exchange markets about future progress towards EMU and about some countries' ability to sustain their currencies against the mark. With Britain still in a deep recession (so that any increase in interest rates would have been disastrous) and sterling thought to be overvalued, the pound came under intense pressure. Throughout the developing crisis, however, the prime minister and Norman Lamont, now chancellor of the exchequer, publicly maintained that there would be no devaluation and no realignment of currencies within the ERM. By the beginning of September sterling was trading near to its lowest permitted level against the mark, and on 3 September the government announced that it was borrowing £7.2 billion to maintain sterling's position. On 5 September, Lamont chaired a meeting of European finance ministers and bank governors at Bath at which he refused to admit to sterling's weakness, again ruled out a general realignment, and, in a rather maladroit fashion, tried to pressure the mighty Bundesbank into lowering German interest rates. On 10 September, John Major was still insisting in a speech to the Scottish CBI that "it's a cold world outside the ERM. . . . There is going to be no revaluation, no realignment." He went on to describe devaluation as "a betrayal of the future."[4]

On 14 September, the Bundesbank shaved 0.25 percent off German interest rates, but this was not enough to convince the markets that the pound could be rescued, and on 16 September ("Black Wednesday") the exchange rate of sterling against other currencies plummeted despite massive intervention by the Bank of England and despite successive hikes in interest rates from 10 percent to 12 percent and then to 15 percent in the space of only a few hours. Throughout a dramatic day the government struggled to defend the pound, but in the evening, looking pale and exhausted, Chancellor Lamont appeared on the steps of the Treasury, blinking in the television lights, to announce that sterling's membership of the ERM had been suspended.

At one level, these events concerned technical matters of high finance that, it might be assumed, would be relatively remote from the concerns of the mass of voters. In fact, however, they involved the complete collapse of the central plank of the government's economic policy. Opposition politicians were quick to point out that the Conservative manifesto at the April 1992 election, only five months before, had stated that "membership of the ERM is now central to our counter-inflation discipline" and that that policy was now in tatters. Moreover, Conservatives had long taunted Labour as being the party of devaluation and hence incompetent managers of the nation's economic affairs. Now *The Times* headline of 17 September conveyed a simple message: "Beaten Lamont Devalues Pound." In terms that all could understand, the media made great play of the money that had been "poured down the drain" by the chancellor in a forlorn attempt to shore up the pound, with *The Times* suggesting that £7 to £12 billion had been wasted. In general, press and television coverage left the voters in little doubt that the episode had been a fiasco, that the government had been humiliated, and that its handling of the crisis had been hopelessly incompetent.

In political terms, the events of September 1992 had four main consequences. First, they sealed the fate of the chancellor. Although he soldiered on for a while—and was reportedly singing in his bath shortly afterwards—Lamont never re-established his reputation. He was also prone to making unguarded remarks implying that he was uncaring about the effects of the recession on ordinary people, and he was finally sacked in May 1993.

Second, the episode emboldened the Eurosceptics among Conservative MPs. The twenty-two MPs who had voted against the government on the Maastricht treaty were die-hards in the anti-European cause, but other sceptics had been persuaded into the government lobby by the "opt-in" to EMU and "opt-out" of the Social Chapter that John Major had negotiated. The other aspects of the treaty were based on the assumption that progress to EMU was unstoppable, but now that the ERM was in ruins the need to support the treaty seemed less urgent. In addition, the short experience of membership of the ERM intensified Tory doubts about closer European integration. The main effects of UK membership of the ERM appeared to have been to prolong the recession, to make it even worse than it otherwise would have been, and to make the Conservative Party unpopular among the electorate. Euroscepticism suddenly became fashionable—and even intellectually respectable. In October the government survived another vote on the issue by only three votes and this time thirty-two Eurosceptics voted against it or abstained.

Third, the prime minister and his government lost the support of most of the Tory press. Although it had enthusiastically supported Major against Kinnock in the general election, the press now turned savagely against him. With the Eurosceptic *Sun* in the vanguard, Major was portrayed as a weak and indecisive muddler, and he never regained even lukewarm support, far less the kind of wholehearted backing that Thatcher had enjoyed.

Finally, Black Wednesday had a dramatic effect on the government's popularity among the electorate. In five opinion polls taken in August and early September the major parties were running neck and neck, with the Conservatives averaging 40 percent of the vote and Labour 41 percent. The first six polls after 16 September produced averages of 43 percent for Labour and 37.5 percent for the Conservatives. In October and November the Conservatives slipped further, to 34 percent and 32 percent respectively, while Labour rose to 47 percent and 49 percent. A Labour lead of one point just before the crisis had been transformed into one of 17 points in a space of only ten weeks (see figure 2.1).

In an emergency House of Commons debate on the ERM affair held on 24 September, the shadow chancellor, Gordon Brown, argued that the government had "lost all claim to economic competence and credibility." His sentiments were evidently shared by a large proportion of the electorate. Traditionally the Conservatives had been regarded by the electorate as the party of economic competence, with Labour seen as prone to misjudgements and even recklessness. At the time of the 1992 election, for example, when asked which party they thought could handle Britain's economic difficulties best, 49 percent of Gallup's respondents opted for the Conservatives and only 36 percent for Labour, despite the fact that the Conservatives had presided over a lengthy recession. In early September 1992 the Conservatives still retained a lead of 5 points over Labour on this question. In October, however, Labour went into an 18-point lead and this stretched to 21 points in November.[5] Although the Labour lead narrowed somewhat during 1993, the Conservatives never regained their reputation as the party that was "sound" on the economy.

Following the ERM fiasco, the government appeared to slide more

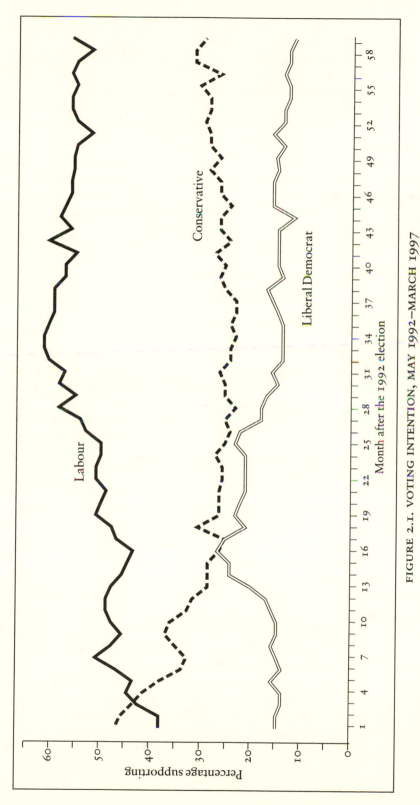

FIGURE 2.1. VOTING INTENTION, MAY 1992–MARCH 1997

NOTE: The graph plots the monthly mean share of unadjusted voting intentions reported in the major opinion polls (Gallup, ICM, MORI, NOP).

and more deeply into a morass, as problems piled on top of one another. As well as being seen as incompetent over the ERM, the government came to be viewed as deceitful over campaign promises, plagued by division and weak leadership, tainted by sleaze, and eager to pursue unpopular policies in the teeth of the electorate's disapproval. These were problems of the government's own making, but they were compounded by the election of Tony Blair as Labour leader in July 1994. In what follows I discuss separately the various developments contributing to the government's unpopularity, but it was their combined and cumulative effects that explain the government's unparalleled unpopularity and form the backdrop to the series of local election disasters and spectacular by-election defeats detailed in tables 2.1 (p. 16) and 2.2.

Taxation

Early in the 1992 campaign John Smith, then Labour's shadow chancellor, published an "alternative budget" which suggested that, if elected, Labour would increase direct taxation and national insurance contributions for the better-off. Thereafter the Conservatives relentlessly attacked Labour's taxation policies. The issue dominated eight of their nineteen national morning press conferences and was the subject of a massive national advertising campaign.[6] Their efforts paid off. Significant numbers of voters were persuaded that Labour would raise taxes and were induced to support the Conservatives by the prospect of tax cuts.[7] Such voters were soon disillusioned.

In his March 1993 budget, Norman Lamont increased taxes on alcohol and tobacco by more than the rate of inflation and announced, among other measures, higher national insurance contributions for employees (effectively a tax rise); a freezing of personal tax allowances (effectively a tax rise); reductions in tax allowances for married couples and mortgage holders (effectively a tax rise); and the extension of Value Added Tax (VAT) to domestic fuel and power (a straightforward tax rise). The latter, in particular, seemed to be a direct betrayal of a campaign promise and was widely credited with (or blamed for) the loss of two by-elections to the Liberal Democrats in the next few months (see table 2.2). More of the same followed in November in Kenneth Clarke's first budget, with tax allowances further restricted and two new taxes —on insurance premiums and air travel—introduced. In 1994 the budget was less severe on taxpayers. Clarke at last uprated personal allowances, but he also devised another new tax (on waste dumping).

In the last two budgets of the Parliament Clarke finally announced

TABLE 2.2

TRENDS IN PARTY SUPPORT: SUMMARY OF BY-ELECTION RESULTS, 1992–97

Year	Month	Constituency	Change in share of vote				Result
			Con	Lab	Lib Dem	SNP/PC	
1993	July	Christchurch	−31.5	−9.3	+39.7		Con lost to Lib Dem
1994	May	Rotherham	−13.9	−8.4	+17.4		Lab held
	June	Barking	−23.5	+20.5	−2.5		Lab held
	June	Bradford South	−20.6	+7.7	+10.2		Lab held
	June	Dagenham	−26.4	+19.7	−3.1		Lab held
	June	Eastleigh	−26.6	+6.9	+16.3		Con lost to Lib Dem
	June	Newham NE	−15.9	+16.6	−7.0		Lab held
	June	Monklands East	−13.8	−11.5	−2.0	+26.9	Lab held
	Dec	Dudley West	−30.1	+28.1	−2.9		Con lost to Lab
1995	Feb	Islwyn	−10.9	−5.1	+4.9	+8.8	Lab held
	May	Perth and Kinross	−18.8	+9.7	+0.4	+4.4	Con lost to SNP
	July	Littleborough & Saddleworth	−20.9	+13.6	+2.2		Con lost to Lib Dem
1996	Feb	Hemsworth	−9.8	+1.1	−3.6		Lab held
	April	Staffordshire SE	−22.2	+21.9	−4.9		Con lost to Lab
	Dec	Barnsley East	−6.9	−0.8	−0.2		Lab held
1997	Feb	Wirral South	−16.4	+18.0	−3.1		Con lost to Lab

NOTE: A June 1995 by-election in Northern Ireland is excluded from the table.

the long-promised reductions in the standard rate of income tax—by one penny in 1995 and another in 1996. But by this time it was a case of too little too late, and the voters saw the income tax reductions as a blatant attempt to bribe them.[8] Even these budgets included large rises in duty on cars, petrol, and tobacco, as well as increases in the taxes on insurance premiums and air travel, and a new tax on travel insurance. After the 1996 budget it was still the case that, as a proportion of gross domestic product, the overall tax burden was greater than it had been in 1979 when Thatcher came to power.

At the time of the 1992 election the Conservative Party was unquestionably seen as the "low tax" party. In May 1992, 49 percent of Gallup respondents thought that the Conservatives had the best policies on taxation, compared with 27 percent who thought the same of Labour. This advantage was rapidly lost after the March 1993 budget. In April Gallup reported that only 16 percent of respondents thought that the Conservatives had told the truth about taxation during the election, with 76 percent saying that they had been misled; by a record margin of 75 percent to 19 percent they thought that the budget was unfair, and, again by a record margin (70 percent to 18 percent), they thought the chancellor was doing a "bad job." Labour now went into the lead as the best party on taxation, by 42 percent to 33 percent and never lost its lead on this question for the rest of the Parliament. The Tories' much publicised attacks on Labour's tax plans in 1992 rebounded on them. From 1993 onwards they were no longer viewed as the "low tax" party and were clearly not forgiven by the electorate for the way in which they had failed to deliver on their campaign promises on taxes.

Conservative Divisions

The existence of sharp and very public divisions within the Conservative Party, especially over European policy, was an ongoing problem for John Major and the government between 1992 and 1997. According to Baker et al., writing in 1994, the Conservatives in Parliament were "divided from top to bottom over Europe" and the question of sovereignty versus interdependence, rather than left versus right or "wet" versus "dry," was the crucial source of the party's internal difficulties.[9]

Party divisions on Europe intensified in 1993, and the government was twice defeated on Maastricht-related issues by substantial backbench rebellions. Although the treaty was finally ratified in August 1993, disputes among the Conservatives had been in the headlines for more than a year. Disaffection extended well beyond the relatively small group of anti-European die-hards who were prepared to vote against the government on almost any European issue. The former prime minister, Baroness Thatcher, attacked the Maastricht treaty in her maiden speech in the House of Lords and later said that she would never have signed it. Former ministers Norman Tebbit, Cecil Parkinson, and Kenneth Baker made clear their sympathy with the rebels. In July the prime minister's anger and frustration became public when he referred to the Eurosceptic ministers in his own cabinet as "bastards" in a taped conversation with an ITN journalist.

The ratification of the treaty failed to heal the rifts over Europe. At the 1994 party conference Michael Portillo delivered a populist attack on the European Commission to loud cheers from the delegates.[10] In November the government, fearing defeat on the second reading of the European Finance Bill, made the vote an issue of confidence. Despite extreme pressure from the party whips, eight Euro-rebels abstained, and in an unprecedented move, John Major removed the whip from them the next day. In effect they were expelled from the parliamentary party, technically putting the government in a minority in the House of Commons. Another MP sympathetic to the rebels resigned the whip voluntarily and "the whipless nine," previously obscure backbenchers, suddenly found themselves famous. They formed their own organisation and proceeded to defy the government not just on Europe but on other issues, including the imposition of VAT on domestic fuel. Despite stern warnings about discipline, there was nothing the government could do, and in April 1995 the prime minister unconditionally restored the whip to all nine. The climb-down was humiliating and yet another sign of disarray.

Divisions over Europe continued to bedevil the Conservatives, however, and contributed to the widespread view of John Major as a weak leader. Never very inspiring at best, and with a peculiarly flat and old-fashioned oratorical style, Major suffered by comparison with the dashing Blair. Talk of dumping him in favour of a more charismatic figure became commonplace. Events took a dramatic turn, however, in June 1995 when he unexpectedly resigned as Conservative leader in order to force a leadership contest. He called on his critics to "put up or shut up," probably believing that they would shut up and that their silence would secure his position for the rest of the Parliament. Instead, the Welsh secretary, John Redwood, put up, resigning his post and campaigning against the prime minister on a Thatcherite and Eurosceptic platform.

Nicknamed "The Vulcan" (i.e. "the man from another planet"), Redwood, with his slogan "No change, no chance," played on the fears of a growing number of Tory MPs that Major was bound to lose the next election. In the event, Major was reelected on the first ballot, obtaining 218 votes compared with 89 for Redwood; 22 MPs abstained or spoiled their ballots. Although Major claimed a clear-cut victory, one third of the Conservative parliamentary party had refused to support him.[11] Nonetheless, after the election there was no more talk of dumping the prime minister. On the other hand, if Major had hoped that his victory would clear the air on Europe and make life easier, he was sadly mistaken. At the October party conference Michael Portillo, the defence secretary, launched yet another fierce (some might say "wild"; the president of the European Commission did say "grotesque") populist attack on the EU. In December another vote on Europe, concerned with fishing quotas, was lost in the House. Even in the dying days of the Parliament, cabinet ministers were squabbling in public over Europe. In February 1996 the foreign secretary, Malcolm Rifkind, suggested in an interview that the cabinet was hostile to a single currency, but the strongly pro-European chancellor, Kenneth Clarke, quickly responded by asserting that Rifkind's remark had been "a slip of the tongue." Stephen Dorrell, the health secretary, provoked another furore over the issue when he too claimed that the cabinet was moving against monetary union.

Throughout the 1992–97 period, the Conservatives' divisions over Europe were deep, public, and enduring. And the electorate noticed. Table 2.3 shows that at the end of 1992, following Black Wednesday, the proportion of Gallup's respondents thinking that the Conservatives were divided shot up to 77 percent. There was some recovery at the start of 1993, but the battles over Maastricht took their toll and by the end of the year only small minorities believed that the Conservatives were united. This situation persisted until the 1997 election. Although substantial minorities still saw the Labour Party as divided, for most of the period more electors thought they were united, in marked contrast to the voters' views during the 1980s when Labour had been rent by bitter internal feuding. Commentators generally assume that the electorate prefer parties to be united, and there seems little doubt that Conservative disunity made the party and the government look shambolic.[12]

Sleaze

A recurrent theme in the politics of 1992–97, especially from late 1994 onwards, was the accusation that the behaviour of the government and of many individual Conservative politicians was "sleazy": "squalid," "disreputable," "tawdry," "of low moral standards," or "slatternly" (to cite dictionary definitions). Although commonly applied to sexual matters, "sleaze" quickly came to be applied more widely to cover areas

TABLE 2.3

PERCEPTIONS OF THE PARTIES AS UNITED

OR DIVIDED, 1992–97

(IN PERCENTAGES)

	Conservatives		Labour	
	United	Divided	United	Divided
1992				
May–Jun	65	26	20	72
Jul–Sep	32	56	45	44
Oct–Dec	15	77	48	41
1993				
Jan–Mar	27	65	39	47
Apr–Jun	22	69	46	42
Jul–Sep	12	80	41	47
Oct–Dec	17	74	42	44
1994				
Jan–Mar	13	77	54	32
Apr–Jun	9	83	55	31
Jul–Sep	13	78	56	32
Oct–Dec	12	78	54	31
1995				
Jan–Mar	9	84	49	38
Apr–Jun	9	83	56	32
Jul–Sep	13	81	54	35
Oct–Dec	19	71	48	38
1996				
Jan–Mar	10	82	50	38
Apr–Jun	11	78	43	43
Jul–Sep	12	77	33	55
Oct–Dec	15	75	43	45
1997				
Jan–Mar	16	80	59	35

SOURCE: *Gallup Political and Economic Index.*

NOTE: These are responses to the question, "Do you think that the - - - - - party is united or divided at the present time?" The figures shown are quarterly averages.

such as the consultancy earnings and activities of MPs and the salaries paid to the bosses of newly privatised industries. Some commentators extend the definition of sleaze to include the practice of "packing" public bodies with government supporters, the secrecy surrounding financial donations to the Conservative Party, and the granting of honours to people associated with companies that made donations.[13] At a general level, however, a belief that "those in public life are pursuing personal gratification, advancement or enrichment against a background of an official facade of respectability, rectitude and probity"[14] became widespread and dogged the Conservatives for most of the Parliament. Four particular areas that contributed to the image of sleaze were sex, "cash for questions," boardroom greed and the "revolving door" ushering politicians into lucrative jobs in the private sector, and the abuse of ministerial power exemplified by the Matrix Churchill affair.

SEX SCANDALS

Between September 1992 and June 1996 no fewer than nine members of the government resigned and another died in the context of a sex scandal. The fate of the first and most prominent casualty, David Mellor, has already been described. In the first few months of 1994 there were four more resignations. Tim Yeo, a junior minister, admitted to a long-running affair with a prominent Conservative councillor by whom he had had an illegitimate child; the wife of the Earl of Caithness, another junior minister, committed suicide, having been depressed, it was alleged, because of her husband's involvement with another woman; Hartley Booth, a parliamentary private secretary and Methodist lay preacher, confessed to a (comparatively tame) relationship with a young female researcher; and an assistant whip, Michael Brown, resigned following revelations concerning a sexual relationship between him, a civil servant, and a student (both male). In addition, in February 1994 the body of Stephen Milligan, another PPS, was discovered in circumstances suggesting spectacularly bizarre autoerotic sexual practices.

In the course of the following year two more junior ministers, Robert Hughes and Richard Spring, resigned in connection with, respectively, a previous extramarital affair and what the *Guardian* (not a tabloid) later described as "a three-in-a-bed romp involving a tycoon friend and a Sunday school teacher."[15] David Ashby, another PPS, also left amid (hotly denied) allegations of homosexuality. Finally, in June 1996 Rod Richards, a junior minister at the Welsh Office, resigned when his extramarital affair was publicised.

Needless to say, sex scandals are nothing new in British politics. What is unusual about this list, however, is the number of government members who were exposed and then forced to quit. In general the British public is fairly tolerant of MPs' private behaviour. Paddy Ashdown, the Liberal Democrat leader, admitted in early 1992 that he had had an affair with his secretary (the *Sun* dubbed him "Paddy Pantsdown") and immediately saw his popularity increase. The context of the Tory sex scandals was different, however. For one thing, at the 1993 Conservative

Party conference John Major advocated a reaffirmation of core Conservative values and, in a celebrated phrase, called for British society to go "Back to Basics." The media, not surprisingly, interpreted the speech as a call for a reassertion of traditional moral values. The Conservatives had also made great play of being the party that championed family values. Indeed Rod Richards, one of the adulterous ministers, had listed "family" as among his recreations in *Dod's Parliamentary Companion*. Not least, as part of their promotion of family values, leading Conservatives had criticised the lack of moral fibre among such people as homeless beggars and single parents, apparently blaming the latter for serious social problems. The sexual sleaze attaching to the government in this context had exceptionally strong overtones of hypocrisy.

"CASH FOR QUESTIONS"

Survey data suggest that, while the British public tends to be relatively tolerant of sexual misdemeanours, it is extremely intolerant of politicians who abuse their positions to feather their own nests.[16] Financial scandals also beset the government and the Tory Party with consequences that will continue to affect the conduct of British politics.

In the summer of 1993 Michael Mates resigned as minister of state at the Northern Ireland Office over his friendship with Asil Nadir, a businessman who was under investigation by the Serious Fraud Office and on whose behalf he had sought to intervene. Nadir had given Mates an expensive watch inscribed, "Don't let the bastards get you down." A few months later, Alan Duncan resigned his position as PPS to the health secretary over an ethically dubious deal involving the purchase and sale of a council house. A more serious case of financial sleaze was exposed in the summer of 1994 when two more PPSs, David Tredinnick and Graham Riddick, were suspended from their posts after the *Sunday Times* revealed that they had been willing to accept a "fee" of £1,000 to ask questions in the House of Commons on behalf of clients. Although the two had been set up by the paper, they were subsequently (April 1995) suspended from the House following an investigation by the Privileges Committee.

The climax came in October 1994. Tim Smith, a junior minister at the Northern Ireland Office, resigned when it emerged that he had failed to disclose payments from Mohamed al-Fayed, the owner of Harrods who was currently seeking British citizenship, in the register of members' interests. More or less simultaneously Jonathan Aitken, chief secretary to the Treasury and a member of the cabinet, was accused of accepting free hospitality at the Ritz Hotel in Paris from al-Fayed and, in the most celebrated case of all, Neil Hamilton resigned as a minister following allega-

tions in the *Guardian* of undisclosed consultancy payments also involving al- Fayed, as well as a lobbying firm owned and run by a man named
Ian Greer. Hamilton and Greer sued the *Guardian* for libel, and the government amended the seventeenth-century Bill of Rights, which regulates
the relationship between Parliament and the courts, to allow Hamilton
to do so. In June 1995 a report by the Commons Committee on Members' Interests decided that some aspects of Hamilton's activities had
been imprudent but recommended no further action. In September 1996,
however, Hamilton and Greer suddenly withdrew their action at the last
minute. The *Guardian* promptly labelled Hamilton "A Liar and a Cheat"
and printed copious details of his use of his position to obtain money.[17]

But this was not the end of the matter. Evidence was then produced
that David Willetts, who had been a junior whip in October 1994, had
sought improperly to influence the Members' Interests Committee to secure a speedy and favourable outcome of the Hamilton investigation
—or, less formally, to arrange a cover-up. Now paymaster general,
Willetts appeared before the new Committee on Standards and Privileges
at the end of 1996. Under intense questioning, especially from fellow
Tory Quentin Davies, he tried to explain away a memo he had written,
following a conversation with the chairman of the Members' Interests
Committee, in which he had referred to "exploiting the good Tory majority" on the committee. The new committee was less than impressed
and reported that Willetts had "dissembled" in giving his account of the
incident and thus aggravated the original offence. The committee also
decided that in its future investigations it would take evidence under
oath. Willetts promptly resigned from the government.

The events of October 1994, together with the preceding sex scandals, led many to believe that misconduct by ministers and MPs was now
on a previously unheard-of scale. John Major responded by announcing
the establishment of a new Standing Committee on Standards in Public
Life under the initial chairmanship of a respected law lord, Lord Nolan.
Following a series of televised public hearings, the committee issued its
first report in May 1995.[18]

The report turned out to be far more radical than most politicians
expected. Many Conservative MPs, in particular, were furious at the report's implications—and furious with the prime minister for having set
the committee up. According to Nolan, the activities of some MPs in re-
lation to lobbyists had undermined respect for the House of Commons,
and the ability of MPs to discharge their duties free from conflicts of interest had been called into question. Nolan recommended that MPs
should remain free to have paid employment related to their duties as
MPs but should be prevented from providing services for multiclient or-

ganisations (a clear reference to lobbying firms). There should be a new code of conduct for MPs, and those with outside jobs should have to register the terms of their contracts and declare, within broad bands, how much they were paid. The two House of Commons Committees on Privileges and Members' Interests should be merged into a new Committee on Standards and Privileges, and an independent parliamentary commissioner for Standards should be appointed to investigate complaints against MPs. This last recommendation challenged the long-standing principle that the House of Commons alone is responsible for regulating, investigating, and judging its own members.

The House debated the Nolan report in May 1995, with some of its recommendations meeting fierce resistance from Conservative backbenchers. Nonetheless, a select committee was appointed to prepare proposals for implementing the recommendations. This committee was agreed about the appointment of a commissioner for standards, merging the Privileges and Members' Interests Committees, and the introduction of a code of conduct, and these proposals met little opposition in the House when the committee reported back in July. But the questions of multiclient consultancies and disclosure of earnings, which had started off the whole process of reform, remained unresolved. The problem re-emerged in November when the special select committee presented a report which argued that the proposed Nolan ban on MPs working for multiclient organisations was unworkable and that, rather, there should be a ban on "paid advocacy" by MPs. Crucially, however, the committee decided that the disclosure of MPs' outside earnings should not be made mandatory. According to the *Sunday Times,* mandatory disclosure was supported by the great majority of the electorate and the case for it was "so compelling, so self-evident, it ought to make any debate redundant."[19] Nonetheless, the prime minister decided to back the committee report and oppose disclosure of earnings. In the debate that followed, he and the government suffered a humiliating defeat as 23 Tories supported a Labour amendment requiring that all fees be declared.

The course of events arising out of the cash for questions affair signally failed to dispel the image of Tory sleaze. Having set up the Nolan Committee to clear the air (which displeased some of his backbenchers), Major then backtracked on the main issue (which displeased others). Conservative opponents of Nolan could easily be portrayed as greedy and self-seeking. Moreover, the issue rumbled on into 1996 with reports of Conservative MPs seeking to avoid declaring their incomes by various ruses, and others, including David Mellor, refusing to do so despite requests from the newly appointed parliamentary commissioner for standards, Sir Gordon Downey. Other Tory MPs announced that they would leave the

Commons at the next election since they could no longer command an adequate income, thereby reinforcing public suspicion that near-corruption was rife among politicians, especially on the Conservative side.

BOARDROOM GREED AND THE
"REVOLVING DOOR"

John Major inherited from Margaret Thatcher, and subsequently extended, the policy of privatising previously publicly owned industries. Unfortunately for him, he also inherited one of the most unpopular aspects of privatisation, namely, the way in which the managers and executives of the new companies (who in most cases had also been managers before privatisation) appeared to be able to award themselves huge salaries and gigantic financial benefits by way of share options, bonuses, payoffs, and the like. There was also much public discontent about "boardroom greed" in other companies, but it was the recently privatised industries, especially gas, water, and electricity, that aroused particular anger. These were, in most cases, private monopolies that had been created by deliberate Conservative policy, and it was easy to compare post-privatisation salaries and benefits with the situation before.

Although not a new issue, boardroom greed leapt to public prominence in November 1994 when British Gas revealed that Cedric Brown, its chief executive, was to receive a 76-percent salary increase, taking his earnings to £450,000 per year. This announcement was made just a week after increases in gas prices had been announced and Major had stated that there was "no doubting the resentment that large and unjustified salary increases can cause."[20] The prime minister was said to have been livid when he heard of Brown's increase, and others variously described it as "grotesque," "obscene," and "crass." In a public relations disaster, British Gas followed up by announcing a few weeks later that its showroom staff could expect cuts in pay and holiday entitlements.

The Labour Party—in particular the shadow chancellor, Gordon Brown—took up the issue with gusto, and more revelations followed. For example, Bryan Weston, a nonexecutive director of MANWEB, a regional electricity company, had retired in August 1994 with a package worth almost a million pounds despite having worked only two days a week for the previous two years; and the appropriately named Desmond Pitcher of North West Water was reported to earn five times more than his predecessor before privatisation. Labour politicians, "scoring copious populist points," according to The Times,[21] called for regulation of directors' financial rewards, pointing out that the remuneration committees that determined them were themselves mainly composed of directors from other companies, who had no interest in stopping the pay spiral.

Major reacted to the furore over Cedric Brown's salary rise by setting up a cabinet committee to examine ways of curbing boardroom excesses, but it never reached a conclusion and the government remained opposed to regulation. Such was the extent of public concern, however, that in January 1995 the Institute of Directors set up its own committee to make recommendations about salaries and other perks. This was chaired by Sir Richard Greenbury, chairman of Marks and Spencer (who himself earned almost £800,000 per annum). As a result, the government was able to respond "Wait for Greenbury" when pressed on the issue. But other incidents kept executive greed on the front pages.

The Commons Employment Committee started public hearings on pay in the privatised industries. When they gave evidence, Cedric Brown claimed that he was being paid "the rate for the job," and Sir Iain Vallance, chairman of BT on a salary of £633,000, disputed whether there was any public concern about executive pay. Vallance commented, "I would quite like a job as a junior doctor in the NHS. It might be quite relaxing"[22]—a remark that provoked public outrage. Meanwhile, Greenbury had publicly attacked water company chiefs as the main culprits in the furore over pay and suggested that some of the extravagant payoffs had rewarded failure and mediocrity. It was also reported that Ed Wallis and John Baker, chairmen of Powergen and National Power respectively, had each earned more than £1,000,000 in 1994—about 1,000 percent more than the highest paid executive of the Central Electricity Generating Board before privatisation in 1989. In response, John Major unexpectedly changed his stance on the issue. Replying to Tony Blair's questioning on a pay package of £2,000,000 for David Jeffries, chairman of the national grid, Major said that such rewards were "distasteful" and that the government was prepared to back up any recommendations of the Greenbury committee with appropriate legislation. Later, the annual general meeting of British Gas was attended by 4,500 angry small shareholders (and a 30-stone pig named Cedric eating from "the trough of privatisation") determined to vote against the reappointment of four directors, including Brown and Richard Giordano, the £450,000 per annum part-time chairman. In the event, they were easily outvoted by large City institutions, which held 97 percent of the shares.

When it finally appeared, the Greenbury Report rejected statutory controls on executive rewards, suggesting, however, that the water and energy industries should review and voluntarily adjust their recent financial packages. Also recommended were "transparency" in the process of setting salaries and other benefits, a code of practice to be followed in such cases, and the taxing of share options as income rather than capital. The chancellor moved immediately to implement the latter recommendation only to discover that the new arrangements would hit lower-level employees harder than the "fat cats" at whom it was directed. Yet again it seemed that everything the government touched turned to dust.

From this point onwards, the issue of executive pay gradually dropped out of the headlines, but the damage to the prime minister and the government had already been done. During the 1980s the privatisation of nationalised industries had been one of the Thatcher government's most distinctive policies, and the public rushed to buy shares. By the mid-1990s privatisation had become a term of abuse, inextricably associated in the public mind with vastly overpaid managers who sacked workers and increased prices while helping themselves to fortunes. The changing balance of opinion about the privatised industries is illustrated in table 2.4. The privatisations of gas, electricity, and, especially, water had never been very popular. By November 1994, however, very large majorities of the electorate said that these privatisations had been "a bad thing." This change in attitude was important because privatisation remained a large and highly visible part of the government's programme.

From the government's point of view it could be claimed that boardroom excesses were not its fault, since only private companies were involved. But senior Conservative politicians found themselves directly in the firing line because of the ease and frequency with which they themselves moved through the "revolving door" from the cabinet to City boardrooms. It was not just that they accepted lucrative jobs but that many of the firms concerned had benefited from the privatisation programme carried through by these self-same ministers. As Richard Littlejohn commented in the *Sun*, "What is really sleazy is the number of Tories sticking their snouts in a trough of their own making."[23]

It was easy to find examples to illustrate the point. Lord Tebbit was appointed to the board of British Telecom, whose privatisation he had

TABLE 2.4

ATTITUDES TOWARDS PRIVATISED INDUSTRIES

	British Telecom	Gas	Water	Electricity
Jan 1993	−2	−5	−40	−15
Jun 1993	−7	−16	−56	−24
Nov 1994	−2	−35	−56	−34

SOURCE: *Gallup Political and Economic Index.*

NOTE: The figures shown are the percentages thinking that the relevant privatisation was "a bad thing" subtracted from the percentages thinking it was "a good thing."

steered; Norman Fowler, a former transport secretary, joined the board of the National Freight Consortium, which he had targeted for privatisation; John MacGregor, another former transport minister, joined Hill Samuel, a bank that had been chosen to advise on the building of the Channel Tunnel rail link; Norman Lamont and Lord Wakeham both joined Rothschild, which had advised on the privatisation of electricity; Richard Needham, a former trade minister, became a director of GEC. In all cases the rules developed to regulate the employment of ex-ministers were followed. Nonetheless, as *The Times* commented: "When a defence minister goes to an arms contractor, an energy minister to an electricity company or a transport minister to a road haulier, the public smell a rat."[24]

ABUSE OF MINISTERIAL POWER:
THE MATRIX CHURCHILL AFFAIR
AND THE SCOTT REPORT

In October 1992 three executives of Matrix Churchill, a Midlands machine tools manufacturer, went on trial on charges connected with breaking government regulations relating to the export of "lethal equipment" to Iraq. The three insisted that the government had known about the exports in question and had, indeed, connived at breaching its own publicly stated ban; and then the trial was halted in dramatic circumstances when a former junior trade minister, Alan Clark, agreed in court that he had given a "nod and a wink" to the company, signifying that the government would turn a blind eye to Matrix Churchill's export activities. In response to the ensuing outcry over Clark's admission, Major set up a public inquiry chaired by Lord Justice Scott. The inquiry held public hearings from May 1993 until March 1994. Civil servants, ministers, ex-ministers, Baroness Thatcher, and the prime minister himself were called to give evidence, and the subsequent report was published in February 1996.

It may be stretching the definition of sleaze to include the revelations that emerged in the course of the Scott inquiry. It is also the case that much of the discussion that took place was technical, detailed, obscure, and unlikely to command the attention of the average voter. Nonetheless, the broad story that emerged over the months was not flattering to the government. Ministers, for whatever reason, had altered the guidelines for dealing with arms exports to Iraq without revealing the fact publicly. They had misled the House of Commons on the matter. Perhaps most important to the electorate at large, ministers appeared to have been willing to see innocent people go to jail for actions that the government had condoned. Indeed, several of them had signed Public Interest

Immunity Certificates ("gagging orders") to prevent material documents from being used by the defence in the original trial. Whatever the rights and wrongs of the whole affair, their actions reeked of a cover-up. The revelation that "gagging orders" were still being signed in similar cases during 1995 led Bernard Levin to complain in *The Times* about the "overpowering stench of Tory sleaze that is at this moment drifting heavenward."[25]

When the Scott Report, running to 1,800 pages, was eventually published, the government organised a huge "spin doctoring" operation to convince people that ministers had been exonerated. Others interpreted the report differently. Hugo Young of the *Guardian,* for example, suggested that it showed that the world inhabited by ministers "is not exactly an amoral world. It merely gives dissembling a higher priority than other worlds. But it countenances apologias which would be intolerable in any other field of human conduct."[26]

It is difficult to know how far the Matrix Churchill affair contributed to the image of sleaze that attached to the Tories. Certainly the topic was of much less interest to the popular press than the sex scandals discussed earlier. But the steady drip of allegations and counterallegations throughout the public hearings, and the more wide-ranging media interest in June 1995, when an early draft of the report was leaked, and again on its final publication, almost certainly meant that some mud stuck to the government and the Conservative Party.

Whatever the contribution of all these different elements, opinion poll data leave no doubt that the voters came to regard the Conservatives as tainted by sleaze. In January 1994 Gallup for the first time asked respondents whether they agreed or disagreed that "the Conservatives these days give the impression of being very sleazy and disreputable." As table 2.5 shows, even at this stage electors agreed by a majority of more than two to one. Later in 1994 and during the first half of 1995 the majority increased to more than three to one; and, although things improved somewhat for the Conservatives after that, substantial majorities of the electorate continued to believe that they were a sleazy lot. When the same Gallup question was asked about Labour between July 1994 and November 1996, an average of only 20 percent of respondents agreed that Labour gave the same impression, while an average of 67 percent disagreed.

Given the background of sleaze in its various manifestations, as well as the other difficulties besetting the government, it is not surprising that the Conservative performance in local and European elections, and in parliamentary by-elections during 1994 and 1995 was woeful. In April 1995 Scotland voted for a new set of local authorities. The Conserva-

TABLE 2.5

PERCEPTIONS OF THE CONSERVATIVES AS SLEAZY
AND DISREPUTABLE (IN PERCENTAGES)

	Agree	Dis-agree		Agree	Dis-agree		Agree	Dis-agree
Jan 94	64	29	Apr 95	71	22	Mar 96	71	21
Jul 94	60	29	Jun 95	75	19	May 96	67	25
Sep 94	59	31	Oct 95	67	25	Aug 96	68	27
Oct 94	73	20				Oct 96	61	29
Dec 94	73	21				Nov 96	66	28

SOURCE: *Gallup Political and Economic Index.*

NOTE: These are answers to the question, "Do you agree or disagree with the following statement: 'The Conservatives these days give the impression of being very sleazy and disreputable.'"

tives won only 11 percent of the vote—their worst-ever performance in Scotland—and ended up with only 82 out of 1,161 seats. In May, when all districts in England and Wales outside London held elections, the Conservatives received their lowest-ever share of the popular vote and their seat losses reached staggering proportions. In their analysis of the 1995 elections, Colin Rallings and Michael Thrasher commented that "the Conservative Party, once dominant in local government, now has the appearance of a minor party with many fewer councillors than Labour and even trails behind the Liberal Democrats. Across Great Britain a meagre total of 13 councils, responsible for administering local services for less than 4 percent of the population, are under Tory control."[27]

In December 1994 the Tories lost the Dudley West by-election to Labour on a massive swing of 29 percent. It began to appear that there was no seat, with the possible exception of John Major's Huntingdon, that the Conservatives could successfully defend, and speculation mounted concerning the mortality of Tory MPs and the chances that a combination of deaths and by-election defeats, not to mention defections from their own ranks,[28] could eventually wipe out the government's majority in the House of Commons.[29]

By contrast with local elections and by-elections, the elections for the European Parliament in June 1994 provided an opportunity for the entire electorate to pass judgement on the Conservatives. They ended up with only 27.9 percent of the popular vote—their lowest vote share of the century in a national election—and a mere 18 of the 84 British Euroseats. Labour, on the other hand, achieved its best vote since 1966—

44.2 percent. A clear sign of the scale of Labour's electoral recovery was the fact that the party won six Euro-seats in the South East outside London, a region where it had trailed in third place behind the Liberal Democrats in the 1992 general election. The Liberal Democrats themselves gained a somewhat disappointing 16.7 percent of the vote but could derive consolation from the fact that they won two seats—their first in the European Parliament.

These results were bad enough for the Conservatives, but shortly after the European elections, something even worse occurred. The Labour Party elected a new leader, Tony Blair.

A "New" Opposition: The "Blair Effect"

Although Labour lost the 1992 general election by a substantial margin, lagging 7.5 points behind the Conservatives in terms of vote share, the party had been in much better shape going in to that election than it had been for much of the previous decade. In the early 1980s, in particular, Labour had been wracked by conflict between left and right (with the left usually coming out on top), saddled with a clutch of unpopular policies, and perceived by the electorate as being divided and extreme. In the 1983 election, under a leader, Michael Foot, who was regarded with something approaching derision by a majority of the electorate, and following a notably inept campaign, Labour suffered a humiliating defeat. Under Neil Kinnock, who replaced Foot in October 1983, the authority of the parliamentary leadership was reasserted, unpopular policies jettisoned, campaigning professionalised, Trotskyite infiltrators expelled, and the "hard Left" marginalised. Following another, if less severe, defeat in 1987, a thoroughgoing policy review was also instituted in an attempt to increase Labour's electoral appeal.[30]

Nonetheless, Labour still lost in 1992, and it was widely believed that a contributory factor to the party's defeat was the relative unpopularity of its leader. Although he was more attractive to the voters than Michael Foot had been, Kinnock was never able to shake off the impression that he was something of a lightweight, prone to rambling in interviews and speeches. His rating as a potential prime minister (percentage saying he would be the best minus percentage saying he would be the worst) was −37 compared with +30 for John Major.

Immediately after the 1992 election, Kinnock announced that he would resign as Labour leader, and in July John Smith was elected to replace him. Smith was a Presbyterian Scot who had a reputation for being somewhat staid but solid and reliable—a heavyweight compared to Kinnock. In the month following his election Labour's support in the polls jumped to 43 percent, having stood at only 37 percent in both May and June, and this improvement was sustained. Over the twenty-one months of Smith's leadership, Labour averaged 46 percent in the polls, compared with 30 percent for the Conservatives. That this improvement in Labour's standing was in some measure due to Smith's personal popularity is suggested by the monthly Gallup 9000 data on the electorate's views as to which party leader would make the best prime minister. At the time of the 1992 election, Major outscored Kinnock by 39 percent to 28 percent. Within three months of his taking over as leader, however, Smith overtook Major as the preferred prime minister, and over his term as leader he was preferred, on average, by 32 percent of Gallup's respondents, compared with 22 percent for Major and 20 percent for Paddy Ashdown, the Liberal Democrat leader.

John Smith's sudden death in May 1994 elicited an extraordinary display of public grief and affection and appeared to have robbed Labour of its first widely respected and popular leader for a generation. In July, however, Tony Blair was elected Labour leader, and he proved even more popular. At forty-one, he was the youngest Labour leader ever, and he proceeded to transform the Labour Party and its electoral prospects. Patrick Seyd provides a detailed account of Labour's transformation in chapter 3, but it can be summarised briefly here. Under Blair, the sorts of changes initiated by Kinnock accelerated. The role of the party conference in policymaking was reduced in favour of new policy forums, the influence of trade unions was reduced by decreasing their share of conference voting power, membership ballots rather than activist decision making became standard practice in the constituencies, policy changes moved the party decisively to the right, and the formerly all-conquering left was reduced to impotence. Blair dominated the party with almost unquestioned authority and was, indeed, accused of authoritarianism by left-wing critics.

In his drive to modernise the party and to refashion its image, the success of his campaign to rewrite Clause 4 of the party's constitution was perhaps Blair's most significant achievement. The clause, committing Labour to public ownership, had assumed the status of Holy Writ for many in the Labour Party, but in his first major speech as leader to the party conference in October 1994 Blair totally unexpectedly announced that "it is time we had a clear, up-to-date statement of the objects and objectives of our party." His action seemed bold to the point of rashness. Hugh Gaitskell had sought to amend the clause following defeat in the 1959 election and had been savagely rebuffed. After stumping the country, however, Blair was overwhelmingly supported in constituency membership ballots, and in April 1995 a special party conference approved a new, more anodyne version of the offending clause.[31]

Blair's success in getting rid of the old Clause 4 had little significance in terms of practical policy, but in symbolic terms its significance was enormous.[32] Labour could now depict itself, plausibly, as "New Labour," a transformed party with a modern decision-making structure, new policies, and new leaders. Thanks to Blair, the baggage of the past no longer encumbered the party so heavily.

Tony Blair's accession to the leadership and the changes that he wrought thereafter provided a significant fillip to Labour support. During the last four months of John Smith's leadership (January–April 1994) Labour's support in the polls averaged 48 percent, while from August to December 1994 the average was 56 percent. Although this improvement was partly at the expense of the Conservatives (27 percent January–April; 25 percent August–December), it was more at the expense of the Liberal Democrats (21 percent January–April; 16 percent August–December). Moreover, almost as soon as Blair was elected, he established a commanding lead over his rivals as the party leader thought likely to make the best prime minister. From August to December 1994 Blair was preferred on average by 41 percent of the Gallup 9000 compared with 16 percent for Major and 14 percent for Ashdown. During the next twelve months the figures were 42 percent for Blair, 17 percent for Major, and 13 percent for Ashdown, while for 1996 they were 39 percent for Blair, 19 percent for Major, and 14 percent for Ashdown. Blair's personal ascendancy was a central fact of British politics from 1994 onwards.

It seems clear that there was a genuine "Blair effect," which importantly influenced the pattern of party popularity between 1992 and 1997. This was not the usual kind of random shock—such as Major's supplanting of Thatcher—the effect of which quickly fades. Instead, the effect was sustained through to the 1997 election. In assessing the significance of Tony Blair for Labour's electoral prospects, two points should be borne in mind. First, at each of the three general elections between 1983 and 1992 Labour had been saddled with a leader who was clearly less attractive to the electorate than his main rivals. Second, there is evidence to suggest that as long-term influences on party choice have declined in strength, the qualities, characteristics, and personalities of party leaders have come to figure more prominently among the various considerations that voters have in mind when deciding which party to support.[33] In these circumstances, the knowledge that their leader was popular greatly boosted the morale of Labour politicians, party workers, and loyal supporters.

It is difficult to know with any precision what it is about a party leader that makes him or her attractive or unattractive to voters. Blair was young—he had been in a rock band when he was a student, unimaginable in John Major's case—and telegenic, with a beaming smile; he wore stylish clothes even when casually dressed. Whereas Major appeared grey, old-fashioned, and boring, Blair seemed modern, lively, and exciting. The impact of these sorts of differences on voters is difficult to measure, but some clues to the ways in which they perceived the party leaders are given in tables 2.6 and 2.7. The MORI data from late 1996 (table 2.6) suggest that, despite being seen as relatively inexperienced, Blair was thought to be more capable than Major and was much more widely perceived to have a lot of "personality." Much smaller proportions than in Major's case believed Blair was out of touch with ordinary people, narrow-minded, and inflexible. Gallup data on the personal qualities of the party leaders (table 2.7) tell a similar story, with Blair outscoring Major on every dimension—on being competent, effective, tough, decisive, firmly in charge, likely to unite the country, likeable as a person, and so on. The perceived contrast between Blair and the hapless John Major was almost certainly a substantial electoral bonus for Labour.

Railways, Mad Cows, and Dogs That Didn't Bark

Black Wednesday, tax increases, internal divisions, sleaze, and the emergence of Tony Blair created huge electoral problems for the Conservatives between 1992 and 1997. But they had other problems as well, including the policy of railway privatisation and the crisis over "mad cow disease." In addition, even when their policies appeared to work—as in the case of the economy—they cut no ice among a sceptical and disillusioned electorate.

RAILWAYS

I have already discussed how the salaries paid to "fat cats" brought the policy of privatisation into disrepute. But this was not the only reason for the unpopularity of the privatised utilities. During the summer of 1996, with the election less than a year away, the Yorkshire Water Company came to symbolise all that seemed to have gone wrong with privatisation.

Faced with a drought in the region, the company was unable to keep consumers supplied, despite increased charges, large management salaries, and healthy profits. Water had to be brought in to affected areas in

TABLE 2.6
IMAGES OF PARTY LEADERS, OCTOBER 1996
(IN PERCENTAGES)

	Blair	Major
Understands the problems facing Britain	34	21
A capable leader	33	19
Has got a lot of personality	33	5
Rather inexperienced	27	9
Down to earth	22	16
Has sound judgement	19	11
Tends to talk down to people	11	18
Out of touch with ordinary people	9	47
Rather narrow minded	7	21
Too inflexible	7	19

SOURCE: MORI.

NOTE: Respondents were presented with the above statements and asked to indicate which fitted Mr. Major and which Mr. Blair.

TABLE 2.7
QUALITIES OF PARTY LEADERS, 1996
(IN PERCENTAGES)

	Blair	Major
Caring/not caring	+65	+9
Tough/not tough	+25	−49
Effective/not effective	+38	−46
Can/cannot be trusted	+25	−18
Competent/not competent	+61	−17
Winner/loser	+56	−33
Firmly in charge/not firmly in charge	+27	−60
Decisive/indecisive	+40	−36
Likeable/not likeable as a person	+57	+20
Listens/does not listen to reason	+44	+2
Likely/not likely to unite the country	+20	−67

SOURCE: *Gallup Political and Economic Index,* Reports No. 427, 431.

NOTE: The figures for Blair are from June 1996 and for Major from March 1996. Respondents were asked whether the positive or the negative statement applied to the leader in question. The figures shown are the percentages of negative choices subtracted from the percentages of positive choices.

tankers, and company executives urged the local population to cut down on baths. For weeks on end, the company, and by implication the whole policy of privatisation, was ridiculed and vilified in the media.

The Major government's most significant new privatisation—the breaking up and selling off of British Rail—also did little to restore the electorate's faith in the government's policies. This hugely complex privatisation was vigorously opposed by a pressure group, Save Our Railways, formed for the purpose and, according to polls, was consistently disliked by a large majority of the public. Despite this, and despite misgivings on its own back benches (the Conservative chairman of the Commons Transport Select Committee voted against the privatisation bill in February 1993), the government pressed ahead. In April 1994 Railtrack took over British Rail's stations, signalling, and tracks, and in May 1996 the company was sold to the private sector. Thereafter, franchises to run individual train services were sold to an assortment of companies.

But familiar troubles soon began to appear. Early in 1997 a privatised company, Eversholt Leasing, which rented rolling stock to franchise holders, was sold off at an enormous profit. The managing director, who had invested £110,000 when it was bought from the state, was said to be making £20 million from the subsequent resale, with other directors cashing in on a similar scale. While this was in the news (and being described as "profiteering" by Tony Blair in the House of Commons), South West Rail was cancelling hundreds of train services, to the irritation of thousands of commuters, because it had sacked too many train drivers. In the North West huge job losses were being forecast in two regional railway companies. Astonishingly, the government chose this moment to announce that it intended to privatise the London Underground—although this announcement had previously been delayed because of the unpopularity of privatisation!

The British had had a love–hate relationship with the railways under nationalisation. But the breakup of British Rail into a variety of companies appeared to many people to be lacking in logic or even common sense. The huge costs associated with privatisation could have been invested in the system; the bureaucracy involved in coordination between the companies seemed expensive and wasteful; the lack of integration on ticketing, pricing, and customer enquiries was an irritant. To a large body of opinion, this was a privatisation too far.

MAD COWS

In the mid-1980s "mad cow disease" (bovine spongiform encephalopathy—BSE) appeared among British cattle and was linked to the use of the carcasses of dead sheep in the production of cattle feed. This latter practice was banned in 1989, and despite considerable public unease, government ministers gave assurances that British beef was perfectly safe to eat. In March 1996, however, Stephen Dorrell and Douglas Hogg, the health and agriculture ministers, conceded that there was a possible link between BSE in cattle and Creutzfeld-Jakob disease in humans, and a "beef crisis" ensued. Consumers at home turned away from British beef, while the European Commission imposed a worldwide ban on its export. In the months that followed, the hapless Hogg shuttled hopelessly back and forth between Britain and Europe. The government railed against the ban but, despite some minor relaxations, was unable to get it lifted.

In some ways, "mad cow disease" might be seen as just another piece of bad luck for an unusually accident-prone government. On the other hand, it was the Thatcher government's enthusiasm for deregulation that had allowed dead sheep to be used in cattle feed in the first place, and it was the drive to maximise profits that had encouraged the practice. Moreover, the Major government's handling of the issue appeared weak and indecisive. Its inability to influence its European partners was plain, and the use of threats to disrupt EU business left Britain more isolated than ever in Europe. Consumers and beef farmers were alienated, and the costs of the cull of British cattle instituted by the government led to accusations of money being wasted through incompetence. Hogg had to carry the can. He was pilloried in the media, received a frosty reception at the National Farmers' Union conference, and was the subject of two debates in the House of Commons, when first the Liberal Democrats and then Labour proposed resolutions to cut his salary. Whoever was to blame for the "beef crisis," the government's handling of it confirmed the view, widespread by 1997, that it seemed unable to get anything right.

DOGS THAT DIDN'T BARK

On the country's previous experience of mid-term slumps, John Major's government should have begun to recover as the 1997 election loomed. In fact, nothing that he and his colleagues did seemed to dent Labour's huge lead—not cuts in income tax, not expensive advertising campaigns, not apparently successful party conferences, not Major's successful reelection as Tory leader. Even strikes by railway workers during the summer of 1994 and postal workers in 1996, which would normally have led to an increase in anti-union and hence anti-Labour feeling, failed to change the public's mood.

However, by far the most important dog that didn't bark during the 1992–97 electoral cycle was the economy. Following Britain's withdrawal from the ERM (some would say because of it), and especially under Kenneth Clarke's stewardship, the standard economic indicators steadily improved. Table 2.8 shows that gross domestic product finally exceeded its 1990 level in 1994 and continued to grow thereafter. Inflation rates and mortgage rates were consistently low, and real personal disposable income increased. Perhaps most significantly, the rate of unemployment fell steadily. The number of people counted as unemployed reached a peak of just under 3 million in December 1992. By February 1997 that number had fallen to 1.75 million. Moreover, throughout 1996 the monthly figures for unemployment, gross domestic product, and real personal disposable income all continued to show steady improvement.

Especially as compared with other European countries, the government could—and did—take some pride in the country's economic performance in the latter part of its term of office. Analyses of previous cycles of government popularity and unpopularity have shown that to a large extent they can be explained by fluctuations in the level of economic optimism among the electorate, these in turn being related to the actual performance of the economy.[34] Conservative Party strategists therefore had good reason to expect that favourable economic trends would eventually be reflected in the electorate's "feeling good" and hence in an increase in the government's popularity. But they were not. For reasons to be discussed in chapter 7, the apparent improvement in economic performance completely failed to rescue the government.

TABLE 2.8

ECONOMIC INDICATORS

	GDP	Unemployment rate	Inflation rate	Mortgage rate	RPDI
1992	97.4	9.8	3.7	10.7	102.0
1993	99.6	10.3	1.6	8.1	103.8
1994	103.5	9.3	2.4	7.8	105.1
1995	106.2	8.2	3.5	8.2	108.5
1996	108.6	7.5	2.4	7.5	112.2

SOURCE: Office for National Statistics, *Economic Trends, Annual Supplement 1996–97.*

NOTE: In all cases the figures shown are annual monthly averages.
   GDP = gross domestic product at factor cost, 1990= 100.
   Unemployment = seasonally adjusted percentage of the workforce defined as unemployed. The current definition is used to estimate the whole series.
   Inflation rate is the percentage increase in the Retail Price Index compared with the same month in the previous year.
   Mortgage rates are based upon the lending rates of selected retail banks; for 1996 the figure is the average from January to May.
   RPDI = Real Personal Disposable Income, 1990 = 100.

Conclusion

All British governments become unpopular; the perils of government await any incoming party. Governing successfully is probably more difficult today than it once was (although it is a salutary thought that the 1945–50 Labour government had to cope with the dissolution of the Empire and the postwar settlement in Europe as well as enormous domestic pressures). Relentless media attention and pressure, and the globalisation of the world economy and financial markets, give rise to major problems for modern governments in their attempts to placate an electorate that appears increasingly difficult to satisfy. Even so, the Major government proved singularly unable to restore its fortunes after the ERM disaster. The emergence of Tony Blair, internal divisions, sleaze, and assorted policy failures were enough to ensure that the real improvements in the economy no longer worked their old electoral magic. But there is another factor to consider. When the Conservatives were hammered in the Wirral South by-election at the end of February 1997, the scale of their defeat confirmed that, apart from all the other considerations, the electorate was simply weary of them. The government was almost visibly floundering, and the voters appeared to have decided that it was, at long last, time for a change.

Notes

1. Quoted in Alan Doig and John Wilson, "Untangling the Threads of Sleaze: The Slide into Nolan," *Parliamentary Affairs* 48 (October 1995): 568.
2. Helen Thomson, "Economic Policy under Thatcher and Major," in *Contemporary British Conservatism,* edited by Steve Ludlam and Martin Smith (London: Macmillan, 1995), 172.
3. Ibid., 172–73.
4. *The Times,* 11 September 1992.
5. For further discussion of the effect of Black Wednesday on public opinion, see Ivor Crewe, "Electoral Behaviour," in *The Major Effect,* edited by Dennis Kavanagh and Anthony Seldon (London: Macmillan, 1994), 107–10.
6. See David Butler and Dennis Kavanagh, *The British General Election of 1992* (Basingstoke: Macmillan, 1992), chap. 6.
7. See David Sanders, "Why the Conservative Party Won—Again" in *Britain at the Polls 1992,* edited by Anthony King (Chatham N.J.: Chatham House, 1993), 205–7.
8. *Daily Telegraph,* 6 December 1996.
9. David Baker, Imogen Fountain, Andrew Gamble, and Steve Ludlam, "The Blue Map of Europe: Conservative Parliamentarians and European Integration," in *British Elections and Parties Yearbook 1995,* edited by Colin

Rallings, David Farrell, David Denver, and David Broughton (London: Frank Cass, 1995), 51.

10. In the words of Steve Ludlam, the conference "feasted on anti-European Commission jibes, delivered to noisy cheers by Michael Portillo." See Steve Ludlam, "The Spectre Haunting Conservatism: Europe and Backbench Rebellion," in Ludlam and Smith, *Contemporary British Conservatism,* 115.

11. For an account and analysis of the Conservative leadership election, see Philip Cowley, "The 1995 Conservative Leadership Election," *Politics* 16 (May 1996):79–86.

12. Geoff Evans has shown that Conservative divisions on Europe lost them support, even though the electorate became more Eurosceptic between 1992 and 1996. Voters who were pro-European were alienated by the Europhobes in the Conservative Party, while anti-EU voters were alienated by the Europhiles. Increasing Conservative Euroscepticism could have been an electoral asset, but divisions in the party turned it into a liability. See Geoff Evans, "Euroscepticism and Conservative Electoral Support, 1992–96: How an Asset Became a Liability," paper presented at CREST conference on "Understanding the Next Election," October 1996.

13. Patrick Dunleavy and Stuart Weir with Gita Subrahmanyam, "Public Response and Constitutional Significance," *Parliamentary Affairs* 48 (October 1995):603.

14. Doig and Wilson, "Untangling the Threads of Sleaze," 573.

15. *Guardian,* 3 June 1996.

16. See Roger Mortimore, "Public Perceptions of Sleaze in Britain," *Parliamentary Affairs* 48 (October 1995).

17. An account of the Hamilton-Greer affair is given in David Leigh and Ed Vulliamy, *Sleaze: The Corruption of Parliament* (London: Fourth Estate, 1997). Aitken also sued the *Guardian* for libel, but when the case was heard, after the 1997 election, evidence was produced that disproved his version of events. Aitken withdrew his action and resigned as a privy councillor amid calls that he should be prosecuted for perjury.

18. See Dawn Oliver, "The Committee on Standards in Public Life: Regulating the Conduct of Members of Parliament," *Parliamentary Affairs* 48 (October 1995).

19. *Sunday Times,* 5 November 1995.

20. *The Times,* 22 November 1994.

21. *The Times,* 17 January 1995.

22. *The Times,* 2 February 1995.

23. *Sun,* 19 January 1993.

24. *The Times,* 8 February 1995.

25. *The Times,* 7 July 1995.

26. *Guardian,* 17 February 1996.

27. Colin Rallings and Michael Thrasher, *Local Elections Handbook 1995* (Plymouth: Local Government Chronicle Elections Centre, 1995), v.

28. Four Conservative MPs defected to other parties during the Parliament: Alan Howarth (to Labour) in October 1995, Emma Nicholson (to the Liberal Democrats) in December 1995, Peter Thurnham (to Independent and

later the Liberal Democrats) in February 1996, and George Gardiner (to the Referendum Party) in February 1997 following his deselection as candidate by his local Reigate association.

29. See Philip Cowley, "Marginality, Mortality and Majority: The Effect of By-elections on Government Majorities," *Politics* 15 (May 1995): 89–95.

30. See Eric Shaw, *The Labour Party since 1979* (London: Routledge, 1994).

31. *Guardian* cartoonist Steve Bell parodied the content of the new Clause 4 as "To secure for the many the choice for responsible partnership in casting out discriminatory unpleasantness. To stand firm in solidarity against sin in a kind of fullish sort of work opportunity society just insofar as and for as long as that's all right with the few."

32. See Tim Bale, " 'The Death of the Past': Symbolic Politics and the Changing of Clause IV," in *British Elections and Parties Yearbook 1996,* edited by David Farrell, David Broughton, David Denver, and Justin Fisher (London: Frank Cass, 1996).

33. See Anthony Mughan, "Party Leaders and Presidentialism in the 1992 Election: A Post-War Perspective," in *British Elections and Parties Yearbook 1993,* edited by David Denver, Pippa Norris, David Broughton, and Colin Rallings (Hemel Hempstead, Herts.: Harvester Wheatsheaf, 1993).

34. See David Sanders, "Forecasting the 1992 British General Election Outcome: The Performance of an 'Economic' Model," in Denver, Norris, Broughton, and Rallings, *British Elections and Parties Yearbook 1993.*

3

Tony Blair and New Labour

Patrick Seyd

The new Labour Party is a different political party, not only in its policies but also in its structures.

> — Tony Blair, *Money Programme,* BBC2, 25 September 1995

There has been a revolution inside the Labour Party. We have rejected the worst of our past and rediscovered the best.

> — Tony Blair, *Independent,* 5 July 1996

I did not come into this Labour Party to join a pressure group. I didn't become leader of this party to lead a protest movement. Power without principle is barren, but principle without power is futile. This is a party of government or it is nothing, and I will lead it as a party of government.

> — Tony Blair, Report of the Labour Party special conference,
> 29 April 1995

On all fundamental issues that affect our lives and our society, New Labour has adopted policies that cannot be supported by those who call themselves socialists.

> — Arthur Scargill, *Guardian,* 15 June 1996

In his leader's speech to the 1995 Labour Party conference, Tony Blair used the word *new* on fifty-nine occasions, sixteen of them with reference to "New Labour." In contrast, he referred to socialism just once and to the working class not at all. A distinctive political project was in the making. Just fifteen months after his election as leader, Blair was engaged in initiating changes to his party more fundamental than any since Labour adopted a new constitution and programme in 1918. By the time the Labour Party was elected to government in May 1997 it had a new constitution, new policies, new internal structures, and a new image. The party had been changed out of all recognition. A revolution had occurred in British party politics more significant than anything since the Conservative Party's postwar adaptation to social democracy.

Since Labour's crushing electoral defeat in 1983, the party had been engaged in change, first of its organisation and then of its policies. By the time of the 1992 general election the party had abandoned all those policy commitments that had been reckoned to have cost it votes in 1983, such as the extension of public ownership, commitment to unilateral nuclear disarmament, restoration of trade union collective bargaining rights, and withdrawal from the European Community. Neil Kinnock bequeathed to John Smith, Labour's new leader after its 1992 election defeat, a party committed to the market economy. Whether the party's electoral defeat in 1992 had been due primarily to Kinnock's unpopularity with the voters, to Smith's proposals, as shadow chancellor, to impose a 50 percent tax on all incomes over £40,000 per annum and to extend the national insurance levy on incomes over £22,000 per annum, or to campaign mistakes such as the Sheffield rally and the "Jennifer's ear" election broadcast, was open to dispute within the party; but Smith's opinion was that further fundamental changes to the party were unnecessary.

John Smith's Leadership

Smith had been overwhelmingly elected as leader in the immediate aftermath of the party's 1992 defeat.[1] His only major rival for the post had been Bryan Gould, whose campaign was based upon the need for the party to rethink radically both its structure and its electoral strategy. In contrast, Smith's campaign reflected the man—a rather cautious, pragmatic social democrat committed to redistribution. In his election address he asserted that the principles on which the party had fought the 1992 election had been correct. He reaffirmed the party's commitment to social justice and the need for the burden of tax to be shared more fairly. Recognising, however, the dilemmas facing a party committed to universal social welfare, he proposed that the nature of the balance between universal and selective welfare benefits, and how progressive taxation could attract public approval, should be the subject of a wide-ranging review. And on the question of the relationship between the party and the trade unions he stated that "Labour must not and will not sever its links with the trade union movement."[2] Smith was closely associated with the "one final heave" school of thought that believed Labour could win the next election with little change to party policies. His period as party leader between July 1992 and his sudden death in May 1994 was one in which Labour capitalised upon the Conservatives' political misfortunes and appeared to be on course for eventual electoral success.[3] Future electoral victory seemed further assured by the party's relatively harmonious intraparty relations, largely generated by Smith's encouragement of younger colleagues and his inclusive style of political leadership, in which he was willing to transcend previous personal and political differences. For example, Margaret Beckett's previous left attachments were seen as no barrier to her becoming deputy leader. There were only the faintest murmurings of discontent at his leadership from a group of party modernisers who felt that there was no guarantee of firm voter support and noted that individual party membership had dropped since the election. But such critical murmurings were at the margins: overall, the modernising project initiated by Kinnock was deemed to have reached its zenith.

After four consecutive general election defeats, however, the last after an economic recession between 1990 and 1992 from which the Labour Party might have been expected to reap real electoral benefits, perhaps more fundamental change was necessary to reassure the voters of the party's governing capabilities. Certainly the party's director of communications, David Hill, appeared to take such a view. After private polling immediately following the 1992 general election and again at the end of that same year revealed that, among wavering Conservative voters, the Labour Party was regarded as "too old fashioned, too tied to the past, too linked to minorities rather than majorities, and too associated with old images of the trades unions,"[4] Hill wrote that the party lacked clear identity and was "the party of the past."[5] The view that, notwithstanding any opinion poll leads Labour might gain, the party would not win an election unless it reassessed itself in a fundamental manner was held among a group of party modernisers, including Tony Blair, Gordon Brown, Harriet Harman, Peter Mandelson, and Philip Gould. The 1992 defeat confirmed these modernisers' view that fundamental changes were necessary.[6] Their target included both the left and the right of the party. Harold Wilson, James Callaghan, Tony Crosland, and Tony Benn were all equally identified with the flawed politics of old Labour. In Blair's view, "Labour needed a quantum leap to become a serious party of government again."[7] His project, as first publicly articulated in his 1995 party conference speech, was to eradicate all aspects of party doctrine and ethos, of policies and strategies, that were of the past.

The lead that Blair gave to this modernising project should not be underestimated. The process of political change in the Labour Party had commenced after the 1983 electoral debacle when, on assuming the party leadership from Michael Foot, Neil Kinnock had reminded his party to "remember at all times . . . how you . . . felt on that dreadful morning of

10 June. Just remember how you felt then and think to yourselves: 'June the Ninth 1982 [*sic*]; never again will we experience that.' "[8] This drive to restore the party's electoral fortunes motivated Kinnock in his internal party reforms, particularly the expulsion of the extreme left-wing Militant Tendency prior to the 1987 election and then the policy review after the further defeat.[9] The changes then introduced had enabled Mandelson to claim as the party's director of communications in 1990 that "we have now effectively completed the building of the new model party."[10] That idea would have remained in place, and the party would have altered little before 1997, but for the election of Blair as party leader in 1994.

Blair as Party Leader

Blair was elected with a convincing majority in all three sections of the party.[11] He had first been elected to the House of Commons in 1983, and in his early years as an MP he had been identified with the "soft" left of the party. Elected to the shadow cabinet in 1988, he became the party's energy spokesperson and from there was promoted to assume responsibility for employment and later for home affairs. His political profile, however, beyond the confines of Parliament was limited. For example, only 3 percent of party members, when asked in 1992 who should replace Neil Kinnock as leader, suggested Tony Blair.[12] After eleven years in opposition, and after the electoral successes of both Bill Clinton and the Australian Labor party, Blair had developed into a convinced moderniser believing that only a moderate, left-of-centre, pro-European party, independent of the trade unions, would be elected to office. But within the group of modernisers Gordon Brown was regarded as the senior figure. In 1992 he had topped the shadow cabinet elections for the third time in four years and, in the same year, at his first attempt, came third in the National Executive Committee (NEC) elections, while Blair followed in fifth place. Nevertheless, after Smith's sudden death Tony Blair had no hesitation in seeking election as his successor, and somewhat reluctantly Gordon Brown, after meeting with his friend and hitherto modernising subordinate, formally withdrew.[13]

In his biography of the Labour leader, John Rentoul suggests three reasons why Blair became the modernisers' leadership candidate rather than Brown. First, Blair's impressive parliamentary performances as shadow home secretary, when he succeeded in wresting the inbuilt Conservative advantage in penal affairs towards Labour by stressing the need to be "tough on crime and tough on the causes of crime," won admiration. Second, Brown's performance as shadow chancellor was perceived by many of his parliamentary colleagues as too cautious, too financially orthodox, and too austere. Brown suffered through his unwillingness to commit the party to full employment or to make public spending commitments and also through his attachment to the ERM, where only Norman Lamont and the Conservative government's problems masked Labour's own difficulties. According to Rentoul, Brown "sacrificed his prospects of becoming leader on the altar of monetary rectitude."[14] Third, Blair's greater prominence in advocating a one-member, one-vote party structure won him support beyond his initially small group of parliamentary colleagues.[15]

For the first time, the new party leader and deputy leader were to be elected by one person, one vote with Labour MPs and members of the European Parliament, individual party members, and political levy payers within the affiliated organisations, mainly the trade unions, making up the three parts of the electorate. The three leadership candidates—Blair, John Prescott, and Beckett—revealed few policy differences in their campaigns. The differences that did emerge were mainly ones of style, with Blair emphasising the case for a dynamic market economy, Prescott stressing the need for collective, state action to attain the goal of full employment, and Beckett reaffirming the importance of social cohesion and unity.[16] A sense of the underlying apprehension among some left-wingers at Blair's political agenda was revealed by Michael Meacher. Writing in *Tribune*, he argued that the party could win elections only "by inspiring people with a strong and clear vision of a different and better society." He wanted the new leader to make specific commitments to a statutory minimum wage fixed at 50 percent of male, median earnings and higher taxes on those earning more than £60,000 a year.[17]

Blair may have worried some of the party's left-wingers, but he certainly attracted strong support from among newspaper editors and columnists. For example, a leader writer in the *Guardian* argued that

> Tony Blair's strengths complement but transcend those of John Prescott. He, too, is innovative and willing to confront real problems. He is a good communicator, relaxed with the media and modern culture, able to appeal to people well beyond Labour's core constituency. But these virtues . . . are only useful extras. His strongest claim is that he has systematically rethought the basis of Labour's appeal and project in the light of modern imperatives and realities. He is the only candidate in this election who has attempted to redefine the nature and boundaries of the party itself. His recent speeches and published statements place the progressive project on an ethical and practical basis which combines the agenda of the immediate present with a tradition of socialist value-based thinking which can be

traced from Winstanley through Owen, Morris and Tawney to contemporary communitarian ideas.[18]

Support such as that led to accusations that Blair was the media's
candidate, a view reinforced by the fact that he had few links or attachments to either the labour movement or its traditions. He was young,
forty-one, when he became party leader, not yet a teenager when Wilson
formed his first Labour cabinet in 1964, and only just out of university
when Callaghan's government lost office in 1979. He had been brought
up in a Conservative family and had attended a public school and then
Oxford. In that he differed little from other past Labour leaders, except
that Blair made little attempt to involve himself in the labour movement
by becoming active in either local government or trade unionism. Defending trade unions as a young barrister in employment law disputes
was the closest he came to the traditional labour movement as he progressed via a by-election candidature in 1982 into Parliament as the MP
for Sedgefield in County Durham in 1983. An angry public outburst six
months after Blair's election from Ken Coates, a Labour MEP and a man
steeped in Labour history and politics, in which he stated that "He
[Blair] is, quite simply, a Liberal. . . . This young man has not the faintest
idea of how socialists think, and does not begin to understand the men-
tality of the party which he has been elected to lead,"[19] reflects the considerable sense of suspicion among older party stalwarts about their
leader. In contrast, John Smith, although a university graduate and a barrister closely identified with the right of the party, had been immersed in
Labour traditions and was therefore more easily accepted.

Blair was the first postwar Labour Party leader to make so public
and explicit the link between his practising Christianity and his political
beliefs. His Christianity and his attachment to family and community are
the basis of his political ideas. For him, the family is the basic building
block of society and, if the family is strengthened, then so will be the
community. He has written that

> it is largely from family discipline that social discipline and a sense of re-
> sponsibility is learnt. A modern notion of society—where rights and re-
> sponsibilities go together—requires responsibility to be nurtured. Out of a
> family grows the sense of community. The family is the starting place.[20]

Blair has also placed considerable stress upon individual rather than collective interests. He has argued that society has a responsibility and a
duty to give people the hope of a better life, but in return individuals
have a responsibility and duty to the community. Family, community, re-

sponsibility, and duty have not been the most familiar terms in the political rhetoric of previous Labour leaders, and in that sense the voters in Labour's new electoral college, whether or not they were aware of it at the time, had taken a decision of considerable consequence in choosing such a young outsider to lead them. And it was not long before the radical nature of their decision became apparent.

Blair's first significant initiative as party leader came shortly after his election when he chose to tackle the most symbolic of party icons —Clause 4 of the party constitution—the one that had remained immune to the efforts of one of his predecessors, Hugh Gaitskell, to reform.[21]

The Revision of Clause 4

April 29, 1995 will become the day when Labour turned itself into a social democratic party.

— Roy Hattersley, *Guardian,* 27 April 1995

Since 1918, the only policy objective enshrined in Labour's constitution had been contained within a subsection of one of the constitution's fifteen clauses, known simply and universally as Clause 4. This committed the party to "secure for the workers by hand or by brain the full fruits of their industry and the most equitable distribution thereof that may be possible upon the basis of the common ownership of the means of production, distribution and exchange, and the best obtainable system of popular administration and control of each industry or service."[22] Notwithstanding the ambiguities contained in the clause, which reflected the contrasting motives of those engaged in rewriting the party constitution in 1918,[23] equality, common ownership, and industrial democracy had clearly been defined as party objectives. The extent of the party's attachment in practice to Clause 4 should not be exaggerated. Nevertheless, until the 1950s there was a broad consensus in the party that public ownership was an essential part of its programme. Once the major utilities had been nationalised by the postwar Labour government, however, a debate opened up over whether public ownership should be extended and, if so, which particular industries should be taken over. Even though Hugh Gaitskell failed in his bid to drop Clause 4 from the party's constitution in 1959, public ownership by the 1960s appeared to be of only limited practical importance. The party's election manifestos between 1964 and 1970 contained few specific nationalisation commitments.[24] The Labour left's temporary political ascendancy in the 1970s and early

1980s resulted in election manifestos more assertive of the benefits of public ownership in general and more specific about industries to be nationalised.[25] Between 1964 and 1979 Labour governments still regarded state intervention and ownership as the means to restructure parts of the steel, shipbuilding, ship-repairing, aerospace, and motor industries. All the same, Labour's crushing electoral defeats in 1983 and again in 1987 meant that by the time of the 1992 election the party had retreated from any commitments to public ownership.

As Gaitskell discovered in 1959, Clause 4 was a potent political symbol, not central to the party's policymaking or electioneering but not easily jettisoned. After the party's fourth successive defeat in 1992, however, a few individuals argued that it should be dropped. Jack Straw published a pamphlet devoted entirely to arguing that it should be rewritten, Giles Radice proposed that the clause be revised as part of the party's updated electoral strategy, and a senior trade union leader, Bill Jordan of the Amalgamated Union of Engineering Workers, said it should be removed.[26]

At the close of his first leader's speech to an annual conference in 1994, Blair, without mentioning Clause 4 by name, nevertheless suggested that it was time for the party to adopt an up-to-date statement of its objectives. Hardly had he sat down when press officers made certain that the media understood that reform of this particular clause was what he had in mind. The audacity of his challenge to the party's most important symbolic totem is confirmed when one remembers that delegates to the 1993 conference had reaffirmed their commitment to Clause 4; and only two days after Blair's 1994 speech delegates agreed, albeit by a narrow margin, that "the popular objective of public ownership be fully incorporated into the party's policies."[27] Some of those most actively involved in the party saw no need for any constitutional rethink. Nor did delegates who attended their local party general committees after Blair had delivered his speech. By the end of the year, *Tribune* reported that fifty constituency Labor parties had voted to retain Clause 4. Much of the opposition to change was grounded in the conviction that common ownership should remain one of Labour's core beliefs.[28] Furthermore, with Labour well ahead in the opinion polls, it was argued that Blair's proposal was both badly timed and irrelevant; it was not an issue raised on the doorsteps by voters.[29] Nevertheless, a problem for Blair's opponents was that they were divided between those wanting no change and those admitting the need for some form of update alongside the original clause.[30] For example, both *Tribune* and the *New Statesman,* initial opponents of change, combined in publishing a possible new version.[31]

In response to this opposition, which by the end of 1994 seemed to be gathering support and momentum, Blair bypassed the more committed activists and appealed directly to the individual membership. In this, as throughout the total exercise, John Prescott's support was of considerable importance, since he remained the authentic voice of old Labour within the leadership. Prescott had been closely consulted about the proposed change in the summer months before the 1994 conference, and now he and Blair prepared a consultation document, *Labour's Objects: Socialist Values in the Modern World,* that was the basis on which the campaign for change was based. Blair then had a questionnaire sent out to every local party branch, affiliated trade union, and socialist society, and had it enclosed in an issue of *Labour Party News,* asking for opinions on Labour's aims and values. The badly designed and unwieldy questionnaire produced just over 8,000 responses. These revealed that, although there was clear evidence of dissatisfaction with Clause 4, because it did not place enough stress on equality and social justice as key values and ignored various themes such as democracy, opportunity, and the environment, a significant number of CLPs nevertheless were content with it.[32]

Apart from this postal consultation, Blair over the four months between January and April 1995 addressed some 30,000 party members at thirty-five meetings. Rather than rely on the trade union bloc vote to see him through, Blair went directly to the individual membership to argue his case.

Finally, prior to the special party conference that had been arranged to debate the new constitution, party members were sent a paper ballot asking them whether or not they agreed with the proposed new clause on Labour's aims and values. Party headquarters then released in the days just before the conference the results of a selected number of CLP ballots (136 out of 500+), all favourable to change. Considerable pressure was also brought to bear on opponents of change in the trade unions—primarily the leaderships of Unison and the Transport and General Workers' Union—who were accused of being undemocratic. They had not held ballots and were therefore unrepresentative of their rank-and-file membership.[33] This last tactic involved criticism of the notion of delegatory democracy, on which the British labour movement had historically been based, and revealed the first signs of the new leadership's commitment to a form of plebiscitarianism that would be developed further during the next two years.

Seven months after Blair's original proposal to rewrite Clause 4, the party agreed, at the special conference held in London on 29 April 1995, to a new five-part clause, entitled *Labour's Aims and Values,* which defined the party's democratic socialism as follows:

1. The Labour Party is a democratic socialist party. It believes that by the strength of our common endeavour we achieve more than we achieve alone, so as to create for each of us the means to realise our true potential and for all of us a community in which power, wealth and opportunity are in the hands of the many not the few, where the rights we enjoy reflect the duties we owe, and where we live together, freely, in a spirit of solidarity, tolerance and respect.

2. To these ends we work for:

A dynamic economy serving the public interest, in which the enterprise of the market and the rigour of competition are joined with the forces of partnership and co-operation to produce the wealth the nation needs and the opportunity for all to work and prosper, with a thriving private sector and high quality public services, where those undertakings essential to the common good are either owned by the public or accountable to them;

A just society, which judges its strength by the condition of the weak as much as the strong, provides security against fear, and justice at work; which nurtures families, promotes equality of opportunity and delivers people from the tyranny of poverty, prejudice and the abuse of power;

An open democracy, in which the government is held to account by the people; decisions are taken as far as practicable by the communities they effect; and where fundamental human rights are guaranteed;

A healthy environment, which we protect, enhance and hold in trust for future generations.

3. Labour is committed to the defence and security of the British people, and to co-operating in European institutions, the United Nations, the Commonwealth and other international bodies to secure peace, freedom, democracy, economic security and environmental protection for all.

4. Labour will work in pursuit of these aims with trade unions, co-operative societies and other affiliated organisations, consumer groups and other representative bodies.

5. On the basis of these principles, Labour seeks the trust of the people to govern.

Ninety percent of the local party delegates present at the conference, and two-thirds of all the delegates, voted for "a thriving private sector" and for the trade unions to be placed on a par with other organisations in society rather than being accorded any special status. Substantial support had been given to changes that marked a significant shift from almost eighty years of party history and doctrine.

Much was made at the time—and has been since—of the overwhelming support for change among the party's individual membership.[34] In the 1995 ballot, 73,288 (85 percent) voted for the proposed new clause and only 12,588 (15 percent) against. Less notice was taken of how few members participated. Only 27 percent bothered to vote, out of an individual membership of 320,000,[35] suggesting that many were either uninterested, uncertain about the importance of the entire debate, or of the opinion that the old clause was purely symbolic.

Electoral Strategy

New Labour will be a government of the radical centre.... A modern party, to be successful in the modern world, must be in the centre speaking for the mainstream majority.

Tony Blair, speaking to the British-American Chamber of Commerce in New York, *Guardian,* 12 April 1996

Be under no illusion. It was New Labour wot won it.

Tony Blair, speaking to the first meeting of the newly assembled PLP, *Guardian,* 8 May 1997

Immediately after the party's defeat in 1992 the Fabian Society commissioned a study of white-collar and skilled manual workers in southern England. These were "swing" voters in the sense that they had voted Conservative but had seriously considered voting Labour. The results showed that these voters had been "scared off voting Labour because of their distrust of its general competence and its ability to manage the economy."[36] They were hostile to the party's commitments to income redistribution, higher taxation, support for the trade unions, and its failure to emphasise achievement and standards in education. The report argued that, on electoral grounds, a new Labour Party was needed that would appeal to upwardly mobile voters, one that would be seen to encourage individual talent and opportunity and would stress opportunity for all rather than equality of outcomes.

The Fabian research, and similar focus-group research commissioned for the Labour Party by Philip Gould, which concentrated upon these "swing" voters, provided the basis for the election strategy devised by Blair and his close team of advisers. The party's target voters were to be those in "middle income, middle Britain,"[37] a shorthand term capturing the essence of a socioeconomic and spatial strategy aimed at moving the party away from its traditional concentrations of support among manual workers in solidly industrial communities. The strategy was to appeal to voters with economic and social aspirations rather than to the poor and disadvantaged. Labour would aim to represent the great majority of the public, not an assemblage of minorities.

In addition to this qualitative research among Labour's formerly "missing millions," note was also taken of Bill Clinton's success in 1992, when he successfully forged a new identity for the Democratic Party. Gould argued that Clinton had listened to disillusioned Democratic voters and had modified his policies to ensure that such voters returned to their traditional home.[38] References to Clinton's successful electoral strategy were dismissed by Blair's critics as "the Clintonisation of the Labour Party."

Moderation and caution were the essence of New Labour's appeal to the voters. Both were reflected in the five specific but very limited pledges that the party guaranteed to honour if returned to office. These were to cut class sizes to thirty or under for five- , six- , and seven-year-olds; to speed up punishment for persistent young offenders by halving the time taken from arrest to sentencing; to cut NHS waiting lists by treating an extra 100,000 patients by saving money in the health service spent on bureaucracy; to take 250,000 young people off benefits and into work by using money from a "windfall" levy on the privatised utilities; and, finally, to set tough rules on government spending and borrowing.

Further to these limited promises, many of the party's other policies were transformed in the drive to appeal to middle-income, middle Britain. Two areas in particular, where the leadership felt the party was particularly vulnerable, were its high-tax image and its close links with the trade unions.

Taxation and the Economy

... we are pledged not to raise the basic or top rates of income tax throughout the next Parliament.
New Labour Because Britain Deserves Better, 1997

For the next two years Labour will work within the departmental ceilings for spending already announced.
New Labour Because Britain Deserves Better, 1997

Throughout the period between the 1992 and 1997 elections Gordon Brown remained shadow chancellor and dominated economic policy-making. His shadow cabinet colleagues were forbidden from making any public spending commitments, and those who attempted to challenge his financial orthodoxy found themselves with new portfolios.[39] Whatever the particular economic policy differences within the party, and whoever his critics were, Brown's views almost always prevailed. Disputes occurred over whether to replace the six-month job seekers' allowance with a twelve-month unemployment benefit; whether to withdraw the payment of child benefits to some sixteen- to eighteen-year-olds; whether to levy a tax on employers to pay for youth training; whether to raise the level of state pensions by linking them to earnings rather than to prices; whether to fix a particular level of the minimum wage; and, finally, whether to expand employment opportunities. Some of his shadow cabinet colleagues, ex-senior party figures like Roy Hattersley and Barbara Castle, and some from *Tribune* left, made efforts to force a change in his policies but to little or no avail.

Brown's economic strategy was predicated on the assumption that the party was constrained by two factors: one international, globalisation; the other domestic, taxpayer revolt. Globalisation would restrict a Labour government's ability to control and direct capital and, in particular, to use public expenditure to stimulate growth in employment. The voters' dislike of high taxes would restrict its redistributive objectives. Faced with these pressures, Brown was more intent on controlling inflation in order to improve Britain's economic competitiveness than on expanding employment. Whereas in 1993, in *Labour's Economic Approach,* he had argued that there needed to be a balance between supply-side and demand-management policies, increasingly as time went on he placed more emphasis upon supply-side economics.[40]

Labour's postwar social democracy had been based upon Keynesian macro demand management combined with progressive taxation and redistributive public expenditure.[41] The first of these commitments had been undermined by Denis Healey as Labour's chancellor of the exchequer in the mid-1970s, and Brown now proceeded to withdraw from the other two. Brown believed that tax and spend had been the "double whammy" that had cost Labour the 1992 election. Four months before the 1997 election Brown announced that a Labour government would neither increase rates of income tax in the lifetime of a Parliament nor would it alter the Conservative government's spending commitments during its first two years in office. The election manifesto also made it clear that public spending was no longer regarded as the means to resolve economic and social problems by stating that "the level of public spending is no longer the best measure of the effectiveness of government action in the public interest."[42] Read in conjunction with David Blunkett's assertion that "any government entering the twenty-first century cannot hope to create a more equal or egalitarian society simply by taking money from one set of people and redistributing it to others,"[43] it revealed a view of social democracy far removed from that expounded even five years earlier. Unlike in 1945, New Labour was not offering the public a radically new political economy. The Thatcherite project would remain in place. Market individualism was the orthodoxy for Brown and his shadow Treasury team, not the egalitarianism of the past.

This fundamental shift in the party's economic thinking did not go unchallenged. Critics included trade union leaders Bill Morris and John Edmonds and Labour MPs Roy Hattersley, Roger Berry, Peter Hain, and Bryan Gould.[44] They argued that the party should retain its traditional Keynesian approach and be prepared to use a combination of public expenditure and taxation to generate employment and redistribute wealth. But a general belief in the party that a "culture of contentment" prevailed among the electorate enabled Brown to prevail. Brown's determined stance made it almost impossible for the Conservative Party to launch the kind of electoral onslaught on Labour that it had in 1992.

The Trade Unions and the Labour Party

Labour's second area of potential vulnerability was its close links with the trade unions. Blair's strategy, therefore, was to distance the party from the unions by insisting that no special relationship with the unions existed and by making no effort to woo trade union leaders; the trade unions would be consulted by a future Labour government only in the same way as other groups. Blair used every opportunity to make it clear that if Labour came to power the unions would receive "fairness not favours."[45] Not surprisingly, this strategy caused tensions, and differences of opinion emerged between trade unionists and the party leadership on a range of issues including the priority to be given to expanding employment, the level of any future minimum wage, whether the privatised rail network would be renationalised, and whether employers should have to pay a compulsory levy to fund industrial training. The party leadership's refusal to support trade unions in individual industrial disputes caused further aggravation. David Blunkett's proposal, in 1996, to introduce binding no-strike agreements for public-sector workers further cooled the somewhat frosty relationship between the leaders of the political and industrial wings of the movement.

A series of internal party reforms affecting the party-union relationship made the task of demonstrating to swing voters that Labour had distanced itself from the unions all the easier. The most significant came in February 1993 when John Smith proposed at an NEC meeting that the trade unions' collective presence in the party should be ended, both for the election of the party leader and for the selection of parliamentary candidates. Instead, trade unionists should participate in party affairs only as individual members. His original idea was that the party leader should be elected by an electoral college in which the votes would be divided equally between MPs and individual members with no trade union involvement. Later, however, in the face of opposition, he proposed that trade unionists who were individual party members would be given a place in the electoral college. Smith's new proposal again ran into considerable union opposition, and with the trade unions' share of the vote at the annual party conference at that time still standing at 70 percent, there was every likelihood of its being defeated. After an intense summer of conflict at the trade union conferences, only a variety of compromises and procedural devices enabled the change to be introduced. John Prescott's role in securing the reform was considerable: first, by proposing that individual trade union levy payers should be entitled to join the party as full members at a reduced rate of subscription (the levy-plus proposal); and, second, by making an impassioned speech at the party's annual conference demanding that delegates back their leader. Smith was further assisted by a last-minute delegation decision of the Manufacturing, Science and Finance Union to abstain in the crucial conference vote, and by the linking of the introduction of all-women short lists for parliamentary selections in safe Labour seats with the trade union issue.[46]

In the future selection of parliamentary candidates and party leaders, trade unionists would be one part of the party but would not be in any position to dominate it. As an inducement to the recruitment of individual members, the party agreed in 1993 that, once membership reached 300,000, the relative balance of trade union and CLP votes at the party conference would be reviewed. So at the 1995 conference the existing 70:30 ratio of trade union and CLP votes was altered to a 50:50 ratio. By reducing to 50 percent the collective voting strength of the trade unions at the party's annual conference, the trade unions had become in the eyes of the party leadership a limited asset rather than an electoral liability.

Further Policy Developments

By making these changes to its taxing and spending policies and its relationship with the unions, the party leadership hoped to reassure voters that it was safe to vote for change. In further moves aimed at reassuring middle-income, middle Britain, Labour introduced policies that emphasised its commitment to improving pupils' standards of performance and discipline in schools, to maintaining law and order by adopting punitive policies to deal with convicted criminals, and to reducing welfare dependency by treating welfare benefits as a means to work rather than a permanent right. As a result, regular testing of pupils and the publication of school league tables, the preservation of grant-maintained schools, the adoption of a zero-tolerance policy towards young offenders and stricter punishment for serious repeat offenders, a proactive employment service to help single parents off benefits, and schemes to encourage unemployed people back to work were all proposals included in the party's election manifesto. Much of the Conservative Party's political clothing was stolen in the bid to reassure voters that a vote for change would not be a vote for instability or political lunacy.

One area of policy, however, where clear water did emerge between Labour and its Conservative opponents was constitutional reform. Labour had always in the past adopted a deeply conservative position on the state and its institutions, essentially wanting to capture but not to transform the British state. During the 1990s, however, a significant shift occurred, with the party becoming committed to major reform. Labour now proposed to abolish the right of hereditary peers to sit in the House of Lords, to devolve powers to Scottish and Welsh assemblies, to introduce a Freedom of Information Act, to incorporate the European Convention on Human Rights into law, and to hold a referendum on the future of the electoral system.

The shift in policy was remarkable. During most of the late 1980s and early 1990s, conventional wisdom among the Labour leadership appeared to be that constitutional reform was an issue of interest only to the "chattering classes" and therefore of little electoral significance. There are a variety of explanations for this transformation. One is that Labour had been out of power for so long that it developed a greater interest in dispersing power more widely in the political system, and it viewed the workings of the British state with a greater detachment than in previous times. Another is that, with the abandonment of social democracy, Labour had little to offer in the economic and social field; institutional reforms provided a substitute sense of radicalism, required to satisfy part of its electoral constituency. A further explanation is the powerful impact that those campaigning for institutional reform, notably Charter 88, had upon a section of the public and the party. Among those campaigning for institutional reforms, Will Hutton's voice was perhaps the most persuasive; his argument that economic success was closely linked to political modernisation, and that too many characteristics of an *ancien régime* prevailed in Britain, was taken seriously.[47] It certainly suited Blair during the 1997 campaign to portray the Conservatives as part of an *ancien régime* unable and unwilling to modernise the country.

A strategy of convincing the voters of the party's governing competence involved developing policies in the manner just referred to, but it also necessitated eliminating any traces of the 1980s "loony left" syndrome. There were to be no loose cannons, whether in the PLP, among parliamentary candidates, or in Labour-controlled local authorities. Discipline was to be imposed at all levels of the party, an objective not easy to achieve given the fragmented structures and habits of dissent that had prevailed in the past. Effective party management was made even more important by the fact that a major feature of Conservative propaganda was the insistence that, while Blair might be the moderate face of Labour, stalking in the background were extremists who would take over again if the party were ever elected.

Internal Party Reorganisation

We have member power now. We are not block-vote driven, not unrepresentative-activist driven, not MP driven. We're membership driven.
— Peter Mandelson, *New Statesman,* 24 January 1997

My absolute priority is that we get away from the position where you had small groups of people not representative of the party at large trying to run the show.
— Tony Blair, *Daily Telegraph,* 30 January 1997

Blair made much of the fact during the election campaign that he had modernised his party. He had, but the party reorganisation that occurred was more than a public relations exercise. It was an important feature of the modernisers' political project that they wished to change the party from one that they believed had been talking to itself and had been dominated by activists and locked into the past into one that was modern, outward-looking, and a part of the community. The party should be linked more closely to the community and should not be dominated by unrepresentative activists. Blair's own constituency party in Sedgefield was a perfect model.[48]

Much of the literature on parties in western Europe assumes the inevitable decline of their individual membership and their shift towards more professional, electoral organisations dominated by party leaders and bureaucrats in which the party members are unimportant.[49] In fact, the number of individual Labour Party members rose from 266,000 in 1993 to more than 400,000 in 1997. Critics claimed that the Labour Party increasingly became an autocracy under Blair. Strict control of the party all the way from Parliament down to local authorities and the local branches prevailed. Annual conferences were ruthlessly stage managed. The policies announced by the leadership often ran counter to previous commitments, with little prior consultation.[50] Perhaps, but the opportunities for consultation and participation by the membership became far greater under Blair's leadership. Blair was the first party leader to be elected by a ballot of all individual party members and political levy payers. Members were balloted for their views on both the reform of Clause 4 and the party's 1997 manifesto. Organised question-and-answer sessions were arranged around the country, involving Blair and Prescott and ordinary party members. For the first time in the party's history, political education was given both a high profile and the commensurate resources, with large numbers of members participating in political education events.[51] Not least, the possibilities for real debate on the party's policies were extended with the establishment in 1993 of a National Policy Forum.

Ensuring party unity was a major priority, and both the shadow cabinet and the PLP were run in a strictly controlled manner from 1994 onwards. In his choice of potential cabinet colleagues, Blair had little room for manœuvre because the PLP elected his shadow cabinet and there was almost no turnover between 1992 and 1997. His only real freedom of choice lay in allocating shadow portfolios. This freedom he used to distance Robin Cook from economic affairs; to appoint David Blunkett, with views similar to his own on schooling, to education; and to demote Michael Meacher, one of the few remaining critics of the modernisation programme.

With regard to the management of the PLP, Blair's powers were strengthened when in 1995 it agreed to the appointment rather than the election of the chief whip. In addition, a new set of standing orders, introduced in 1996, ensured that it was to be "a serious, professional and disciplined organisation."[52] It would be an offence for any Labour MP to do anything that would bring the party into disrepute (though an amendment was also accepted that the new standing orders would not be interpreted "in such a way as to stifle democratic debate on policy matters or weaken the spirit of tolerance and respect referred to in Clause Four of the Labour Party constitution").[53] On the one hand, the party leadership clearly wished to introduce stricter controls over the backbenchers; on the other hand, both the shadow cabinet and the PLP demonstrated the most extraordinary unity during these years. The scars of the early 1980s, when the party had torn itself apart, had left a permanent mark. The voicing of public disagreements, so long a Labour tradition, gave way to a disciplined silence. Most Labour MPs were desperate for victory. But the price of such strict discipline was a clampdown on discussion of important issues: for example, the future of the monarchy, the legalisation of soft drugs, and the possibility of higher rates of income tax.[54] Even some moderates felt the clampdown was excessive.

In party management terms, the National Executive Committee was no longer a problem. Neil Kinnock had downgraded its policymaking role in the 1980s, and after 1992 Smith and Blair reinforced the dominant role of the parliamentary party and, especially, the shadow cabinet. While the NEC remained formally responsible for party policy in opposition, a newly established Joint Policy Committee, made up of equal numbers from the NEC and the shadow cabinet, with additional representation from the European Parliamentary Labour Party and the party in local government, became the significant policymaking body. Six policy commissions (covering democracy and citizenship, economic affairs, environment, social policy, equality, and foreign affairs and security) reported to it; in addition, the National Policy Forum acted as the first stage of consultation, and the last stage of ratification, before policy documents were submitted to the annual conference. These new procedures and institutions were all part of an attempt to create a more informal, more discussion-based and less rule-bound party culture. Tom Sawyer, appointed as party general secretary when Blair became leader, was committed to the changes. The new procedures nevertheless offered considerable scope for elite domination of the policy process. Only a small and diminishing hard left consistently voted against the leadership on the NEC.[55]

Where the NEC did remain significant was in its use of its powers to control parliamentary candidates both at by-elections and for the general election. At by-elections an NEC subcommittee drew up the short list of candidates for local party consideration, ensuring that only candidates able to withstand media pressure and sympathetic to New Labour politics were available for selection by local members. The NEC ensured, for example, that a National Union of Mineworkers' sponsored candidate, and therefore someone associated with Arthur Scargill, was not short-listed for the Hemsworth by-election, even though he had local party support. The NEC also used its powers to refuse to endorse locally selected general election candidates in Leeds North East (Liz Davies) and

Exeter (John Lloyd). Finally, the NEC determined the short lists in seven
constituencies where the sitting Labour MP anounced his resignation immediately before the general election, leading to the suspicion that this
had been done to ensure the election of certain "Blairites."[56]

One other reform of long-term significance for the nature of the PLP
was the agreement at the 1993 party conference that women should fight
50 percent of the most winnable Labour seats and those where Labour
MPs were retiring. To make sure this happened, women-only short lists
were to be introduced where appropriate by local parties. The decision
was the culmination of a long campaign, not by the modernisers, but by
many female Labour activists. Women-only short lists provoked considerable opposition in some of the more traditional parts of the country,
however, and two male party members eventually succeeded in winning
a ruling by a Leeds Industrial Tribunal in 1996 that the policy was contrary to the 1975 Sex Discrimination Act. Even so, 159 women stood as
Labour candidates at the election.

From the moment of Blair's election as leader, the party's individual
membership started to grow—a significant achievement when contrasted
with the drop that occurred following the 1992 election (see figure 3.1)
and with the spiralling decline in Conservative Party membership.

Various claims have been made about these new members. They
have been described as "armchair supporters" and "distinctly old Labour in their views on policy,"[57] as "upwardly mobile yuppies, reminis-

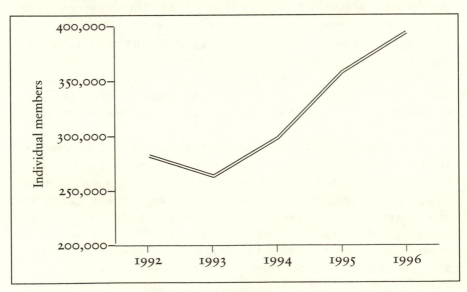

FIGURE 3.1

INDIVIDUAL LABOUR PARTY MEMBERSHIP, 1992–96

cent of the old SDP, save that they now clutch mobile telephones rather than filofaxes,"[58] and as "increasingly middle class [and] inactive."[59] There is no firm evidence for any of these claims.[60] But the increasing use of membership ballots both to elect party personnel (leader and deputy leader, parliamentary candidates, and constituency representatives on the NEC) and to affirm party policies (Clause 4 and the election manifesto) is predicated on the belief that individual members will be more representative, and perhaps more malleable to leadership promptings, than party activists.

To some extent under Blair a tension developed between two very distinct models of grassroots party. One was the "electoral-professional" party in which policymaking and campaigning were increasingly professionalised and run by MPs and full-time officials, and members' role was to assist in centrally directed and targetted election campaigning, with the opportunity to participate in member ballots as their reward. This is very much a top-down model. The other was the "grassroots-campaigner" party in which education and campaigning in communities was carried out by party members. This possibility was represented by the party regeneration project initiated in 1994, which resulted in the expansion of the party's political education activities, referred to earlier, and was about "changing the Labour Party . . . about making [it] a campaigning party . . . [in which] branches attract members to attend lively policy discussions. . . ."[61] This is a more bottom-up model of party politics. Which model will prevail with Labour now in power remains to be seen.

Conclusions

By failing to win in 1992 the Labour Party undermined a common political assumption that no government could preside over a deep economic recession and be reelected. Voters then had taken other factors into account in casting their ballots, notably each party's degree of managerial competence. On this criterion Labour suffered in comparison to the Conservatives. Reestablishing its governing credentials was therefore Labour's first priority under both John Smith and Tony Blair. Both men recognised the necessity of reassuring both the financial markets and the voters. Whereas, however, Smith, apart from eliminating the trade unions from their collective role in electing party leaders and selecting parliamentary candidates, demonstrated no further commitment to fundamental reform, believing that the party as it stood could exploit the Conservative government's electoral weakness, Blair felt wholesale party change was essential. Blair wanted to retain power as well as attain it, and this required reforms in both institutions and policy. The sharp drop in Conservative support following Black Wednesday, along with John Major's permanent difficulties in maintaining Conservative Party unity, made it likely that Labour even under John Smith's leadership would have won in 1997, but not by a landslide. Blair's success lay in transforming the Labour Party in such a manner as to convince hundreds of thousands of voters that the party was now both competent to govern and safe to support. Blair's New Labour project was based on a mixture of belief and fear: on the one hand, belief in free markets, private enterprise, individual choice, "family values," and law and order. On the other hand, fear of the Conservatives' ability to frighten voters of the consequences if they voted Labour and fear of the Conservative press. The leadership's fears were reflected in an election campaign in which the party leadership rigidly adhered to its predetermined positions, in particular on taxation, public expenditure, law and order, and welfare, and in which it appealed more to the voters' desire for a change after eighteen years of Conservative governments than stimulating their desire for something radically different. And the party at all levels, from individual members to MPs, from trade union leaders to members of the NEC, were all so hungry for victory that they were willing, over almost a whole Parliament, to submit to this single-minded regime. Once elected to power, the challenge is whether Blair and his colleagues can put aside those fears and implement the beliefs in such a manner that New Labour does in fact lead to new Britain.

Notes

1. Smith won 90.9 percent of the votes in the electoral college. Margaret Beckett was elected deputy leader with 57.3 percent of the vote.
2. See John Smith's election manifesto, *New Paths to Victory*, 9.
3. In May 1994 Labour's opinion poll lead over the Conservatives was 19.5 percent (Labour 36.0, Conservatives 17.5).
4. *Guardian*, 6 June 1992.
5. *Guardian*, 5 January 1993.
6. See Jon Sopel, *Tony Blair: The Moderniser* (London: Bantam, 1995), chap. 7; John Rentoul, *Tony Blair* (London: Little, Brown, 1995), chap. 11.
7. *New Statesman*, 19 April 1996.
8. *Report of the Annual Conference of the Labour Party*, 1983, 30.
9. For an analysis of the party's changes between 1987 and 1992 see Patrick Seyd, "Labour: The Great Transformation," in *Britain at the Polls 1992*, edited by Anthony King (Chatham, N.J.: Chatham House, 1993): 70–100.
10. *Guardian*, 16 February 1990.

11. Blair won the election with the votes of 52.30 percent in the affiliated organisations section, 60.55 in the MPs and MEPs section, and 51.17 percent in the individual party member section. John Prescott was elected deputy leader.

12. In 1992 Paul Whiteley and the author reinterviewed the party members first interviewed in 1990. The results of those interviews were published in Patrick Seyd and Paul Whiteley, *Labour's Grassroots: The Politics of Party Membership* (Oxford: Clarendon Press, 1992). For further details of the 1992 survey, see Paul Whiteley and Patrick Seyd, *The Dynamics of Party Change* (Ann Arbor: University of Michigan Press, forthcoming).

13. For a detailed description of the events immediately following Smith's death and Blair's decision to stand as party leader, see Sopel, *Tony Blair,* chaps. 8 and 9, and Rentoul, *Tony Blair,* chaps. 16 and 17.

14. Rentoul, *Tony Blair,* 268.

15. This claim is debatable, since Brown had been involved in attempts to reform the party since the late 1980s and had written a pamphlet (*Making Mass Membership Work*) advocating one member, one vote in 1993.

16. See, in particular, Tony Blair's personal manifesto, *Change and National Renewal.*

17. *Tribune,* 22 July 1994.

18. *Guardian,* 2 July 1994.

19. *Daily Telegraph,* 13 January 1995. Colin Leys stresses that Blair's personal upbringing and relationship with the Labour Party is vital to an understanding of Labour's politics. See "Labour versus Labour," *Red Pepper,* February 1996, 21–24.

20. Quoted in Rentoul, *Tony Blair,* 292.

21. On the importance of symbols in party behaviour, see Tim Bale, "Symbolic Politics and the Changing of Clause 4," in *British Elections and Parties Yearbook 1996,* edited by David Farrell, David Broughton, David Denver, and Justin Fisher (London: Frank Cass, 1996), 158–77.

22. Clause IV(4), *The Constitution of the Labour Party,* Labour Party 1994.

23. See R. Harrison, "The War Emergency Workers' National Committee, 1914–1920," in *Essays in Labour History 1886–1923,* edited by Asa Briggs and John Saville (London: Macmillan, 1971), 257.

24. Steel, water supply, and building land in 1964; a regional ports authority in 1966; and a national port authority in 1970.

25. Labour's election manifesto in February 1974 specifically referred to ship building, ship repairing, ports, airframes and aero engines, and sections of the pharmaceuticals, road haulage, construction, machine tools, and oil industries. Even banking, insurance, and building societies were mentioned as being considered.

26. Jack Straw, *Policy and Ideology,* Blackburn Labour Party, 1993; Giles Radice, *Southern Discomfort,* Fabian Society, September 1992; *Guardian,* 28 April 1992.

27. *Report of the Annual Conference of the Labour Party,* 1994, 199. Blair admitted in a later interview that the proposal to reform Clause 4 had been "a hell of a risk." *Guardian,* 1 May 1995.

28. See, for example, the advertisement placed by 32 Labour MEPs in the *Guardian,* 10 January 1995.

29. "I would not have chosen to rewrite Clause 4 at this point in the electoral cycle." Clare Short, *Guardian,* 12 January 1995.

30. Articulated by the Keep Clause Four Campaign.

31. *Tribune,* 11 November 1995.

32. Of the 210 CLPs responding to the questionnaire, 49 disagreed with the statement that "the current Clause IV does not set out Labour's actual values in a clear and concise manner." *Labour's Aims and Values: The Consultation Report,* Labour Party, 1995.

33. A MORI poll, published in the *Today* newspaper the day before the special conference met, claimed that 66 percent of TGWU members supported the move to rewrite Clause 4. No details were provided of how the sample of trade union members had been selected. *Today,* 28 April 1995.

34. For example, "Ninety percent of the party membership approved the change [to Clause 4]." Tony Blair, *Guardian,* 19 September 1996.

35. According to Peter Coleman, Labour's national organiser, this was the membership figure at that time. See *Tribune,* 31 March 1995.

36. Radice, *Southern Discomfort,* 5.

37. Tony Blair, *Guardian,* 25 February 1995.

38. Patricia Hewitt and Philip Gould, "Lessons from America: Learning from Success—Labour and Clinton's New Democrats," *Renewal* 1, no. 1 (January 1993):45–51.

39. Chris Smith was moved from Social Security to Health in 1996.

40. In 1993 the party had argued that "the key stimulus to investment is of course the prospect of growing demand. To pretend that supply side measures alone are sufficient to secure the level of investment that Britain needs is to neglect this basic fact." *Labour's Economic Approach* (London: Labour Party, 1993), 10.

41. See Eric Shaw, *The Labour Party since 1945* (Oxford: Blackwell, 1996), chap. 8.

42. *New Labour Because Britain Deserves Better* (London: Labour Party, 1997), 11.

43. David Blunkett, Julius Silverman Memorial Lecture, 20 February 1997.

44. "New Labour must not assume that lower taxes are the automatic path to power. . . . It will not win in 1997 unless it is clearly identified with the better Britain which crucially depends on improved education, health and infrastructure. Those improvements cost money. On the evidence of the British Social Attitudes Survey, the British people are certainly willing (and possibly anxious) to pay the bill through their taxes. It would be strangely self-destructive for Labour to deprive them of that opportunity. The party leadership ought to build on the national inclination to finance improved services by arguing the case for higher taxes on top incomes." Roy Hattersley, *Guardian,* 28 November 1995. See also R. Berry and P. Hain, *Labour and the Economy* (London: Tribune Publications, 1993); and Bryan Gould, *Guardian,* 10 February 1994.

45. Speech to the Trades Union Congress, September 1995.

46. The conference agreed to individual votes from affiliated organisations by 48.926 to 48.127; to one member, one vote for parliamentary selections by 47.509 to 44.388; and to quotas for women by 53.840 to 34.923. *Report of the Annual Conference of the Labour Party, 1993*, 179.

47. For example, "Britain's production problem and state structures are at the heart of the present malaise . . ."; and "Bills of rights, constitutional reform and proportional representation are not ends in themselves—they are means of attacking the economics and politics of exclusion upon which the British state is founded." Will Hutton, *Guardian*, 19 July 1993.

48. See Peter Mandelson and Roger Liddle, *The Blair Revolution* (London: Faber, 1996), chap. 9.

49. A. Panebianco, *Political Parties: Organization and Power* (Cambridge: Cambridge University Press, 1988).

50. The most consistent advocate of the autocracy argument has been the political commentator of *Tribune*, Hugh Macpherson. A good example of the switching of policy without prior consultation would be Scottish devolution and, in particular, the leadership's announcement that the party would hold two referendums, one on the principle of devolution and the other on the taxing powers of a Scottish assembly.

51. Between 1994 and 1997 political education meetings were held in various parts of the country. New members, in particular, were invited and attendances were very often around 400 to 500. The emphasis at these meetings was on small-group discussions, giving everyone the opportunity to discuss party policies in detail.

52. Tony Blair, *Guardian*, 5 December 1996. The new standing orders were proposed by the PLP Review Committee in its report *Preparing for Government*.

53. *Guardian*, 5 December 1996.

54. Clare Short was one who suffered from this disciplined regime, leading to her public attack on Blair's political advisers ("the people who live in the dark"). See *New Statesman*, 9 August 1996.

55. Among the constituency party representatives on the NEC only Dennis Skinner and Diane Abbott were consistent critics.

56. Doug Hoyle (Warrington North), John Evans (St. Helens North), Geoffrey Lofthouse (Pontefract and Castleford), John Gilbert (Dudley East), Stuart Randall (Hull West), William McElvey (Kilmarnock and Loudoun), and Norman Hogg (Cumbernauld and Kilsyth) all retired with such short notice that the NEC invoked its special powers. A notable moderniser, however, who failed to make the selection short lists in any of these constituencies was Jack Dromey, husband of Harriet Harman.

57. Sarah Baxter, *New Statesman*, December 1995.

58. *Tribune*, 28 July/14 August 1995.

59. *Independent*, 4 January 1997.

60. An ESRC-funded study of new Labour members is currently being conducted by the author and Paul Whiteley.

61. *Active Labour: Towards 2000*, Labour Party Regeneration Project, 1994, 1.

4

The Conservative Party: "In Office but Not in Power"

Philip Norton

The results of the general election in April 1992 surprised many Conservatives as much as they dismayed most Labour politicians. The Conservative victory at the polls appeared to confirm the wisdom of the parliamentary party in replacing Margaret Thatcher with John Major. The Major government was seen by electors as new, and John Major had proved to be something of a Teflon prime minister during his first sixteen months of office.[1] He had had a good Gulf War. He had helped negotiate a treaty on European union at the intergovernmental conference at Maastricht that his party could live with, thereby achieving an outcome that probably could not have been achieved by his predecessor. His vigorous campaign during the general election—taking his message to the people and delivering speeches from a soapbox—was derided by some commentators but attracted praise after the results were announced. With the return of a Conservative government for an unprecedented fourth term, with an overall majority of twenty-one, the stature of the prime minister appeared to be confirmed. Some commentators expected another five years of Conservative government to create a crisis for the Labour Party while the Conservatives prepared the ground for economic recovery and a possible fifth term.

In the event, the new Parliament heralded five years of almost unremitting gloom for the Tories. While Labour began to regroup, emerging afresh as New Labour, the Conservatives regressed into a state almost of "Old Conservative," resembling the party during the early years of the century when it was riven internally by divisions over free trade. The party trailed in the opinion polls for virtually the whole of the Parliament, experienced bitter feuding within its own ranks, and staggered from one crisis to another. John Major frequently came under attack from some of his own backbenchers and actually resigned his leadership in 1995 in order to force an election, which he contested and won, though not by an overwhelming margin. The Queen described 1992 as an *annus horribilis* (horrible year, or "bum year" in the translation of one tabloid headline writer) for the royal family. For the Conservative Party, every year from 1992 onwards proved to be an *annus horribilis*. There was no respite from internal divisions and almost universal unpopularity.

By the beginning of 1997, with an election imminent, party members were dispirited and expecting defeat. If the Labour Party's lead in the opinion polls fell below 20 points it was regarded as a success, albeit one rarely achieved. Given that the Conservatives needed to be ahead by several points to retain office with an overall majority, few saw cause for optimism. Shortly before Parliament was dissolved in March 1997, one junior minister seeking reelection in a marginal seat met a newspaper's political editor in one of the corridors of the House of Commons. "Good-bye," said the junior minister, "I shan't be seeing you again. I won't be coming back." His view was shared by many others; and he, and they, were right.

What Went Wrong?

What explains the Conservative Party's sudden fall from public favour and its consistent unpopularity during the lifetime of the 1992 Parliament? Was it, as many of his critics suggested, the result of poor leadership by John Major, or was it something more fundamental to the Conservative Party? Or was it simply a matter of bad luck, being in office at a time of deep and extended economic recession?

To explain the party's unpopularity, one has to look to the reasons for the party's previous success. The Conservative Party has a record of unparalleled success in British electoral politics.[2] For most of the period of modern mass politics, it has been the "in" party in Britain. There are several explanations for this success. It has been fortunate in its opponents, who have split at times opportune for the Conservatives (as with the Liberals over Home Rule at the end of the nineteenth century and over Lloyd George's leadership early in this century, and the Labour Party over public expenditure cuts in 1931). It has benefited at times from the prevailing climate of expectation (as in 1979). But perhaps most fundamental has been its capacity to convey to the world that it is a party of governance. The party has always emphasised its capacity to govern and this emphasis was central to the party's appeal in the 1980s. It was not so much Thatcherism—the philosophy espoused by party leader Margaret Thatcher—that made the party so electable during that decade but rather Margaret Thatcher as an individual and her style of leadership.[3] Electors did not always agree with Thatcherite policies, but they were prepared to support a government that appeared competent and knew what it wanted to achieve.

What, then, are the essential attributes of a party of governance? Four essential components stand out. One is being competent in handling the affairs of the nation, especially its public finances. This does not necessarily mean delivering prosperity, at least not immediately, but it does mean demonstrating what electors regard as a "safe pair of hands" in dealing with the problems facing the nation. It entails knowing what policies to pursue and, equally if not more importantly, knowing what policies not to pursue.[4] The party came close to jeopardising this claim to competence in 1990 with the introduction of the community charge (the poll tax) but regained its position by abandoning both the tax and the leader responsible for its introduction.

The second component is that of unity. Electors do not reward divided parties. The Conservative Party has split on a number of occasions but has traditionally appeared a party united on the essential aims of Conservative governments. It has rallied round at times of difficulty and especially in the period leading up to a general election. The desire for office has generally been a powerful incentive to unite. This has traditionally been contrasted with the position in the Labour Party, where the desire to be right rather than in office has predominated. Electors have consistently viewed the Labour Party as more divided than the Conservatives.

The third component is that of strong leadership. The Conservative Party places particular emphasis on the role of the leader.[5] The leader is the fount of all policy within the party. Leading positions within the party are within the gift of the leader. The leader is expected to lead, imparting a sense of direction. If things go well, the leader is praised. If things go badly, the leader is blamed. Though strong leadership can generate tensions within the party, as under the premierships of Edward Heath (1970–74) and Margaret Thatcher (1979–90), the Tory preference is for strong rather than weak leadership. Margaret Thatcher's strong leadership and her capacity to impart a sense of direction appeared to resonate with electors and indeed with her opponents, many of whom wanted a leader who could lead in a similar style (and they appeared to be rewarded when Tony Blair was elected Labour leader in 1994). The leader is expected to listen—a failure to do so may result in a leadership challenge (as happened to Margaret Thatcher in 1989 and 1990)—but is also expected to act.

The fourth component is public service. The members of the party in government are there to serve their constituents and their country, not themselves. Benjamin Disraeli, during his leadership of the party from 1868 to 1881, transformed the party from a sectional into a national party, appealing to all sections of society. He extended the appeal of the party beyond that of the privileged to the working class. The concept of the Tory paternalist has been a notable feature of British politics, the Tory grandee serving to ameliorate the condition of the workers. Conservatives in positions of public office have viewed public service as a duty and have conducted themselves according to largely unwritten rules of conduct. Some rules have found expression in writing—for example, motions of the House of Commons forbidding acceptance of money for raising issues in Parliament—but most have not. When Conservatives in government appear to depart from the standards expected of them, with MPs appearing out of touch, arrogant, or keen to pursue personal gain, this fact in itself contributes to electoral unpopularity. The closing years of the Macmillan premiership (1957–63) suffered from perceptions of a government that seemed arrogant and out of touch, with some members behaving in ways that attracted the headlines.[6]

When these four components have come together, the Conservative Party has been in a strong position; when combined with a weak opposition, as in 1983, the electoral rewards have been substantial. The problem for the party in the period from 1992 to 1997 was, brutally, that none of the four components was present.

First, the party effectively lost its appeal as a party of governance, doing so early in the life of the Parliament following Britain's ignominious withdrawal from the European Exchange Rate Mechanism (ERM) in September 1992. The effect was to prove both deep and lasting. The events of the Parliament appeared to confirm that the party had lost its traditional skill of managing effectively the nation's affairs.

Second, the party lost its image as a united party, principally—indeed, almost exclusively—because of deep and continuing divisions over European integration. The 1992 European Communities (Amendment) Bill, to ratify and give effect to certain provisions of the Maastricht treaty, served to emphasise those divisions, later superseded by debate over a single European currency.

Third, the leadership of the party was a subject of continuing debate. The prime minister was frequently accused of following, rather than leading, and the political agenda appeared to be set by his critics within the party. Following his dismissal as chancellor of the exchequer in 1993, Norman Lamont made a damning resignation speech, accusing the government of giving the impression of "being in office but not in power."

And, fourth, as we saw in chapter 2, the government was beset throughout the Parliament by scandal affecting both ministers and government backbenchers.

These developments, coupled with a Labour Party that was transformed into a "new" and seemingly electable party, rendered the Conservatives unpopular and on a consistent and unprecedented scale. Throughout the Parliament, the situation rarely improved and, more often than not, worsened. When the prime minister announced on 17 March 1997 that a general election was to be held on 1 May, there seemed little that could save the Tories from disaster at the polls.

Let us, then, explore—and explain—the elements of Conservative unpopularity. Each—the departure from the ERM, splits over Europe, controversy over the leadership, and scandals (subsumed under the heading of "sleaze")—can be taken in turn, not least because they occurred roughly, though not precisely, in that order.

Departure from the ERM

The circumstances of Britain's ignominious departure from the ERM have already been described, and there is no need to go into detail here.[7] When the House of Commons was recalled for a two-day debate on 24 and 25 September—one day to discuss the economic crisis, the other to discuss the Bosnian crisis—it was the first time the House had been specially recalled since sitting on a Saturday morning in 1982 to discuss the Argentinian invasion of the Falkland Islands. The new Labour leader, John Smith, in his first speech at the dispatch box as leader of the opposition, delivered a powerful attack on the government, following a lacklustre speech by the prime minister.

Withdrawal from the ERM, and the manner of its announcement —a "pale and drawn"[8] chancellor of the exchequer rushing out on to a pavement in darkness at 7.45 P.M.—was a humiliation for the government. Membership of the ERM had been the cornerstone of its economic policy, and it was now without a policy. Sterling was left to its own devices and depreciated over the following weeks. Interest rates, which had been scheduled to increase to 15 percent, were reduced and soon fell further. An interest rate reduction, however, did little to affect the public's reaction to the government's withdrawal from the ERM.

Indeed, if one had to identify a single event that destroyed public confidence in John Major's government, it was the suspension of Britain's membership of the ERM. Until that point, the Conservative Party had been seen by electors as a competent party in handling the affairs of the nation, more competent than Labour. As David Sanders has argued, that perception of competence was an important electoral resource, particularly at times of uncertainty. "From the time of the ERM crisis in September 1992, that resource appears to have dissolved."[9] As Sanders observes, it is not clear whether the ERM crisis itself provoked a change in perception or whether it triggered a change that, as a result of three years of recession, was waiting to happen. Whichever, Conservative support in the polls plummeted.[10] Economic optimism collapsed, and the percentage of respondents who approved of the government's record to date was halved; so too was the proportion expressing satisfaction with the prime minister (see table 4.1). As David Denver says, respondents now judged Labour as the best party to handle the economy, a reversal of the normal position. For the rest of the Parliament, the gap between the two parties remained substantial.

The government seemed incapable of regaining its claim to competence in economic affairs. It had no obvious policy to succeed the ERM. Some ministers favoured rejoining the ERM as soon as possible; others, including the chancellor, preferred to stay out. Various other measures undermined public support. To counter a massive budget deficit, various taxes were raised. As chancellor, Norman Lamont in 1993 announced the imposition of Value Added Tax (VAT) on domestic fuel, to take ef-

TABLE 4.1

THE IMPACT OF BLACK WEDNESDAY

(IN PERCENTAGES)

	Jun–Aug 1992	Oct–Dec 1992	Change	Jan–Dec 1993
Percentage satisfied with the prime minister	49	25	−24	23
Percentage saying Major would make best prime minister	41	23	−18	20
Percentage who "approve of the government's record to date"	30	15	−15	14
Optimism index about "general economic situation"[a]	−3	−27	−24	−4
Optimism index about "financial situation of your household"[a]	0	−13	−13	−8

SOURCE: Gallup polls, reproduced in Ivor Crewe, "Electoral Behaviour," in *The Major Effect*, ed. Dennis Kavanagh and Anthony Seldon (London: Macmillan, 1994), 109.

a. Percent replying will get "a lot better" or "a little better" minus percent replying will get "a little worse" or "a lot worse."

fect in two stages—a rate of 8 percent and then one of 17.5 percent. This constituted only one of a total of nineteen tax increases introduced in the Parliament;[11] it was also the most unpopular. To counter extensive criticism, including that from Conservative backbenchers, the chancellor announced measures to offset the cost of the increase to senior citizens. The tax nonetheless remained unpopular, and in the 1994 budget debate the Opposition tabled a motion designed to prevent the second-stage increase going ahead. The government lost the vote by 319 votes to 311, 10 Conservatives voting with the Opposition and a further 13 abstaining.[12] The government accepted the defeat and cancelled the second-stage increase. The chancellor of the exchequer, Kenneth Clarke, then returned to the House to present a minibudget. Though there was popular support for the cancellation of the VAT increase, the manner in which it was achieved further undermined the government's standing in the polls.

The government's actions were compounded by what was seen as insensitivity on the part of ministers. At a time of economic uncertainty, even many people with jobs felt insecure. During 1992 many small businesses had collapsed, unable to cope with high interest rates. In 1993 house prices fell, leaving many homeowners with negative equity (paying interest on a mortgage that was more than their house was now worth). Despite saying at the time of the 1992 general election that there were no circumstances in which he could envisage increasing VAT, John Major presided over a government that found itself forced to increase VAT. When put under pressure by the Opposition to apologise, ministers adopted a defensive posture. At one point, the prime minister commented that there was "no gain without pain."

The comments that attracted the most negative reaction came from Norman Lamont. Not only did he admit to "singing in his bath" at Britain's withdrawal from the ERM. When he was asked at a by-election press conference if he regretted what he had done as chancellor, he replied "Je ne regrette rien." Despite calls for his dismissal, John Major retained him in office for another nine months following Black Wednesday. Lamont was only dismissed, following a media campaign against him, in May 1993—he refused to take another, lesser office—and on 9 June he made a bitter and devastating resignation speech. "There is something wrong with the way in which we make our decisions," he declared. "The Government listen too much to the pollsters and the party managers.... As a result, there is too much short-termism, too much reacting to events, and not enough shaping of events. We give the impression of being in office but not in power."[13] Thereafter, he criticised government policy from the backbenches and considered challenging Major for the leadership. His successor as chancellor, Kenneth Clarke, proved a popular figure, and economic indicators improved significantly during the remainder of the Parliament (in April 1993, one month before Lamont's dismissal, the inflation rate fell to its lowest level since 1964); but those improvements failed to make inroads into popular perceptions of a government that had lost its claim to be a competent party of economic management.

Europe

The issue of European integration constitutes the permanent fault line of British politics. It has done so ever since the end of the Second World War. Both major parties have been split on the issue.[14] At times, it has lain dormant—but rarely for long. The eruptions have sometimes been seismic, as in 1972 at the time of the debate on Britain's entry into the European Community. Another such seismic eruption occurred in 1992, and the volcano continued to erupt for the rest of the Parliament.

THE MAASTRICHT BILL

The seismic eruptions were not foreseen at the beginning of the Parliament. The treaty on European union negotiated at Maastricht in 1991 had been hailed as a success for John Major, achieving concessions for Britain (such as an opt-out on a single European currency) and the inclusion of the principle of subsidiarity, with decisions to be taken at the most appropriate level, rather than automatically in Brussels. Following Conservative success in the 1992 election, the government expected to achieve the necessary legislation without too much difficulty.

The Queen's Speech at the opening of the Parliament, on 6 May 1992, signalled the government's commitment to "lay before Parliament the treaty of Maastricht and introduce a bill to implement it."[15] Within a matter of days, ministers introduced a short, three-clause bill, the European Communities (Amendment) Bill, more commonly known as the Maastricht Bill. Although criticised by a number of Eurosceptic Conservative MPs opposed to further European integration, the bill achieved its second reading on 21 May by a comfortable majority. The House rejected an Opposition amendment by 360 votes to 261 and then gave the bill its second reading by 336 votes to 92.[16] Twenty-two Tories joined with dissident Labour MPs to vote against it.

The bill's committee stage was scheduled to begin on 4 June, but on 2 June the Maastricht treaty was rejected in a referendum in Denmark. The following day, the government decided to postpone the committee stage pending clarification of the legal and practical implications of the

Danish vote. The prime minister conceded that some form of report should be made to the House before the committee stage was resumed; on 8 June the foreign secretary, Douglas Hurd, said that the government accepted that there should be a debate on the implications of the Danish referendum before the bill was discussed again in committee.

The Danish vote emboldened Conservative critics of European integration. The day after the "no" vote in Denmark, 69 Conservative MPs—approximately one-fifth of the membership of the parliamentary party—signed a Commons early day motion (EDM No. 174) urging the government to use the opportunity to make a "fresh start with the future development of the EEC," emphasising the need to pursue an extension of the borders of the EEC "and to create a fully competitive common market."

The Eurosceptics also seized upon Britain's withdrawal from the ERM in September as a means of attacking the government's European policy. The "fresh start" EDM had not been signed by any senior ex-ministers, but in the debate on 24 September a former home secretary, Kenneth Baker, attacked the treaty. "It seems irrefutable," he declared, "that last week tore a gaping hole in the Maastricht treaty. . . . The Danes have given us an opportunity to think again about the next step forward."[17] He was joined by various other Conservative critics, including a leading opponent of Britain's membership of the EC, another former cabinet minister, John Biffen.

The government decided to resume the committee stage of the bill in the autumn. The "paving" debate that the prime minister had promised was scheduled for 4 November. As the day of the debate drew nearer, commentators began to speculate on the possibility of a government defeat if, as seemed likely, Tory Eurosceptics voted with the Opposition. Members of the premier's staff intimated that the prime minister might treat the vote as a vote of confidence in himself.[18] After a tense debate, the House rejected an Opposition amendment by 319 votes to 313. Subsequent reports suggested that, as voting got under way on the government motion (which reaffirmed Britain's commitment to Europe and invited the government to proceed with the bill), the prime minister and the president of the board of trade, Michael Heseltine, assured Tory rebels that the third reading of the bill would be delayed until after a second Danish referendum had taken place.[19] In the event, 26 Conservatives still went ahead and voted against the government, and a further 6 abstained. But their numbers were not sufficient to deny the government a majority. The government had the Liberal Democrats' support and achieved victory, albeit by the slimmest of margins: 319 votes to 316.[20]

The bill then resumed its committee stage, taking up part of December and resuming the following January. The principal period of committee deliberation occupied a total of 22 parliamentary days—a total of 163 hours—between 13 January and 22 April. Proceedings were marked by uncertainty, bordering on farce at times, as the government issued different interpretations as to whether or not the treaty could be ratified if a particular amendment on the social chapter was carried; the amendment was ruled out of order at committee stage but a vote was then allowed on it at report stage.[21]

The government had hoped to get the bill through committee without amendment. In the event, it failed. On 8 March, "amid scenes of uproar . . . and calls on the government to resign, a Labour amendment was carried by 314 votes to 292."[22] No fewer than 45 Tory MPs rebelled; 26 voted for the amendment, with 19 abstaining.[23] The defeat was not only a political embarrassment for the government but also had an important procedural consequence. A bill that is taken for its committee stage in committee of the whole House and is not amended does not then have a report stage. If it is amended, then a report stage is necessary. The defeat triggered a report stage, thus further prolonging its passage.

The defeat on the amendment showed that the Tories opposed to the bill were serious and now had the numbers to embarrass the government. When another defeat looked likely, on a new clause to the bill stipulating that the act would come into force only after the House "has come to a Resolution on a motion tabled by a Minister of the Crown concerning the question of adopting the Protocol on Social Policy" (the social chapter of the Maastricht treaty), the government accepted the clause rather than risk losing the vote. By accepting the clause, the government unknowingly created further problems for itself. It also accepted a number of other amendments, the purpose of resisting them having now disappeared.

The bill successfully completed its report stage, and MPs gave it a third reading on 20 May—more than a year after its introduction. The Opposition abstained from voting, and the bill passed by 292 votes to 112.[24] Those voting against the bill included 66 Labour MPs and 41 Tories. A further 5 Tories abstained.

The bill then went to the House of Lords, where it occupied nine days of parliamentary time. Despite being attacked by some senior Conservative peers, including the former leader, Baroness Thatcher, the large Conservative majority in the upper house ensured its successful passage. Peers rejected by a decisive margin (445 votes to 176)[25] an attempt to require a consultative referendum on the treaty, the government whips bringing in the massed ranks of loyal Tory peers to ensure the desired outcome.

The bill completed its third reading in the House of Lords on 20 July and received the royal assent the same day. Before the act could come into effect, though, the House had to come to a resolution on the social chapter. The government tabled a motion "noting" the policy of Her Majesty's Government on the social policy. The Opposition tabled an amendment declaring that ratification should not take place until the government notified the European Community that it intended to adopt the social chapter. Although the Opposition amendment was not likely to attract the support of the Conservative rebels, there was no guarantee that the government could muster a majority for its motion.

The debate, on 22 July 1993, took place in an atmosphere of total uncertainty. At 10.00 P.M. MPs voted on the Opposition amendment. The tellers announced that the voting was tied: 317 votes to 317. In accordance with precedent, the Speaker cast her vote against the amendment.[26] Members then trooped into the lobbies to vote on the government motion. When the tellers returned to the chamber, it was clear the government had lost. (The tellers for the winning side always stand to the right, facing the Speaker.) The motion had been negated by 324 votes to 316. Although Ulster Unionist MPs had voted with the government (amid allegations of a secret deal), their number proved insufficient to stave off defeat: 22 Conservatives voted in the Opposition lobby. With the amendment and the motion both defeated, the conditions for putting the act into effect had not been met.

Immediately after the voting figures had been announced, the prime minister rose to say that another motion would be put before the House the following day, a Friday, and that the vote would be one of confidence. If the government lost, it would request a dissolution. (Downing Street had already checked with Buckingham Palace that the Queen would grant a dissolution in those circumstances.) The following day, the House debated a motion expressing confidence in the government's policy on the adoption of the social chapter. The House rejected an Opposition amendment by 339 votes to 301 and carried the government's motion by 339 votes to 299. No Conservative voted against the government in either division and only one—Rupert Allason, the MP for Torbay—failed to vote at all. The following week, the Conservative whip was withdrawn from Allason, though accompanied by an indication that it would be restored in the event of good behaviour. It was restored a year later.

Although Tory Eurosceptics proved unwilling to vote against the government on a confidence motion, they resented the government's tactics and discussed ways of preventing the treaty from being ratified. During the debate on 23 July, a number of them, at the instigation of Sir Richard Body, met to consider an immediate challenge in the courts to the government's motion on the grounds that, by seeking to overturn the decision of the House the previous evening, it had acted illegally. The idea was to go immediately by taxi to the High Court in the Strand. "To make the strategy effective and put the wind up the Whips we really needed a dozen people to come with us. There were not enough."[27]

A legal challenge to the treaty was, however, already under way in the High Court, mounted by the Tory peer (and former editor of *The Times*) Lord Rees-Mogg, with financial backing from Sir James Goldsmith, previously a major contributor to Tory party funds. The challenge rested on three grounds, including that the Queen had no power to transfer her prerogative powers to another body. On 30 July, a unanimous court rejected each of the challenges advanced by Rees-Mogg's counsel. When Rees-Mogg subsequently decided not to appeal against the decision, the government moved promptly to ratify the treaty.

It was publicly and painfully obvious throughout the passage of the bill that the Conservative Party in Parliament was split badly, and the divisions lingered. In the autumn following its enactment, some of the prime minister's supporters tried to purge the executive committee of the 1922 Committee (the body representing backbenchers) of opponents of the bill. About sixty loyalists met and formed themselves into the Mainstream Group. They campaigned against five members of the executive committee who were seeking reelection but proved successful in defeating only one of them—Sir George Gardiner, the MP for Reigate. According to *The Times,* the outcome of the election "suggests that the parliamentary party wants an end to factional infighting."[28] If that was what the party wanted, it was not what it got. A year later, infighting on the issue of Europe again dominated the parliamentary party and was to do so for the rest of the Parliament.

WITHDRAWING THE WHIP

The temporary truce between the competing factions ended at the 1994 party conference, held in October at Bournemouth. The former chancellor, Norman Lamont, addressing a fringe meeting, raised the prospect of British withdrawal from the European Union. The country, he said, had to confront the choices that faced it. "That must mean looking at all the options.... One day it may mean contemplating withdrawal."[29] Former minister and leading Eurosceptic Lord Tebbit also weighed in with a critical speech at another fringe meeting, while in the conference hall itself Douglas Hurd defended the government's stance. Britain's interests, he declared, were best served "by steering Europe our way" rather than "kicking over the table."[30] The conflict was again in the open, and in the following month it was taken to the floor of the House of Commons.

As part of the Maastricht treaty negotiations, the government had committed itself to an increase in its annual contribution to the European Union budget. A bill to give effect to this commitment, the European Communities (Finance) Bill, was announced in the Queen's Speech in the autumn of 1994. The bill came before the House for second reading on 28 November. Given the government's declining overall majority in the House—by this time, as a result of by-election losses, it was down to 14—and the animosity shown towards the bill by Eurosceptics, the government's business managers knew they might have difficulty getting the bill through. Even if the government achieved a majority on second reading, Tory rebels looked likely to cause trouble throughout the bill's remaining stages. In order to ensure its passage, the prime minister announced that the issue was to be one of confidence. If the government lost the bill, he would request a dissolution.

The government's tactics annoyed the committed Eurosceptics, who claimed that it was a "constitutional outrage," with some claiming that it was the personal action of the prime minister and that the cabinet would not allow the prime minister to seek a dissolution,[31] a claim immediately dismissed by the chancellor of the exchequer, Kenneth Clarke.[32] Recognising the government's difficulties, the Opposition tabled a reasoned amendment to reject the bill. (As it supported the principle of the bill, it did not intend to vote against the second reading.) The government persuaded Ulster Unionist MPs to support it in the vote on the Opposition amendment, and with the vote being made one of confidence, a government victory was expected. Even so, the House remained tense during the debate and the subsequent vote. Eventually the tellers emerged, with the government tellers standing the right. The Opposition amendment had been defeated by 330 votes to 303, a comfortable margin even though 7 Conservatives abstained from voting. The House then gave the bill a second reading by 329 votes to 44. The Opposition line had been to abstain, but Labour rebels forced a division. No Conservative joined them, but one, who had voted with the government in the previous division, abstained.

All eight Conservatives who failed to support the government (see table 4.2) then received a letter from the chief whip withdrawing the whip. The action was unprecedented.[33] Another Conservative, Sir Richard Body, promptly resigned the whip in protest. The withdrawal of the whip appeared to achieve the government's immediate goal: it acted as a salutary warning to potential rebels, and the bill passed through its remaining stages without too much difficulty. Nevertheless, it had longer-term consequences. One was procedural. Technically, the government no longer had an overall majority in the House. The other was political. The

TABLE 4.2

MPS TO LOSE THE WHIP, NOVEMBER 1994

Member of Parliament	For	Since
Nicholas Budgen	Wolverhampton South West	Feb. 1974
Michael Carttiss	Great Yarmouth	1983
Christopher Gill	Ludlow	1987
Teresa Gorman	Billericay	1987
Tony Marlow	Northampton North	1979
Richard Shepherd	Aldridge Brownhills	1979
Sir Edward (Teddy) Taylor	Glasgow Cathcart, 1964–79, and for Southend East	1980
John Wilkinson	Bradford West, 1970–74, and for Ruislip-Northwood	1979

nine MPs without the whip formed a grouping of their own and achieved a public prominence that most of them had never before had. The status of being a whipless MP served almost as a badge of pride.

The existence of the whipless MPs soon became a public embarrassment for the government and, within days, a serious political embarrassment. The nine helped defeat the government on 6 December on the second-stage increase of VAT on domestic fuel. Kenneth Clarke announced various concessions during the debate, but they failed to keep Tory rebels from voting with the Opposition. "Labour MPs whooped with glee in extraordinary scenes in the Commons when the vote was announced."[34] Of the seven Conservatives who voted against the government, three were without the whip, and, of the eight who abstained, five were without it. One commentator promptly dubbed the defeat "the revenge of the Euro sceptics."[35]

The clash over Europe proved central to another contest in November 1994: that for the chairmanship of the 1922 Committee. Eurosceptics viewed the incumbent, Sir Marcus Fox, as a prime ministerial loyalist and they persuaded one of their number, Sir Nicholas Bonsor, to challenge him. In the secret ballot, Fox fought off the challenge, and initial reports implied that he had done so with a comfortable majority. Subsequent reports, however, suggested that it had been a tight race, Fox winning by 129 votes to 116.

Conservative rebels continued to make much of the running in the following year. They called for a government commitment to a referendum on a single currency. They criticised the stance of the chancellor, viewed as too sympathetic to European integration, and pressed for the replacement of the Europhile foreign secretary, Douglas Hurd. The whipless MPs adopted an especially prominent role in criticising a single currency and the actions of the European Union. On 19 January 1995, eight of the nine issued their own manifesto on Europe, opposing economic and monetary union. They even provided photo opportunities, visiting ports to express support for fishermen opposed to the European common fisheries policy. The government's business managers wanted to restore the whip to them in order to avoid further embarrassment. Though two of the rebels, Nicholas Budgen and Richard Shepherd, seemed amenable to having the whip restored, the others indicated that they were in no hurry to have it back and that, if it was to be given back, it would be on their terms. In April, the government whips discussed how they could resolve the situation. One senior whip raised the possibility of the chief whip simply writing to them and giving them the whip back.[36] On 25 April, that was what he did. Sir Richard Body, who had resigned the whip of his own volition, refused to apply for the whip to be restored to him, but the other eight returned formally to the fold. It was not until the following January that Body also did so.

CONTINUING CONFLICT

The restoration of the whip provided little respite for the government. Criticism of its stance on EU issues showed no signs of abating. In May and June 1995, backbench critics of the prime minister pushed for a challenge to his leadership in the autumn. As we shall see, the prime minister preempted his critics and forced an election in July, being reelected as party leader. The day after John Major announced the leadership contest, Douglas Hurd confirmed that he was to step down as foreign secretary. Although party officials claimed Major's reelection as a triumph, it nonetheless demonstrated a substantial level of discontent, principally over the handling of European policy. Major's reelection may have secured his position until the general election, but it failed to still party conflict.

The party conference in October 1995 provided the site for further conflict, with fringe meetings held by opponents and supporters of European integration. Although the Queen's Speech in November announced no legislative measures that affected Europe, the issue of the European common fisheries policy came before the House in December. A "take note" motion was defeated, by 299 votes to 297, after 2 Conservatives cross-voted and 11 abstained.[37] Eurosceptics also used the chamber to pursue their opposition to further European integration and their support for a referendum on the issue. In an attempt to meet the criticism from its own backbenches, the government in January 1996 announced that it would issue a consultation paper on European integration, which it duly did, and on 2 April—despite reported opposition in cabinet from the chancellor, Kenneth Clarke—committed itself to a referendum if a Conservative government in the next Parliament recommended British entry into a single currency.

These events took place in the midst of an additional crisis facing the government and one that had a notable EU dimension. The government's concession in March 1996 that there might be a link between bovine spongiform encephalopathy in cows (BSE, commonly called "mad cow disease") and Creutzfeld-Jakob disease in humans led to the collapse of beef sales and the imposition of an EU ban on the export of British beef. The ban infuriated Eurosceptics, and government attempts to have it lifted led to conflict in the Council of Ministers. Attempts by agriculture minister Douglas Hogg to resolve the problem proved fruitless, and the government embarked on an "empty chair" policy at meetings of the Council of Ministers until a compromise was reached that, in the event, delivered little to the UK. John Major stood by his embattled agriculture minister, much to the chagrin of many Tory backbenchers, and his attempts to get tough with the EU garnered the support of the parliamentary party but did little for his reputation with his backbench critics.

During the BSE crisis, Eurosceptics continued to put pressure on government for an ever more hardline policy on Europe. On 23 April 1996, Iain Duncan-Smith, the Eurosceptic MP for Chingford, sought leave to introduce a bill under the ten-minute rule procedure to give Parliament power to overturn rulings of the European Court of Justice. MPs denied leave by a narrow margin: 83 votes to 77.[38] A total of 66 Conservatives (including the two tellers) supported the motion; 6 voted against and the rest stayed away. On 11 June, another Eurosceptic, Bill Cash, used the same procedure to propose a bill "to provide for the holding of a referendum on the need for changes to the treaty on European Union affecting the United Kingdom's continuing membership." Given that the procedure allows an issue to be raised and voted on, but with no real prospect of the bill making further progress, the whips, keen to avoid an embarrassing vote, tried to avoid a division taking place, but were thwarted when two of Cash's supporters agreed to act as tellers against the bill. The whips then urged MPs to abstain. MPs gave Cash leave to introduce his bill by 95 votes to 1, with 74 Tories voting in favour.[39]

The vote on Cash's bill proved an embarrassment for the government. Two more followed in short order. Two days after the vote, the prime minister publicly rebuked his predecessor, Baroness Thatcher, for giving a "substantial donation" to the antifederalist European Foundation run by Bill Cash. "An 'incandescent' Prime Minister ... virtually accused his predecessor of disloyalty."[40] Then on 22 July, the paymaster-general, David Heathcoat-Amory, a little-known but respected minister, resigned from the government. In his resignation letter to the prime minister, he put his reason for doing so bluntly: "I can no longer support the Government's policy towards the European Union." Heathcoat-Amory immediately penned a pamphlet in support of his position. Major responded in an interview in *The Times,* reiterating his commitment to a policy of "negotiate and decide" on the issue of a single currency. "For us to opt out of the debate now would be a dereliction of duty."[41]

In September, the foreign secretary, Malcolm Rifkind, signalled a more Eurosceptic approach. In a speech in Zurich on 18 September, he warned that a single currency could divide the Continent into two groups. He also cautioned against blindly leaping towards ever-greater integration. The following day, the *Independent* carried a letter from six elder statesman of the party—including former prime minister Sir Edward Heath, former deputy prime minister Lord Whitelaw, and three former foreign secretaries (Douglas Hurd, Lord Howe, and Lord Carrington)—putting the case for a more positive engagement in Europe. Britain's future, they declared, lay in seeing the European Union "as an opportunity, not a threat."

The debate continued at the 1996 party conference, the last before the election. On the eve of the conference, former party treasurer Lord McAlpine announced his defection to the recently formed Referendum Party. Critics used fringe meetings to make their case—Lord Tebbit addressed a meeting of 1,200 sceptics and John Redwood one of 300,[42] while Norman Lamont attacked "federalism by stealth" in a debate with European commissioner Sir Leon Brittan[43]—but they were overshadowed by powerful speeches from the conference rostrum by the foreign secretary, the chancellor, and the prime minister himself. The emphasis was on unity, and the prime minister delivered one of his best-ever conference speeches. The mood on the conference floor clearly favoured the leadership's stance. "The hysteria was confined to the hotels."[44] As some ministers acknowledged, however, it was a holding exercise, and conflict resumed when Parliament returned shortly afterwards.

In November, the government faced criticism in the Commons for not allowing debate on three documents recommended for debate by the Select Committee on European Legislation. MPs on both sides of the House alleged that the government had withheld certain documents from the committee, and in order to stem a growing welter of criticism the prime minister sent the chancellor, Kenneth Clarke, to the House on 25 November—the day before his budget speech—to explain the government's actions and to announce that a debate would be held before the Dublin meeting of the European council on 13–14 December.[45]

On 2 December the *Daily Telegraph* carried a report that the prime minister might be prepared to abandon the government's policy of "negotiate and decide" on the issue of a single currency. This was countered by the chancellor, Kenneth Clarke, and the deputy prime minister, Michael Heseltine, the latter declaring publicly that "we are not going to change our position in the election campaign or this Parliament."

Their intervention forced Major to restate government policy. At the dispatch box, Major confirmed that Heseltine's assertion that policy would not change was correct. As Heseltine's biographer recorded,

> Afterwards a foul-tempered John Major told Tory back-benchers in the tea-room that there was no way he could have wrong-footed his deputy in public. Heseltine had played a crucial role in keeping the 'wait-and-see' policy in place, much to the dismay of most of the Cabinet. Many Conservative MPs were even more furious; many of them saw the rejection of a single currency as the one remaining weapon to defeat Labour.[46]

In a television interview on 8 December, Major warned his critics that he could not be held to ransom. His performance was forceful, but "it was clear ... that Mr Major failed to quell the dissatisfaction of Conservative MPs who want him to rule out a single currency in the next Parliament."[47] The following morning, *The Times* carried an advertisement sponsored by the European Movement and signed by pro-European MPs from different parties, including sixteen Conservatives, calling on the prime minister to forge a cross-party alliance for any deal reached at the Dublin summit and warning that progress at the summit should not be blocked.

The debate promised prior to the Dublin summit took place on 11 and 12 December. The opening speech by the chancellor attracted more interruptions from Conservative Eurosceptics than it did from Labour.[48] The debate took place not between parties but between those MPs who supported a single currency and those who did not. At various points, Conservative MPs addressed themselves to the party's internal debate, though calls for unity fell on deaf ears: neither side was going to influence the other. Sir Edward Heath rose to put one side of the argument, Nigel Lawson and John Redwood the other.

The year had proved a disastrous one for the government, John Major having failed to steady the ship and with critics on both sides of the argument eager to fire warning shots across his bows. The government did, however, have one success. It won a vote on the common fisheries policy, which it had failed to win the year before. However, it emerged shortly after the event that, in order to ensure a majority, government whips had double-paired three Tory MPs (each of the three had been paired with a Labour and a Liberal Democrat MP). The Opposition suspended normal pairing arrangements in protest. Ironically, the government would have won even without the double-pairing. One former minister summed up the worsening situation in a note to this writer: "What a shambles!"

The conflict continued into 1997. At a cabinet meeting on 23 January, ministers agreed a line stressing that it was "unlikely" that Britain would join a single currency at the start date in 1999 and that, on the information available, the government considered it unlikely—though not impossible—that other countries would be ready either.[49] Then, in an interview with the *Financial Times,* the chancellor said that Britain could still join in the first wave; the cabinet had not ruled it out. He added, for good measure, that he was not prepared to be part of any "Eurosceptic election campaign."[50] His comments attracted immediate condemnation from Eurosceptics.

The Eurosceptics continued to press the prime minister to rule out British participation in a single currency. Europhiles responded by demanding that no concessions be made to the critics. In Reigate, leading Eurosceptic Sir George Gardiner suffered deselection by his local party because of his continued attacks on the prime minister, and shortly afterwards he defected to the Referendum Party. When the prime minister announced the date of the general election on 17 March, the party was still at war with itself over the issue of a single currency. The cracks over the official policy of "negotiate and decide" were papered over, but they still showed.

THE TAXONOMY OF CONFLICT

The debate over European integration was notable for its length, its ferocity, and increasingly its factional nature. The motivations of Conservative opponents of further European integration differed; some opposed it on economic grounds, some on constitutional grounds.[51] The longstanding opponents of UK membership of the European Community took their stance principally on constitutional grounds. They were joined in the 1980s by those who supported membership in order to achieve a single market but who were opposed to anything that extended beyond that; their viewpoint found its most significant expression in Margaret Thatcher's 1988 Bruges speech. By the 1990s, there was thus a much larger body in the party than before that was critical of any moves towards political and economic union. The motivation of the critics might differ, but they were able to make common cause.

What was different in the 1990s from earlier years was not only the size of the Eurosceptic wing of the party but the extent of its factional organisation. The different viewpoints were not merely expressed by adherents, they were championed by increasingly well-organised groups. By the summer of 1995, several such groups existed.[52] On the Eurosceptic side, the highly critical Fresh Start Group (named after the 1992 early day motion) enjoyed the support of about 80 MPs, and the European Research Group—Eurosceptic but more willing than the Fresh Start Group to support Major's line—could claim about 40 MPs. The Conservative Way Forward, formed to promote Margaret Thatcher's ideas and with about 80 to 100 MPs supporting it (there was a large overlap in membership with the other groups) also promoted an ultrasceptical line. On the pro-Europe side, the Conservative Group for Europe—the principal body supporting further integration—had almost 40 MPs among its membership; former foreign secretary Lord Howe was a leading figure. Also in the pro-Europe camp was the Tory Reform Group, advocating an agenda that went beyond the issue of Europe. It too had about 40 MPs, though the overlap with membership of the Conservative Group for Europe was substantial.

What is clear from these figures is that the Eurosceptic wing of the party outnumbered the pro-European wing. An analysis by this writer of the stance taken by Tory MPs at the end of the Parliament—using three broad categories of Eurosceptic right, party faithful (but further subdividing the category to identify their leanings on Europe), and pro-European integration left—produced the taxonomy shown in table 4.3.[53]

The Eurosceptics in the party enjoyed the most support—on the issue itself, a majority of Tory MPs were sceptical towards further European integration—and the Eurosceptic right were especially vocal and generally made most of the running in debate (or at least grabbed most of the headlines). The pro-Europeans had sufficient numbers, however —about a quarter of the parliamentary party—to ensure that they could not be ignored, and they were prepared on occasion to make their voices heard when they felt the Eurosceptics were close to getting what they

TABLE 4.3

TAXONOMY OF CONSERVATIVE MPS

Eurosceptic right		32%
Party faithful		49%
of which		
Eurosceptic leaning	24%	
Agnostic/don't know	20%	
Pro-European integration leaning	6%	
Pro-European integration left		19%

wanted. Hence, for example, their newspaper advertisement in December 1996, an advertisement that carried the names of some normally loyal MPs such as Sir John Hunt and Patrick Thompson.

Nor was the conflict confined to the backbenches. The cabinet too was divided. Michael Portillo, Peter Lilley, and (during his time in the cabinet) John Redwood championed the Eurosceptic cause, aided by the somewhat more loyal figure of the home secretary, Michael Howard. Supporters of European integration had prominent allies in Michael Heseltine, Kenneth Clarke, and, until his departure in 1995, the foreign secretary, Douglas Hurd. Two other cabinet ministers—the environment secretary, John Gummer, and, ironically (given his clashes with the EU over the BSE crisis), the agriculture minister, Douglas Hogg—were also in the pro-Europe camp. Much of the battle took place not in cabinet but on the public stage or, perhaps more accurately, in the radio or television studios, with ministers countering one another with immediate statements. We have already seen that Clarke appeared to undermine the line agreed in cabinet in January 1997 in an interview given to the *Financial Times*. Three weeks later, on 19 February, the foreign secretary, Malcolm Rifkind, said on the morning *Today* programme that Britain was broadly "hostile" to a single currency. Clarke immediately issued a statement claiming that Rifkind had made "a slip of the tongue" when pressed by a skilful interviewer. Rifkind responded that it was not a slip of the tongue. According to one junior minister, "My press officer says word in the lobby is that Rifkind was freelancing and there was no No. 10 involvement."[54] Ministers freelanced frequently during the Parliament, with the prime minister having difficulty in enforcing discipline for fear of losing powerful figures from his cabinet.

The party in Parliament—and in the country—thus contained people who took conflicting and in some cases mutually exclusive stances (those contemplating withdrawal from the EU and those favouring further integration). For the leadership, the task of ensuring a united party appeared insuperable.

The conflict was both organised and bitter. The animosity shown towards John Major when he attended a meeting of the Fresh Start Group in June 1995 apparently prompted his decision to force a leadership contest. Perhaps most disastrously of all for the Conservatives, the conflict took place in public, and it did so on a continuing basis. The Tories' secret weapon—loyalty—was effectively decommissioned during the lifetime of the Parliament. Even the proximity of a general election in 1997 failed to rally the party behind a single line. Electors have historically viewed the Labour Party as more divided than the Conservative Party. Survey data show that by 1994 the position was reversed, and for the rest of the Parliament voters looked upon the Conservative Party as the more divided party. As the general election neared, those divisions appeared to become more, not less, severe.

The Leadership

John Major was essentially a pragmatist. Whereas Margaret Thatcher as prime minister assumed the role of an innovator, Major emerged as a balancer.[55] He was concerned with the here-and-now of politics rather than with achieving distinct future goals. In the short term, this was an advantage. In the long term, it proved to be a mixed blessing. In the eyes of his critics, it was a disaster.

Major's pragmatism meant that the policies to which Margaret Thatcher was implacably wedded and that were proving damaging to the party's standing in the polls could be jettisoned. The poll tax was abolished shortly after he took office and a more moderate stance taken on the issue of European integration.[56] Some of the principal obstacles to the party's reelection in 1992 were thus dismantled. In the longer term, however, Major's pragmatism meant that he was not able to offer a clear and decisive lead. To many of his critics, this was the problem. They complained that he offered no leadership or, rather, that he offered leadership from the rear, following those who were setting the agenda and then taking action to try to meet their demands. More mundanely, others claimed that he was driven by the demands of his in-tray.

But Major's style was only part of the reason for the party's troubles during the Parliament. Indeed, in some respects it may have prevented the situation from being worse than it was. Julian Amery once observed that "a good jockey rides a difficult horse." The Conservative Party proved a remarkably difficult horse after the 1992 election, and Major did well to stay astride it, perhaps even to prevent it from bolting more often than it did.

The problems for Major during this period derived from a unique confluence of four circumstances. First, there were the sheer and increasing pressures on government. Ministers found it increasingly difficult to discuss policy in strategic terms.[57] They were too busy being ministers to find the time to think as politicians. This meant it was difficult to convey a clear sense of direction because Major and his ministers had not mapped one out. When ministers did assemble at the prime minister's country residence, Chequers, in September 1995 to discuss future plans, no papers were circulated in advance and the meeting concluded by early evening, with ministers departing for other engagements.

Second, there were the circumstances of Major's election to the lead-

ership in 1990. He succeeded Margaret Thatcher and garnered the votes
not only of the party faithful among Conservative MPs but also of most
of the Thatcherites; the votes of those on the left went to Michael Heseltine and Douglas Hurd.[58] Though the Thatcherites constituted a minority
of the parliamentary party, they were a vocal and very intense minority.
They resented the displacement of their eponymous leader and wanted to
ensure that the legacy of Thatcherism endured. In part, it did; some
Thatcherite policies continued, most notably privatisation of firms in the
public sector. The important point—in order to understand what was
happening—however, was not that the policies being continued were
Thatcherite but rather the fact that they were merely being continued.
"The Conservative Party could think of little more than continuing what
Mrs Thatcher had begun."[59] Because ministers had so little time to stand
back and start again from first principles, they carried on as before.
When things went wrong, with the government being knocked off course
by Black Wednesday and by party in-fighting, Major and his ministers
had no philosophical framework to draw on. Their response was pragmatic and, in the eyes of critics, overly responsive to opinion polls. They
were then attacked by the Thatcherites for not keeping to the true faith.

Third, there were the party divisions over Europe. As we have
noted, the issue of European integration constitutes the fault line of British politics. Once Major had entered Downing Street, the issue could not
be avoided. He had to engage in negotiations leading to the Maastricht
treaty and then introduce bills to ratify it and to implement one of the
agreements reached at Maastricht (on increasing contributions to the EC
budget). The issue of a single currency also began to engage the minds of
Eurosceptics as the Parliament progressed. The issue could not be resolved by recourse to the basic articles of Conservative faith. Eurosceptics saw European integration as a threat to British strength and
greatness, handing over sovereignty to a supranational body that Britain
could not control. Pro-Europeans viewed British participation in the EU
as a means of achieving not only peace but renewed British influence on
the world stage. Those on both sides of the argument could thus call in
aid Conservative tenets to justify their cause.

Fourth, there was the practical problem resulting from the government's overall majority—or ultimately lack of it—in the House of
Commons. Though returned to office with an overall majority of 21, the
government gradually saw its majority whittled away as a result of by-
election losses and the unprecedented defection, towards the end of the
Parliament, of four of its MPs: Alan Howarth, to Labour; Emma Nicholson and Peter Thurnham, to the Liberal Democrats (Thurnham sitting
briefly as an Independent Conservative before accepting the Liberal

Democrat whip); and Sir George Gardiner, at the very end of the Parliament, to the Referendum Party. By the end of 1996, the situation veered between a "tied" Parliament, the government having as many MPs as the combined strength of Opposition parties, and its being in a minority of one. John Major thus found himself in a situation not faced by any previous Conservative premier in the twentieth century. Though there had been periods of minority Labour government, no Tory administration had ever had to survive on a single-figure (or no-figure) parliamentary majority. The government thus stood vulnerable to defeat if only a tiny number of its backbenchers voted in the Opposition lobby. As we have seen, it did suffer a number of defeats as a result of that happening. Europe apart, some Tory MPs exhibited a willingness to exploit the government's vulnerability simply in order to get the results they wanted. A small group of backbenchers, for example, forced the government to abandon plans, championed by Michael Heseltine, to privatise the post office. At the end of the Parliament, two MPs even publicly threatened to withdraw their support over the proposed closure of a local hospital.

Each of these developments would have made it difficult for any leader to provide decisive leadership after 1992. Nor were things helped by a series of scandals affecting MPs which, as we shall see, undermined the standing of the government. When all these are put together, the result is a situation that would probably have got the better of any leader. John Major found himself, in the colloquial phrase, between a rock and a hard place.

Throughout the Parliament, Major tried to hold the party together, but the more he tried, the more he was criticised by those looking for leadership, which usually meant leadership that favoured their particular stance. Attempts to steer a middle course on the issue of European integration attracted criticism from both sides. As two of those closest to Major were to record:

> First, the Prime Minister had trouble with the left wing of the party, who jibbed at his scepticism about a single currency and robust defence of the nation state in an article for *The Economist* in 1993. Then he had problems with the right, who wanted him to commit himself to a referendum on Europe. This pattern repeated itself with a hideous predictability.[60]

Former home secretary Kenneth Baker described the decision to withdraw the whip from the eight Conservative rebels in November 1994 as "an act of crass stupidity."[61] The following January, Europhiles attacked Major when he signalled that, if circumstances warranted, a referendum could be held on Europe. Former prime minister Sir Edward Heath weighed in, claiming that the Eurorebels had got the upper hand. "They, in fact, are running the country and the Government. I don't find that acceptable and now is the time to say so quite bluntly."[62]

Nor was the problem just one of upsetting backbenchers. Major failed to carry some cabinet ministers with him. He had to cope with some notable Eurosceptics in his cabinet, whose actions in promoting their cause led to an unscripted outburst by the prime minister following a television interview on 24 July 1993. Chatting to the ITN political editor after the interview, but with the microphone still live, Major complained bitterly about the actions of the Eurosceptic "bastards" in his cabinet. When he warmed to the idea of a referendum in late 1994 and early 1995, he came under pressure from two senior cabinet ministers —Kenneth Clarke and Douglas Hurd—not to advocate one.[63] Another cabinet minister, the Eurosceptic Peter Lilley, went on the public record to support one: "I am prepared to consider it on a single currency," he said on television.

THE LEADERSHIP CONTEST

Major was lauded for leading the party to victory in the 1992 election, but the adulation proved short-lived. The consequences of the Danish referendum "no" vote and of withdrawal from the ERM soon took their effect on his standing among MPs. Following Black Wednesday, according to one report, "Major just disappeared for two days (there were dark tales of an emotional collapse) and then popped up again as if nothing had happened. There was no acknowledgement of the scale of the disaster, no admission of error. He never wiped the slate clean with an angry public and party."[64] The effect on his public standing can be seen in table 4.1 (p. 80). The political kudos of election victory was wiped out within a matter of months.

His subsequent failure to offer the lead that many MPs wanted, primarily but not exclusively on Europe, fuelled criticism and triggered talk of a challenge to his leadership. In March 1994, one backbench rebel, Tony Marlow, urged Major to quit. "Backbenchers from across the party spectrum were openly questioning whether the Prime Minister could survive," reported *The Times,* "if the Tories lose heavily in the European elections in June."[65] In the event, the party did badly in the European Parliament elections, but not quite so disastrously as the media had been predicting. The prospect of a challenge remained. In November, various right-wingers were reported to be attempting to mount a challenge,[66] and former chancellor Norman Lamont indicated his willingness to stand.[67]

Under the rules governing the election of the party leader (revised following the 1990 contest that deposed Margaret Thatcher), a ballot could be forced at the beginning of the new session if 10 percent of the members of the parliamentary party wrote to the chairman of the 1922 Committee demanding one.[68] A challenge in 1994 required the signatures of thirty-four MPs. The prospect of a challenge was one of the reasons advanced by some commentators for the withdrawal of the whip from the eight Conservative rebels. The eight were critics of the prime minister. So long as they were not in receipt of the party whip, they were not eligible to write to the chairman of the 1922 Committee. Without them, the critics of the prime minister probably lacked the numbers necessary to force a ballot. In the event, no challenge took place, the election for the chairman of the 1922 Committee being used instead as a sort of surrogate contest.

The prime minister continued to attract criticism from some of his backbenchers throughout the rest of 1994 and into the spring of 1995. Talk of a leadership challenge again surfaced. Major's handling of the European issue was at the core of the criticism. Major attempted to defuse the situation and in June 1995 attended a meeting of the Fresh Start Group of Conservative MPs. He had a difficult meeting, facing not only hostile questioning but also heckling from some MPs. He appeared to be rattled by the experience and decided that the existing situation could not continue. He discussed the matter with his advisers and then called a press conference for 22 June in the garden of 10 Downing Street.[69] Standing at a small lectern, the prime minister declared that for the past three years he had been opposed by a minority and that during those years there had been repeated threats of a leadership election. "In each year they turned out to be phoney threats. Now the same thing is happening again in 1995." The government was being undermined and the party damaged. "I am not prepared to see the party I care for laid out on the rack like this any longer." He had that afternoon, he said, tendered his resignation as leader of the Conservative Party in order to trigger an election. "I have confirmed ... that I shall be a candidate in that election." And he concluded:

> The Conservative Party must make its choice. Every leader is leader only with the support of his Party. That is true of me too. That is why I am no longer prepared to tolerate the present situation. In short, it is time to put up or shut up.[70]

He probably imagined his cabinet colleagues, at least, would shut up.

The first ballot for the leadership was scheduled for 4 July. Norman Lamont emerged initially as the most likely challenger, but the situation changed dramatically when it emerged that the Welsh secretary, John Redwood, might resign from the cabinet in order to enter the contest. Newspapers on the weekend of 24–25 June ran stories about Redwood's intentions. Some carried reports that at least 80 MPs, and possibly as many as 100, might refuse to back Major.[71] On the Monday, 26 June, Redwood did resign from the cabinet and enter the race. He announced his candidacy in a Commons committee room, surrounded by supporters. His statement attracted serious coverage, though he was not helped by pictures of the occasion, those who stood behind him being among the "awkward squad" at Westminster. He was immediately dubbed a "malcontent" by Major.[72] He made clear his opposition to a single currency and his support for early tax cuts.

Both candidates at once started pitching for the support of MPs. Both addressed the 92 Group. Redwood did the rounds of potential supporters. Major visited the tea room in the House of Commons and saw waverers individually. Major had a campaign team led by four cabinet ministers. The nucleus of Redwood's team comprised several back-benchers, only one of whom had some (minor) ministerial experience. Redwood nonetheless picked up support from some senior ex-ministers, including Norman Lamont and Lord Tebbit.

Redwood's candidacy made the contest a serious one, and as Redwood canvassed support among Eurosceptics there was increasing speculation that Major might not clear the hurdles necessary for victory in the first ballot (an absolute majority plus a majority representing 15 percent of those eligible to vote). "Both sides agree that the contest is finely balanced, with Mr Major struggling to secure enough votes to take him out of danger."[73] To some extent, such stories reflected attempts by Redwood supporters to talk up his support. Other stories circulated, however, that some MPs were contemplating voting for Redwood in order to force a second ballot in which other candidates could then stand. Though cabinet members declared their intention to vote for Major in the first ballot, a number were discreetly, or not so discreetly, making preparations in case the election went to a second ballot.[74] Michael Portillo attracted embarrassing publicity when extra telephone lines were seen being installed at the home of a leading supporter. Backers of Michael Heseltine were reportedly ready to act in support of their candidate. Another cabinet member approached a backbencher to act as campaign manager. On the day of the ballot, rumours circulated of a deal between Major and Heseltine, Heseltine being offered something in return for the backing of his supporters. The day after the contest Heseltine became deputy prime minister, thus appearing to give credence to the rumours.

Voting closed at 5.00 P.M. on 4 July. A tense twenty minutes followed in which the votes were counted, and the results were then announced by the chairman of the 1922 Committee, Sir Marcus Fox. Major received 218 votes and Redwood 89. There were 8 abstentions and 12 spoilt ballot papers. Two MPs (Sir Trevor Skeet, who was seriously ill, and Edwina Currie, who wasn't) failed to vote. Major's vote was sufficient to clear both hurdles required for election on the first ballot. He was declared reelected as party leader. Cabinet ministers, led by Michael Portillo, hailed the result as a triumph for the prime minister. John Redwood conceded defeat.

Despite the victory for Major, the country came very close at 5.20 P.M. that day to witnessing the resignation of the prime minister. Major had been aiming for a "decisive" win. What constituted a decisive win was not defined, but it was generally believed that if as much as a third of the parliamentary party failed to support him he would resign. On the day of the ballot, he was reported to have told colleagues he would go if more than 100 MPs failed to back him. In the event, more than 100 MPs did fail to back him. There is some evidence that Major had to be persuaded by colleagues to stay. According to one newspaper report, a "wobbly" prime minister had to have his resolve stiffened by two cabinet ministers that afternoon.[75] The records of some of those closest to events in Downing Street appear to confirm this interpretation.[76] After the result was announced, there was no immediate statement from Downing Street: the first televised comment came from Portillo. Eventually Major did emerge to claim victory, but at least one of those ministers close to him later conceded, at least by implication, that there had been a problem.[77]

Once Major emerged to claim victory, his campaign team immediately lauded it as a remarkable victory. It was far from that: one-third of the parliamentary party, about half of all backbenchers, had failed to back their own prime minister. Yet the claim of a great victory was accepted and recounted by the media. The claim stuck because of the activities of the Redwood campaign. Major's critics—in the media as well as in the parliamentary party—had talked up the prospect of Redwood's denying Major victory in the first ballot. Leader writers on the *Daily Telegraph* and *The Times* urged Conservative MPs to choose a new leader. Redwood himself talked of victory in the first ballot. When the result was announced, Redwood's supporters were poorly prepared to respond and could hardly deny that it was a clear victory for Major. The prime minister had done far better than his critics had been predicting. The prime minister's honour was saved, ironically, by those who had been keenest to get rid of him.[78]

Major achieved his reelection because his ministers remained predominantly loyal, as did most of the party faithful among backbenchers. Most pro-Europeans are also believed to have backed him because he was preferable to Redwood (though not all apparently voted for him: some who wanted Heseltine as leader are believed to have abstained in the hope of forcing a second ballot). Major also picked up the support of some Eurosceptics, such as Sir Michael Spicer, Bernard Jenkin, and James Cran, who supported his line, though they may also have been influenced by a desire to prevent a Heseltine victory in the event of a second ballot. (Another Eurosceptic, Michael Carttiss, supported Major because Redwood had never spoken to him since he entered the House.) As a result, Redwood failed to maximise his support on the right and notably failed to make significant inroads into the party faithful who had Eurosceptic leanings. Had he done so, then, as is clear from table 4.3 (p. 94), he would have been able to deny Major victory in the first round. Virtually all his support came from Eurosceptics, but not all Eurosceptics supported him.

The result of the election left Major virtually certain to lead the party into the next general election (the 1922 Committee executive subsequently decided not to permit a leadership election in the autumn) but nonetheless emphasised the extent of the party's internal divisions. The voting also revealed the vulnerability of Major as party leader. His support had some breadth but little depth. In the 1990 leadership contest, he had no candidate to the right of him. In the 1995 contest, he had no candidate to the left of him. He thus picked up support from different constituencies without consolidating his support in either. There was no strong body of "Majorites" to bang the drum in support of his beliefs and leadership.

CONTINUING DIFFICULTIES

Major's reelection as leader secured his position but not his authority. The day after his reelection, he reshuffled the cabinet, conceding little if anything to his critics. "Major Swings Cabinet to Left," declared the headline in *The Times*. It was the worst day for the right since Margaret Thatcher was forced out in 1990, declared one young right-wing MP. "The Cabinet will now be judged on how well it reflects the views of the 111 MPs who did not vote for the Prime Minister," declared another.[79] As we have seen, hostilities soon resumed on the issue of Europe, Major failing to unite the party behind any particular line.

Major attracted persistent sniping from critics and was beset by a string of unrelated crises. In February 1996 the Irish Republican Army (IRA) ended their cease-fire. (The cease-fire, the first cessation of hostilities since "the troubles" began in Northern Ireland in the late 1960s, had been announced in August 1994 as a result of the Downing Street Declaration agreed by John Major and Irish premier Albert Reynolds in December 1993 and had been seen as one of Major's notable successes.) The following month, there was the beef crisis following the announcement that BSE might be transmitted to humans. Major's attempts to persuade the Council of Ministers to lift the ban on beef exports attracted initial support from the parliamentary party, but the eventual compromise fell far short of what Eurosceptics wanted. Allegations of sleaze continued. Those that derived from ministers' personal behaviour not only undermined the reputation of the government but rebounded on Major. At the party conference in 1993 he had declared that it was "time for a return to basics."[80] The values he mentioned were those of self-discipline, respect for law, responsibility, and consideration for others, but his words were interpreted by the media as "extolling family values, social discipline and clean living."[81] That interpretation was backed by private briefings by No. 10. Thereafter, whenever a minister fell from grace because of misconduct, it was portrayed as undermining the values of Major's administration.

By early 1997 Major's difficulties in keeping the party together and the party's persistent and marked unpopularity led to persistent discussion about the leadership. There was no way that Major could be removed before the election, but speculation was rife as to what would happen after it. Supporters of potential leadership contenders talked up their candidates' claims to the succession. Many assumed that the party would lose the election and that Major would go or quickly be forced out. Supporters of defence secretary Michael Portillo actively promoted his cause. Unexpected Eurosceptical comments by health secretary Stephen Dorrell were seen as his pitch to the party's right. Some MPs began to organise on behalf of home secretary Michael Howard, including one of those MPs who had been part of Major's campaign team in 1995. Talk of the leadership became a dominant topic of conversation at Westminster and undermined the prime minister's position. Some on the right, such as Sir George Gardiner and David Evans, a member of the 1922 Committee executive, publicly criticised him.

Major thus faced a divided party and, on the issue of Europe, a divided cabinet. He could not afford to sack any of the leading Eurosceptics or pro-Europeans in his cabinet. They had powerful constituencies on the backbenches and were able to conduct a semipublic contest for the leadership. Major led his party into the 1997 campaign divided and dispirited, questions about his own leadership constituting part of the internal party debate.

Sleaze

The word *sleaze* entered the lexicon of political discourse during the 1990s. Sex scandals kept the tabloid newspapers occupied from the beginning of the Parliament to the end. By themselves, these stories would probably have done the government little damage. What damaged it was their collective impact and that they were lumped together with the far more serious cases of alleged political and financial misconduct that David Denver has described.

Links between MPs and outside bodies, including lobbying firms, were well known and in most cases declared in the Register of Members' Interests. Nevertheless, allegations of MPs being paid by outside interests to pursue their causes in Parliament without those interests being declared had been circulating for some time. In July 1994, the *Sunday Times* revealed that two MPs approached by a journalist posing as a businessman had not declined offers of £1,000 to table parliamentary questions. This triggered a major "cash for questions" story. Shortly afterwards, the *Guardian* claimed that two ministers had, when backbenchers, accepted cash to table questions and had not disclosed the arrangements in the Register of Members' Interests. One of the ministers, Tim Smith, admitted the claim and resigned. The other, Neil Hamilton, denied the claim and fought to stay as a minister, eventually being forced to resign. Another resignation, this time of a cabinet minister, came the following year after the chief secretary to the Treasury, Jonathan Aitken, was caught up in allegations—occupying newspaper headlines for weeks —over who paid for a visit he made to the Ritz Hotel in Paris. The upshot was the appointment of the Nolan Committee and the acceptance by the House of Commons of most of its recommendations.

THE HAMILTON AFFAIR

The implementation of the Nolan recommendations did not, however, end the allegations. Indeed, the issue remained in the public eye as the various alleged breaches of the rules were investigated. Attracting most publicity was Neil Hamilton. Following the allegations made by the *Guardian,* he and lobbyist Ian Greer sued the paper.[82] Hamilton achieved a change in the law in order that parliamentary privilege, covering proceedings in Parliament, could be waived. Then, at the end of September, the case collapsed after it emerged that there was a conflict of interest between Hamilton and Greer. Both claimed that they could not afford to continue separate cases. The *Guardian* headline the next day, 1 October 1996, referred to Hamilton as "A Liar and a Cheat."

The inquiry by the parliamentary commissioner for standards into Hamilton and other MPs alleged to have received money from Ian Greer continued. Greer's company, Ian Greer Associates, previously the doyen of lobbying companies, went into voluntary liquidation. In 1997, various MPs were cleared by the commissioner's inquiries, but other investigations were still under way when the prime minister announced the date of prorogation and dissolution. Still under investigation was Neil Hamilton himself, and opposition MPs subsequently criticised the prime minister for proroguing Parliament so early, preventing completion and publication of the commissioner's inquiry into Hamilton. The campaign got under way with the case unresolved.

THE SCOTT INQUIRY

The government suffered further embarrassments during the Parliament because of the inquiry established to consider changes in the rules governing the export of defence-related equipment to Iraq. The inquiry, under a judge, Lord Justice Scott, had been established in November 1992 following the collapse of a prosecution of a firm for obtaining export licenses by deception. The inquiry took place in the full glare of publicity—61 out of 82 witnesses were questioned in public—with minister after minister appearing before the judge in order to explain their roles in changing the guidelines on the export of defence-related and dual-use goods to Iraq and in signing public interest immunity (PII) certificates, certifying that disclosure of documents requested in the trial would be contrary to the public interest. Some ministers had particularly difficult sessions: William Waldegrave, by this time a member of the cabinet, over the change in the guidelines that had been agreed when he was a junior foreign office minister, and Sir Nicholas Lyell, the attorney general, over his advice to ministers to sign the PII certificates.

The inquiry lasted far longer than expected: a total of three years and three months. When the final report was published on 15 February 1996, it revealed confusion and a culture of secrecy in Whitehall.[83] It criticised Waldegrave for deliberately misleading the House of Commons, though Scott accepted that Waldegrave believed he was not doing so. Lyell was criticised for being at fault over his handling of the PII certificates. In Scott's view, the attorney general's view of the law "was unsound" and without "clear prior judicial authority," and he was personally at fault for not passing on the reservations of one minister (Michael Heseltine) to the trial judge. Ministers had not discharged the obligations imposed by the principle of ministerial accountability.

The government moved quickly to defend its position. The prime minister made clear that Waldegrave and Lyell retained his confidence, and in a statement to the House trade and industry secretary Ian Lang emphasised those parts of the report upholding the government's position and asserted that, overall, the report showed that ministers had acted honestly and in good faith. Nonetheless, mistakes had been made and the government would move to rectify them.

The House debated the report on 26 February. At this time, the government had an overall majority of five in the House. A number of Conservative MPs—three in particular, Rupert Allason, Quentin Davies, and Richard Shepherd—were known to be critical of the government's actions. Speaking on television the day before the debate, Davies said there was no way he could vote for the government in present circumstances: "it would mean that what has happened can be forgotten, and we can just carry on regardless."[84] Ministers were reported to be offering concessions to the critics on its own backbenches, and rumours circulated of a deal with Ulster MPs in return for their abstention. The Opposition made clear that, if the government lost the vote, it would table a motion of no confidence.

The debate on the report saw a powerful attack on the government by shadow foreign secretary Robin Cook, who appealed to Conservative MPs to join him in the lobby. No one was sure of the outcome of the vote. The prime minister had seen the leader of the Ulster Unionists, David Trimble, and told him he was not prepared to offer any concessions. The Ulster Unionists voted against the government. Rupert Allason made a last-minute decision to support it, however, and it survived by one vote: 320 to 319.[85]

The victory in the lobbies was a relief for the government, but the whole episode had harmed its credibility. The publication of the Scott Report attracted extensive media coverage, the broadsheet newspapers giving over several pages to its findings. A MORI poll for *The Times*, published on 29 February, found that, by a margin of three to one, those questioned believed that the ministers criticised in the report should have resigned. Of those questioned, 69 percent thought that the government had handled the inquiry badly. Only 8 percent thought the government had handled it well. The activities uncovered in the Scott Report were widely seen as a central part of the catalogue of ministerial misbehaviour and misjudgement that appeared to be overwhelming the government.

Conclusion

The Conservative government of John Major could claim some successes during its period in office. The prime minister's handling of the Northern Ireland issue was generally conceded to be courageous and had produced a period of peace in the province. Despite the disaster of Black Wednesday (or, rather, because of it in the eyes of some Eurosceptics), the government's economic record by the end of the Parliament was a successful one: the country enjoyed low inflation and looked like doing so for some time. Despite controversy over the accuracy of the figures, unemployment was falling. Even in parliamentary terms, the situation was not as bad as it could have been. Despite a tiny and a declining majority, the government experienced few defeats. John Major actually managed to keep his party more or less together in the most inauspicious circumstances. Despite deep and bitter divisions, John Redwood was the only minister to resign from the cabinet because of disagreement with the prime minister. Other than on the issue of Europe, the party in Parliament rarely split and certainly not on any consistent basis. There were rebellions on the closure of the country's remaining coal mines, privatisation of the post office, and the banning of handguns, but such events were the exception rather than the norm. Tory MPs were actually less rebellious in the 1992–97 Parliament than they had been in some earlier Parliaments, and the government suffered fewer defeats than might have been expected given its precarious majority.[86]

The problem for the Conservatives, though, was that the issue of Europe would not go away. The party was publicly divided. The division was compounded by Black Wednesday, controversy over the leadership and a string of scandals and crises. In the first two years of his premiership, as we have noted, Major appeared as the Teflon prime minister: nothing nasty appeared to stick. The period from 1992 to 1997 witnessed the banana-skin premiership: Major was fated to be the victim of virtually every disaster that could happen.

By the end of the Parliament, the Conservative Party had jettisoned all the features that had made it a party of governance. From September 1992 onwards, it never regained its claim to be a party of governance. As we saw in chapter 2, voters took every opportunity to punish it, in parliamentary by-elections, in elections to the European Parliament, and in each year's local elections. The Conservative Party never won a by-election under John Major's leadership. (The last seat it retained in a by-election was Richmond, North Yorkshire, in February 1989.) During the course of the 1992 Parliament, the party defended eight seats in by-elections and lost every one, four to the Liberal Democrats, three to Labour, and one to the Scottish Nationalists. In the elections to the European Parliament, the party won 18 out of 87 seats—reducing significantly its influence within the Parliament—compared with 32 seats in 1989. (In

1984 it had won 45 seats.) By the end of the Parliament, the Tories controlled only one county council (Buckinghamshire) and had been pushed into third place, behind the Liberal Democrats, in terms of the number of council seats it held.

Nothing succeeds like failure. Each electoral loss also added to the party's organisational problems. Once renowned for its organisational strength and efficiency, the party lost thousands of activists from its ranks, with many defeated councillors retiring from political life. Unpopularity and organisational neglect further hit the party's declining, and aging, membership base.[87] By early 1997, with an election imminent, the party was highly unpopular and organisationally dispirited. It faced a Labour Party that was popular, organisationally vibrant and making a claim to the very attributes that had formed the basis of Conservative success for most of the previous century. The excitement generated by the election victory at the beginning of the Parliament had given way to a mood of deep gloom and exasperation by the end of it. The wilderness years beckoned.

Notes

1. See Philip Norton, "The Conservative Party from Thatcher to Major," in *Britain at the Polls 1992*, edited by Anthony King (Chatham N.J.: Chatham House, 1992), 59–65.
2. See Anthony Seldon and Stuart Ball, eds., *Conservative Century* (Oxford: Oxford University Press, 1994); and Philip Norton, ed., *The Conservative Party* (Hemel Hempstead, Herts.: Prentice Hall/Harvester Wheatsheaf, 1996), chaps. 1–4.
3. Norton, "The Conservative Party from Thatcher to Major," 32–33.
4. See James Bulpitt, "The Discipline of the New Democracy: Mrs Thatcher's Domestic Statecraft," *Political Studies* 34 (1986):22.
5. See Norton, *The Conservative Party,* chap. 9.
6. See, for example, Clive Irving, Ron Hall, and Jeremy Wallington, *Scandal '63* (London: Heinemann, 1963); and Wayland Young, *The Profumo Affair: Aspects of Conservatism* (Harmondsworth: Penguin, 1963).
7. See pp. 17–22 above. See also Alan Davies, "Economic Policy and Macro-Economic Developments," in *Contemporary Britain: An Annual Review 1993,* edited by Peter Catterall (Oxford: Blackwell, 1993), 170–71.
8. "Beaten Lamont Devalues Pound," *The Times,* 17 September 1992.
9. David Sanders, " 'It's the Economy, Stupid': The Economy and Support for the Conservative Party," *Talking Politics* 7 (1995):162.
10. The figures are reproduced in Ivor Crewe, "Electoral Behaviour," in *The Major Effect,* edited by Dennis Kavanagh and Anthony Seldon (London: Macmillan, 1994), 109.
11. At the end of the Parliament, the Labour Party claimed—as a result of some

double-counting—that the number was 22. Ministers responded by pointing out that the number of occasions on which tax rates were reduced was even greater, though the tax burden was not brought below its 1992 level.

12. The figures include a number of Conservative MPs who were without the Conservative whip, the reasons for which are discussed below.

13. House of Commons Debates, vol. 226, cols. 282–3.

14. See Philip Norton, "The United Kingdom: Political Conflict, Parliamentary Scrutiny," in *National Parliaments and the European Union*, edited by Philip Norton (London: Frank Cass, 1996), 92–94.

15. Treaties do not require parliamentary ratification. They are negotiated and agreed under the monarch's (in practice, the government's) prerogative powers. However, a clause inserted in the 1978 European Assembly Elections Act requires that any treaty increasing the powers of the European Parliament has to be approved by Parliament.

16. House of Commons Debates, vol. 208, cols. 597–600.

17. House of Commons Debates, vol. 212, col. 57.

18. *Sunday Times,* 25 October 1992.

19. *The Times,* 6 November 1992.

20. House of Commons Debates, vol. 213, cols. 377–85.

21. See David Baker, Andrew Gamble, and Steve Ludlam, "The Parliamentary Siege of Maastricht 1993: Conservative Divisions and British Ratification," *Parliamentary Affairs* 47 (1994):39–42.

22. "Major Humiliated as Rebels Inflict Maastricht Defeat," *The Times,* 9 March 1993. The amendment provided for a different British membership of the European Union Committee of the Regions to that proposed by the government.

23. House of Commons Debates, vol. 220, cols. 715–19.

24. House of Commons Debates, vol. 225, cols. 468–71.

25. House of Lords Debates, vol. 548, cols. 328–32. The tellers announced the numbers as 445 to 176, but the clerks recorded 446 names against and 176 for.

26. The following day it was revealed that the whips had miscounted and that the amendment had been defeated anyway, by 317 votes to 316. According to the story circulating at the time, the government whip in the aye lobby had heard someone shout "all out" and thought that it was an MP's name being shouted and so added an extra one to the final tally.

27. Teresa Gorman, with Heather Kirby, *The Bastards* (London: Pan Books, 1993), 218.

28. "Tories Punish Maastricht Rebel," *The Times,* 26 November 1993.

29. "Lamont Sees No Reason to Stay in Europe," *The Times,* 12 October 1994.

30. "Lamont Ends Tory Truce on Europe," *The Times,* 12 October 1994.

31. "Eurosceptics Renew Threat of Defiance," *The Times,* 23 November 1994.

32. "Cabinet Pact to Resign if Rebels Win," *The Times,* 24 November 1994.

33. Philip Norton, "Whipless MPs," *The House Magazine,* 9 January 1995, 10–11.

34. "Whips Blamed for Scale of Victory by Tory Rebels," *The Times,* 8 December 1994.

35. "Major Defeated by Tory Revolt over Rise in VAT," *Daily Telegraph,* 7 December 1994.

36. Confidential source to author.

37. House of Commons Debates, vol. 268, cols. 1401–5.

38. House of Commons Debates, vol. 276, cols. 202–3.

39. House of Commons Debates, vol. 279, cols. 120–21.

40. "Thatcher Rebuked by Angry Major," *The Times,* 14 June 1996.

41. "We Have an Absolute Right to Say No to a Single Currency," *The Times,* 25 July 1996.

42. "Right Opens Fire on Clarke over Single Currency," *The Times,* 9 October 1996; "Euro-sceptics Spurn Appeal for Unity," *Independent,* 9 October 1996.

43. "Federalism by Stealth Warning from Lamont," *Guardian,* 10 October 1996.

44. "Unity, Unity, Unity—or Just a Tactical Truce?" *Financial Times,* 11 October 1996.

45. House of Commons Debates, vol. 286, cols. 21–24.

46. Michael Crick, *Michael Heseltine: A Biography* (London: Hamish Hamilton, 1997), 432.

47. "Major Tells Sceptics: I Will Not Be Bullied," *The Times,* 9 December 1996.

48. House of Commons Debates, vol. 287, cols. 287–302.

49. "Major Rules Out Joining EMU in 1999," *The Times,* 24 January 1997.

50. *Financial Times,* 29 January 1997.

51. See David Baker, Andrew Gamble, and Steve Ludlam, "Whips or Scorpions? The Maastricht Vote and the Conservative Party," *Parliamentary Affairs* 46 (1993):151–66; Peter Riddell, "Major and Parliament," in Kavanagh and Seldon, *The Major Effect* (London: Macmillan, 1994), 51–53; and Norton, "The United Kingdom," 94–95.

52. The following figures are taken from "Focus," *Sunday Times,* 18 June 1995, 13.

53. These figures were reported on the BBC2 *Newsnight* programme on 2 May 1997 and published in "Fault Lines Hamper Tory Rebuilding," *Guardian,* 3 May 1997.

54. Phillip Oppenheim, "Diary of an Underdog," *Sunday Times,* 4 May 1997.

55. Philip Norton, "Prime Ministerial Power: A Framework for Analysis," *Teaching Politics,* 16 (1987):327–32.

56. Norton, "The Conservative Party from Thatcher to Major," 60–61.

57. Philip Norton, "Conclusion: Where to From Here?" in Norton, *The Conservative Party,* 235–38. See also Philip Norton, *"Think, Minister....":Reinvigorating Government in the UK* (London: Centre for Policy Studies, 1997).

58. Philip Cowley, "How Did He Do That? The Second Round of the 1990 Conservative Leadership Election," in *British Elections and Party Yearbook 1996,* edited by David M. Farrell, David Broughton, David Denver, and Justin Fisher (London: Frank Cass, 1996), 198–216.

59. Hugo Young, "The Prime Minister," in Kavanagh and Seldon, *The Major*

Effect, 22. See also Dennis Kavanagh, "A Major Agenda?" in the same volume.

60. Sarah Hogg and Jonathan Hill, *Too Close to Call: Power and Politics —John Major in No. 10* (London: Little, Brown, 1995), 265.

61. Kenneth Baker, "This Is No Way to Run a Government," *Sunday Telegraph*, 4 December 1994.

62. "Referendum Pledge Will Fuel Party Strife, Major Told," *The Times*, 14 December 1994.

63. "Heseltine and Clarke Unite Against Major," *Sunday Times*, 11 December 1994.

64. "Man in the Psychological Bubble," *Sunday Times*, 4 May 1997.

65. "Major Faces New Struggle for Survival," *The Times*, 30 March 1994.

66. "Major Faces New Plot to Oust Him," *Sunday Times*, 13 November 1994.

67. "Lamont Set to Challenge Major," *Sunday Telegraph*, 27 November 1994.

68. A copy of the revised rules can be found in Leonard P. Stark, *Choosing the Leader* (London: Macmillan, 1996), 173–76.

69. See Hogg and Hill, *Too Close to Call*, 266–70.

70. Press statement by the Prime Minister, 22 June 1995.

71. See, e.g., "Redwood Ready to Enter Tory Race," *Sunday Telegraph*, 25 June 1995.

72. "Major Attacks Redwood as 'Malcontent,'" *The Times*, 27 June 1995.

73. "Back Me or Face Abyss, Says Major," *Daily Telegraph*, 3 July 1995.

74. See "The Endgame: How Major Cut a Deal," *Sunday Times*, 9 July 1995.

75. "Wobbly Major Was Ready to Quit the Race," *Independent on Sunday*, 9 July 1995.

76. Hogg and Hill, *Too Close to Call*, 281.

77. Minister to author. See also Hogg and Hill, *Too Close to Call*, 282.

78. Philip Norton, "A Close Run Thing: The 1995 Conservative Leadership Contest," *British Politics Group Newsletter*, 82 (1995):9–12.

79. "Right Rues 'Worst Day since Thatcher Was Forced Out,'" *The Times*, 6 July 1995.

80. "Back to Basics," *Conservative Newsline*, 336 (November 1993):4.

81. David Leigh and Ed Vulliamy, *Sleaze: The Corruption of Parliament* (London: Fourth Estate, 1997), 149.

82. For the two sides of the case, see Leigh and Vulliamy, *Sleaze*; and Ian Greer, *One Man's Word* (London: André Deutsch, 1997).

83. *Report of the Inquiry into the Export of Defence Equipment and Dual-Use Goods to Iraq and Related Prosecutions*, HC 115 (London: HMSO, 1996).

84. "Major Tries to Buy Off Rebels," *Guardian*, 26 February 1996.

85. See "Tories Hang On by One Vote," *Guardian*, 27 February 1996.

86. Philip Cowley and Philip Norton, *Are Conservative MPs Revolting? Dissension by Government MPs in the British House of Commons 1979–96* (Hull: Centre for Legislative Studies, 1996).

87. See Paul Whiteley, Patrick Seyd, and Jeremy Richardson, *True Blues: The Politics of Conservative Party Membership* (Oxford: Clarendon Press, 1994).

5

The Battle for the Campaign Agenda

Pippa Norris

The 1997 election was a struggle not just for votes but also for control of the campaign agenda. Significant challenges faced the media, the parties, and the public. For the media, the problem was how to spark any interest in the campaign. Ever since Black Wednesday, Labour had seemed assured of victory while the Conservatives floundered. For five years—it seemed even longer—pundits had been writing of the end of the Conservative era, bolstered by the accumulating evidence from opinion polls, by-elections, and local elections. By the start of the six-week campaign, the horse race story was almost lifeless.

Moreover, to the dismay of commentators and columnists, Blair's strategic shift towards the centre-left had removed much dramatic policy conflict between the major parties. Few issues remained on which anyone could discern clear blue water between Labour and the Conservatives —devolution and constitutional reform, perhaps the faint ghost of trade union rights, and spending priorities—but on almost everything else the contest was a classic case of an echo, not a choice. At the outset the campaign promised tight party control, in as gaffe-free an environment as could humanly be managed. At the start the Labour Party seemed insecure and sweaty despite its enormous lead in the polls. The professional Mandelson machine at Millbank Tower left almost nothing to chance, as though the soufflé of Labour support might suddenly collapse. Based on their formidable track record during the 1980s, the Conservatives had a reputation for running highly professional campaigns. Given the palpable sense of public boredom and impatience, a feeling of oh-do-let's-get-on-with-it, the challenge for journalists was to find something fresh and interesting to hold the attention of their readers and viewers. During the six-week campaign there were, on average, about ten hours of regular BBC and ITN television news and current affairs programmes every weekday,[1] not including the plethora of other media coverage. Something had to fill the ravenous news hole.

For the public, the primary urge seemed to be to get it over and done with. But voters also needed to make sense of the choice before them, when policy differences between the parties had shaded from the red-and-blue days of Thatcher versus Foot to a wishy-washy mauve. Many issues confronting the voters were complex, technical, and subtle, with no easy answers.

Parties faced different problems. Given their lead, Labour's primary challenge was to manage the media environment against unexpected crises, in a play-safe reactive mode. The watchword was control. Memories of the 1992 opinion poll fiasco and Neil Kinnock's false expectation of victory in that campaign ("We're all right!") dominated strategy in 1997. The Conservatives needed to boost grassroots morale by emphasising their positive economic performance, by reassuring voters to trust Prime Minister John Major against the inexperienced and unknown Tony Blair, and by attacking Labour on the old bugaboos of taxes and trade unions. To gain traction the Conservatives had to take more risks than Labour. The challenge facing all the minor parties, but particularly the Liberal Democrats, was to avoid being squeezed by Labour's slither to the centre-left.

Who won the battle to control the campaign agenda? This chapter examines the battle and evaluates its outcome. The first section sets out the long-term context by considering how campaigning has been transformed in the postwar era. The 1997 election represented another critical step, it will be argued, in the transition to the postmodern campaign in Britain, characterised by partisan dealignment in the press, growing fragmentation in the electronic media, and strategic communications by the parties. The second section goes on to analyse what was covered in the national press and television during the campaign and whether the pattern of coverage suggests that Labour won the battle of the campaign agenda as well as the actual election. Lastly, we consider how the public reacted to the coverage, whether they felt that journalists generated interesting, fair, and informative coverage, and the implications of our analysis for the struggle over campaign communications.

The Evolution of the Postmodern Campaign

Modernisation theory suggests that during the postwar era the political communication process has been transformed by the decline of direct linkages between citizens and parties and the rise instead of mediated relationships. Similar though not identical developments, Swanson and Mancini argue, are recognisable across the industrialised democracies.[2] In the earliest stage, the premodern campaign in Britain was characterised by the predominance of the partisan press, a loose organisational network of grassroots party volunteers in local constituencies, and a short, ad hoc national campaign run by the party leaders with a few close advisers. This period of campaigning gradually evolved in the mid-nineteenth century, following the development of mass party organisations registering and mobilising the newly enfranchised electorate. Despite the introduction of wireless broadcasting in 1922, this pattern was maintained in largely identifiable form until the late 1950s.[3] The watershed came in 1959, with the first television coverage of a British general election, symbolising the transition to the next stage.

The evolution of the modern campaign was marked by a shift in the central location of electoral communications, from newspapers towards television, from the constituency grassroots to the party leadership and from amateurs towards professionals. The press entered an era of long-term decline: circulation of national newspapers peaked in the late 1950s, and sales have subsequently dropped by one-third (see figure 5.1). The fall was sharpest among tabloids, pushing them further downmarket in the search for readers.[4] This fierce competition transformed the nature of the British press, producing growing sensationalism and more journalism "with attitude," while changes in ownership ratcheted the partisan balance further in the Conservative direction.

A major factor producing declining circulation was the rise of television. The political effects of this new technology were strongly mediated by the regulations governing broadcasting in each country. In Britain the legal framework for the BBC/ITV duopoly was suffused by a strong public-service ethos that required broadcasters to maintain "party balance" and impartiality in news coverage, to "inform, educate and entertain" according to high standards, and to provide an agreed allocation of unpaid airtime to party political broadcasts.[5] Within this familiar context, television centralised the campaign and thereby increased the influence of the party leaders: what appeared on BBC1's flagship *Nine O'Clock News* and ITN's *News at Ten,* and related news and current affairs programmes, were the principal means by which politicians reached the vast majority of voters.

To work effectively within this environment, parties developed a co-ordinated national campaign with professional communications orchestrated by specialists skilled in advertising, marketing, and polling. The "long campaign" in the year or so before polling day became as important strategically as the short, "official" campaign. These changes did not

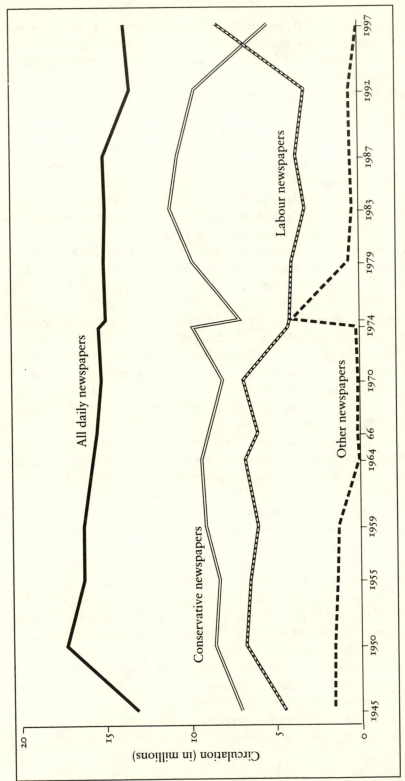

FIGURE 5.1. PARTISAN BALANCE OF THE PRESS, 1945–97

NOTE: Party affiliation defined by editorial endorsements.

occur overnight, nor did they displace grassroots constituency activity, as the timeless ritual of canvassing and leafletting continued. A few trusted experts in polling and political marketing became influential in each party during the campaign, such as Maurice Saatchi, Tim Bell, and Gordon Reece in Conservative Central Office, but their role remained that of part-time outside advisers. They were not integral to the process of government or even to campaigning, which was still run by politicians. Unlike in the United States, no political marketing industry developed, in large part because the only major clients were the Labour and Conservative leaderships. The minor parties had limited resources, while individual parliamentary candidates ran retail campaigns based on grassroots helpers and shoe leather. But the net effect of television during the era of modernisation was to shift the primary focus of the campaign from the ad hoccery of unpaid volunteers and local candidates towards the central party leadership flanked by paid, although not necessarily full-time, professionals.[6]

Lastly, in the late twentieth century Britain seems to have been experiencing the rise of the postmodern campaign, although there remains room for dispute in the interpretation of the central features of this development. The most identifiable characteristics, evident in the 1997 campaign, include the emergence of a more autonomous and less partisan press, following its own "media logic," the growing fragmentation and diversification of electronic media outlets, programmes, and audiences, and, in reaction to all these developments, the attempt by parties to reassert control through strategic communications and media management during the permanent campaign. Politicians realised that the techniques of monitoring the pulse of public opinion and mobilising support outside Westminster needed to be extended beyond the month-long official campaign to everyday politics between elections. In the United States, where this process has gone further, the techniques for electioneering and for governing have become completely intertwined.

Partisan Dealignment in the Press

In the postwar period, parties had long-standing and stable links with the press. In 1945 there was a rough partisan balance, with about 6.7 million readers of pro-Conservative papers and 4.4 million readers of pro-Labour papers. This balance shifted decisively in the early 1970s, with the transformation of the left-leaning *Daily Herald* into the pro-Conservative *Sun* and with the more aggressively right-wing tone of *The Times,* both under Rupert Murdoch's ownership. By 1992 the cards had become overwhelmingly stacked against the left: the circulation of the Conservative-leaning press had risen to about 8.7 million compared with only 3.3 million for Labour-leaning papers (see figure 5.1, p. 116). Throughout the 1980s Margaret Thatcher could campaign assured of a largely sympathetic press that provided a loyal platform for getting her message across.[7] One of the most striking developments of recent years has been the crumbling of these traditional press-party loyalties.

The evidence comes partly from editorial policy. The Conservative press had started to turn against Thatcher in 1989–90, when the economy was in recession and her leadership was becoming increasingly unpopular, and this constant barrage of press criticism probably contributed towards her eventual political demise.[8] During the 1992 election, while the *Sun* and the *Daily Express* continued to beat the Tory drum, comment from some of the other pro-Conservative papers, such as the *Mail* and the *Sunday Times*, was more muted, and four out of eleven daily papers failed to endorse a single party.[9]

The new government enjoyed a brief respite on returning to office, but press criticism of John Major's leadership deepened following the ERM debacle on 16 September 1992, with only the *Daily Express* staying loyal. The *Sun*'s reaction the day after Black Wednesday—"Now we've all been screwed by the government"—blamed the government for losing £9 billion in reserves, to no apparent avail. The *Daily Mirror* described John Major as a political pygmy, while even the *Daily Mail* warned that Major's "flip-flop" government was in danger of becoming no more than a joke. Only later was it revealed that the depths of the damage caused by the ERM debacle had caused John Major seriously to consider resignation, only to be dissuaded by senior cabinet colleagues.

Throughout 1993–94, headlines continued to highlight the government's difficulties over Europe and the Tories' deep internal splits over the debate on the Maastricht treaty. The Conservative backbench rebellion by the "whipless nine" produced irresistible human drama. Moreover, the image of a tired and dispirited government was made worse by a succession of scandals involving Conservative politicians. Sex scandals involving senior ministers and more obscure backbenchers were not only splashed by the tabloids but also covered by the broadsheets and television news. Among the more lurid revelations were those concerning the heritage minister ("the minister for fun"), David Mellor, and his long-standing affair with an unemployed actress, and it was an unfortunate coincidence that Mellor, before he resigned, happened to be the minister responsible for new legislative proposals on press privacy.

As though that were not enough, the tabloids then piled in with two stories about Norman Lamont, one claiming that the chancellor of the exchequer had not paid a credit-card bill and another reporting that he had rented part of his London house to a "sex therapist." When Lamont finally evicted the woman, the government incurred yet more bad publicity by agreeing that some of the chancellor's legal costs should be defrayed by the Treasury—that is, the taxpayer. The *News of the World* headline in April 1993 read "Chancellor's Flat Is Vice Den." The government defended itself where it could. The impecunious *New Statesman* was successfully sued over hints of an affair between John Major and Clair Latimer, and the damages awarded seriously affected its finances. But the tabloids' attack was too sustained to regard this success as more than a minor victory in a bloody war.

Stories like these were compounded by financial scandals, most notably the "cash for questions" issue that was championed by the *Guardian* but covered by all the papers. By the time of the 1997 general election, twenty-three Conservative candidates who were standing again had been involved, at one time or another, in personal scandal. The stain spread from the individual MPs to the party leadership, and editorials in the previously Conservative press regularly denounced the government, particularly the prime minister, for lack of decisive action to reprimand or sack the miscreants.

The flavour of the press as the government floundered in the opinion polls can be vividly illustrated by its coverage of the 1995 Conservative leadership contest. Unable to quell the civil war over Europe within his own party, Major's was a desperate gamble finally to resolve matters one way or another. The rumours and counterrumours about who would and would not back John Redwood and about the chances of Michael Heseltine or Michael Portillo or Norman Lamont entering the race swirled around Palace Green and provided yet more human drama. Typical comment from the previously loyal Tory press came on 25 June 1995 from the *Sunday Times:* "Forget for a moment the question marks over his style of leadership, the hikes in taxation, the failure to tackle welfare spending, the endless stream of sleaze, and the own goals. He has to surprise us by confronting head on the dominant issue of our time: where does the party stand on the future of Britain in Europe? Nothing less will bridge the cavernous rifts within the party." The general tone was reflected in the headline over Andrew Neil's commentary: "Major Is a Loser and He Must Go." Only the *Daily Express* backed Major solidly, with the *Sun,* the *Mail, The Times,* and the *Daily Telegraph* all arguing that it was time for him to go.[10] For the *Sun*'s editorial writer, the prime minister was "damaged goods" with "loser" written all over him: "Major could not lead a cinema queue, let alone a country." The *Mail* tilted its coverage in favour of Redwood, describing Major as "this most likeable of premiers who has become one of the least respected leaders of modern times." And the most Conservative of papers, the *Daily Telegraph,* said Major had "held his government together at the price of ceaseless fudge, muddle, compromise and obfuscation." All these comments proved a considerable embarrassment for Conservative leader writers, given the outcome. After Major's victory there was a short hiatus when press criticism subsided slightly, but in February 1996 the publication of the Scott Report on the "arms to Iraq" affair raised questions about the conduct of William Waldegrave and Sir Nicholas Lyell and provoked attacks on the government's competence in all the papers.

Why did the bulk of the press turn so vehemently against the government and particularly the leadership? A variety of factors probably contributed towards changed loyalties, although it is difficult to know which proved most decisive. In part, the papers may have been following, instead of leading, opinion among their readers. The depths of the government's unpopularity in the opinion polls, evident with Labour's commanding lead ever since Black Wednesday, may have convinced some papers that they would lose some of their market share if they persisted in backing probable losers. Moreover, the sea change in party policies, with Tony Blair's shift to the centre-left, abandonment of the socialist trilogy of nationalisation, unilateralism, and trade union rights, and his modernisation of the party, may have convinced journalists, commentators, and leader writers that New Labour did provide an attractive, energetic, fresh, and newsworthy alternative to the overfamiliar and tired faces on the government front bench.

According to insider accounts, the attitudes of the proprietors, notably Rupert Murdoch, seem to have been influenced by Peter Mandelson's and Alastair Campbell's charm offensive and their strategic courting of the press and by Tony Blair's leadership. Lastly, the most plausible reason for the papers' shifting loyalties seems to have been the general tabloidisation of the press, described below, which led to far greater attention to personal scandal and sensationalism in high places, whether about the younger royals or government ministers. Coverage in the British press in the next few years will help ascertain whether, when Labour popularity slides, its newfound friends in the press will start to desert the government, signifying dealignment, or whether the period from 1992 to 1997 will have portended a longer-term realignment of traditional loyalties among British newspapers.

One question, therefore, in the long run-up to the election was whether the Tory press would return home once the Conservative government's future was under real threat. In the event, the 1997 election represented an historic watershed. In a major break with tradition, six of the ten national dailies, and five of the nine Sundays, endorsed the Labour Party in their final editorials (see table 5.1, p. 122). This was twice the highest previous number, and it reversed the long-standing pro-Conservative leanings in the national press. With impeccable timing, the *Sun* led the way on the very first day of the campaign, with a splash headline "The Sun Backs Blair" and a front-page leader claiming that Blair is a "breath of fresh air," while the Conservatives were "tired, divided and rudderless." The *Sun*'s defection stole the headlines and deeply damaged Tory morale. This stunning change of heart came after assiduous efforts by Labour to court press support, including meetings between Blair and Rupert Murdoch in 1995. Throughout the campaign the *Sun,* with 10 million readers a day, provided largely unswerving support for Blair, although continuing to oppose Labour policy on Europe and the unions; commentators close to Murdoch, such as Andrew Neil, predicted that the switch, based on commercial considerations rather than political affinities, would not last long.[11] Labour's traditional tabloid, the *Daily Mirror,* with 6 million readers, continued to purvey its brand of centre-left journalism ("the paper for Labour's *true* supporters"). On the last Sunday of the campaign, influenced by Murdoch, the *News of the World* decided to follow the lead of its sister paper, the *Sun,* and backed Labour.

Among the broadsheets the *Guardian* called for tactical voting for the Liberal Democrats in seats where that made sense, but broadly it endorsed Labour. The *Independent* was more restrained in its backing, casting its vote for Labour "with a degree of optimism that is not entirely justified by the evidence." The paper was clearly more anti-Tory than pro-anything. *The Times* advised its readers to back Eurosceptic candidates from whatever party, though in practice nearly all the Eurosceptics were Conservatives. Only the *Daily Telegraph* and the *Daily Mail* ("Labour Bully Boys Are Back"; "Labour's Broken Promises") remained strongly in the Tory camp. Even the *Daily Express* was more neutral than in the past: a double-page spread was divided between Lord Hollick, its chief executive, arguing for Labour, and its chairman, Lord Stevens, arguing for the Conservatives. The front page of the election-eve *Daily Mail* carried a colourful Union Jack border and the apocalyptic warning that a Labour victory could "undo 1,000 years of our nation's history."[12]

Yet any comparison of editorial policy probably gives a misleading impression of the balance of partisanship in news coverage before and during the campaign. For example, the *Mail* ostensibly endorsed the Conservatives during the campaign, but in practice it probably damaged the government by headlining sexual scandals within the party and rein-

TABLE 5.1

NATIONAL DAILY PRESS: OWNERSHIP, CIRCULATION, AND PARTISANSHIP

Newspaper	Owner	Editor	Circulation April 1997	Preferred election winner
Daily Express	MAI/United, Lord Hollick	Richard Addis	1,220,000	Conservative
Daily Mail	Associated Newspapers, Lord Rothermere	Paul Dacre	2,151,000	Conservative
Daily Mirror	Mirror Group	Piers Morgan	3,084,000	Labour
Daily Star	MAI/United, Lord Hollick	Phil Walker	648,000	Labour
Daily Telegraph	Hollinger, Conrad Black	Charles Moore	1,134,000	Conservative
Financial Times	Pearson, Lord Blakenham	Richard Lambert	307,000	Labour
Guardian	Scott Trust	Alan Rusbridger	401,000	Labour
Independent	Mirror Group	Andrew Marr	251,000	Labour
Sun	News International, Rupert Murdoch	Stuart Higgins	3,842,000	Labour
The Times	News International, Rupert Murdoch	Peter Stothard	719,000	(Eurosceptic)

SOURCE: Colin Seymour-Ure, "Editorial Opinion in the National Press," *Parliamentary Affairs* 50, no. 4 (1997).

forcing images of disunity, with leading articles highlighting the number of Tory Eurosceptics. With friends like the *Mail,* the Conservatives hardly needed enemies. To appreciate this point fully, we need to go beyond the leaders, which are rarely read and even less heeded, and examine the broader pattern of front-page stories. The most plausible evidence for press dealignment is not just that certain papers like the *Sun,* traditionally pro-Conservative, switched camps but also that front-page stories were often so similar across all the papers, driven by news values irrespective of any paper's ostensible partisanship.

Since the early 1970s, there has been more sensational coverage in the popular press, fuelled by an endless diet of stories about "scandals" (mostly sexual but also financial), film and television stars, and the royals, preferably all three. This process started when Rupert Murdoch bought the *News of the World* in 1968 and the *Sun* a year later. It accelerated as a result of cutthroat competition produced by the launch in 1978 of the *Daily Star,* which sought to outdo the *Sun* in its relentless search for investigative "exclusives" about celebrities, sex, violent crime, and graphic coverage of the bizarre. Those who thought that British newspapers had reached their nadir at this point underestimated the soft-porn *Sunday Sport,* launched in 1986.[13]

The tackiness of the popular press, with its endless gossip about the goings-on of the younger royals, gradually infected and corroded the news culture of the broadsheets as well. By the mid-1990s, the journalism of scandal trumped the journalism of partisanship hands down. This development helped promote the series of sleaze stories about Conservative politicians that ran throughout John Major's years in government, and there was no let-up during the actual campaign. As documented in detail later, the first two weeks of the election were dominated by a succession of stories about corruption in public life and sex scandals, providing a steady diet of negative news for the Conservatives and swamping their message about the economy.

The most plausible reason for this sensationalism is the fierce competition for readers following the plummeting circulation figures: between 1981 and 1995 the proportion of the public reading a daily paper dropped from 76 to 62 percent among men and from 68 to 54 percent among women.[14] In Britain the national press competes for attention headline-to-headline in newsagents' shopwindows, unlike in countries where there are strong regional papers with their own distinct markets.

This drive for readers may also have influenced the papers' shift in partisanship, if indeed they decided to follow rather than lead changes in popular views of the government. At the start of the campaign, according to MORI polls from 1 January to 17 March 1997, only the *Express* and the *Telegraph* out of nineteen daily and Sunday papers had clear majorities of readers who said they would vote Conservative (see table 5.2). Papers may have believed that they could not expect to maintain circulation if they advocated views too far out of line with those of their readers. This possibility was later publicly acknowledged by Lord Rothermere, proprietor of the *Mail.* He was asked whether the editor of the *Daily Mail,* Paul Dacre, would be allowed to continue to express his Euroscepticism. "It is a free country," he replied, "and he is entitled to his views and to express them. But, of course, if they start to affect the circulation, that will be different."[15] In many countries that used to have a strongly partisan press, like the Netherlands, political coverage is now driven more strongly by an autonomous "media logic" in the fierce competition for readers than by traditional allegiances or the proprietor's politics. "Modern media are more powerful, more independent, and more determined to pursue their own interests through a professional culture of their own making."[16] This dealignment has increased the complexity and uncertainty of media management for the parties, which can no longer rely on getting their message out through well-known and sympathetic sources.

The Growing Fragmentation
of the Electronic Media

Although newspaper circulation has shrunk, the electronic media expanded during this same period, with far greater diversification in the 1990s. The erosion of the BBC's and ITV's duopoly of viewers proceeded relatively slowly in Britain, compared with the fall in the networks' share of the audience in wired countries like the United States, the Netherlands, and Canada. Channel 5 covered about two-thirds of Britain when it was launched in March 1997, although with a modest audience; and this added to the existing choice of four terrestrial channels. But today the BBC/ITV duopoly faces its greatest competition from the rapid emergence of digital, cable, and satellite "narrowcasting" and from such new forms of interactive communications as the Internet.

The first satellite services became available in Britain from Sky TV in February 1989, followed by BSB the following year. By 1992, about 3 percent of homes had access to cable TV, while 10 percent had a satellite dish. In contrast, by 1997 almost a fifth of all households could tune into fifty channels on satellite and cable. In these homes, more than a third of all viewing was on these channels. During the election campaign, between 10 and 15 percent of the audience usually watched cable and satel-

TABLE 5.2

CHANGES IN SUPPORT FOR PARTY BY DAILY NEWSPAPERS' READERS, 1992–97
(IN PERCENTAGES)

Newspaper	Conservative			Labour			Liberal Democrat		
	General election 1992	Jan–Mar 1997	Change	General election 1992	Jan–Mar 1997	Change	General election 1992	Jan–Mar 1997	Change
Daily Express	67	52	–15	15	32	+17	14	12	–2
Daily Mail	65	48	–17	15	34	+19	18	13	–5
Daily Mirror	20	12	–8	64	79	+15	14	7	–7
Daily Star	31	19	–12	54	67	+13	12	11	–1
Daily Telegraph	72	57	–15	11	27	+16	16	11	–5
Financial Times	65	43	–22	17	45	+28	16	9	–7
Guardian	15	6	–9	55	75	+20	24	14	–10
Independent	25	15	–10	37	67	+30	34	16	–18
Sun	45	27	–18	36	59	+23	14	8	–6
The Times	64	41	–23	16	38	+22	19	16	–3

SOURCE: MORI.

lite programmes every evening. Occasionally, when there was wall-to-wall coverage on the terrestrial channels, such as on Thursday, 24 April, a week before the election, the proportion of cable and satellite viewers jumped to almost a quarter of the audience. Moreover, *Sky News,* CNN, Channel 5, and BBC Radio's 5 *Live* have altered the pace of the news, offering brief headlines on the hour every hour. The planned launch of about thirty digital television channels in summer 1998, under the consortium British Digital Broadcasting (BDB), will further increase this diversity. The new service promises more channels, interactive services, and access to the Internet. The BBC Multiplex promises a twenty-four-hour TV news channel, and BDB's Multiplex plans *Public Eye,* with documentaries and *Sky News.* Until now British television has been remarkably resistant to fragmentation of television, but the dam now looks as though it is about it break.

While probably only political junkies surfed the Internet in 1997, the easy availability of the BBC's *Election '97,* ITN Online, the online headlines from the Press Association and Reuters, the parties' home pages, as well as electronic versions of *The Times* and the *Telegraph,* dramatically accelerated the news cycle. The BBC's *Politics '97,* giving easy access to RealAudio and RealVideo broadcasts of its major political programmes (such as live web transmission of the budget), promises the shape of things to come. With twenty-four-hour coverage, the acceleration of the news cycle has dramatically increased the need for parties to respond rapidly or get knocked off their feet by a suddenly shifting agenda.

Strategic Party Communications during the Permanent Campaign

As press-party loyalties have declined and the outlets for electronic news have diversified, politicians have been forced to respond to a more complex communications environment. Parties have been transformed by the gradual evolution of the permanent campaign, where the techniques of spin doctors, opinion pollsters, and professional media managers are increasingly applied to everyday routine politics. Peter Mandelson's central role in the Labour campaign and the high-tech developments in media management at Millbank Tower are not isolated phenomena.[17] Supposedly modelled on the "war room" in the Clinton campaign, the Millbank organisation had a tight inner core, including Peter Mandelson, Gordon Brown, the press secretary Alastair Campbell, the pollster Philip Gould, Blair's personal assistant Anji Hunter, Lord Irvine of Lairg, and Jonathan

Powell. The inner circle was surrounded by about 200 staffers connecting via fax, modem, and pagers to key shadow spokepersons and candidates in the marginal constituencies—all in order to keep the party "on-message." Briefings were sent out nightly, sometimes twice a day. The Labour Party designed its communications strategy down to the smallest detail, with a rebuttal unit under the direction of Adrian Mc-Menamin, ready for a rapid response to anticipated attacks.

After 1992, Labour realised that elections are not usually won or lost in the official campaign, and they therefore designed a strategy for the long haul. Labour renewed its interest in constituency campaigns, and local contests became increasingly professionalised by strategic targeting of key voters under the guidance of Millbank Tower. For two years before polling day, a Labour task force was designed to switch 5,000 voters in each of ninety target marginal seats. Those identified as potential Labour converts in these seats were contacted by teams of volunteers on the doorstep and by a canvassing operation run from twenty telephone banks around the country, coordinated from Millbank. In January 1997 "get out the vote" letters were sent to each type of target voter, and young people received a video of Tony Blair.[18] Candidates in marginals were asked to contact at least 1,000 switchers. Information from the canvassing operation, especially on issues of concern raised by voters, was also fed back to Philip Gould, to help shape Labour's presentation.

Labour carried out opinion polling regularly from late 1993, and Philip Gould and Deborah Mattinson conducted a programme of focus-group research to monitor reaction to Labour's policies. Strategy meetings were conducted almost daily from late 1994, tackling Labour's weaknesses on taxation, trade unions, and crime well before the official campaign began. The manifesto *New Labour Because Britain Deserves Better* was designed to focus on five specific pledges: cutting class sizes for under-seven-year-olds; fast-track punishments for persistent young offenders; reducing NHS waiting lists; moving 250,000 young unemployed into work; and cutting VAT on domestic heating fuel. By launching the draft manifesto *New Labour, New Life for Britain* as a dry run a year earlier, Labour had had ample opportunity to iron out any pledges that proved controversial. The main theme of Labour's advertising was "Britain Deserves Better"—bland and safe. To press home the message, Tony Blair visited sixty constituencies, travelling some 10,000 miles by road, rail, and air, providing controlled photo opportunities rather than press conferences for the media. The membership drive that Blair launched was also part of his long-term strategy. It increased rank-and-file membership by almost two-thirds, from 261,000 in 1991 to

420,000 by the time of the election.[19] This achievement was in stark contrast to the Conservatives, whose membership fell, perhaps by half, between 1992 and 1997 to an estimated 350,000 to 400,000.[20] Lastly, Labour's assiduous courting of the City, including the launch of its special business manifesto, was all part of its planning to anticipate and batten down any lines of potential weakness.

In contrast, Conservative Central Office far more often appeared to be knocked off-message by events out of its control, with the topics planned for press conferences torn up at the last minute. The campaign was led by John Major, the party chairman, Brian Mawhinney, the deputy leader, Michael Heseltine, and Danny Finkelstein, head of Tory party research. Lord Saatchi advised Central Office, although up to twenty people attended strategy meetings, each with different priorities. During the long campaign the Conservatives seemed unable to decide whether the most effective strategy was to attack Old Labour (the party of trade unions and taxes) or New Labour (the party of "smarmy," "phoney," and untrustworthy Blair). Tory briefings, and posters, veered back and forth uncertainly.[21] Their most widely used slogans were "Britain Is Booming—Don't Let Labour Blow It" and "New Labour, New Danger," but their advertising was generally regarded as unconvincing (indeed a "Tony and Bill" poster was widely believed to be a Labour advertisement).

Labour suffered a wobbly day or two in early April, over privatisation of the air traffic control service, with Blair and Prescott producing contradictory messages. Some wobbles also occurred in the second week of the campaign, over the unions and Blair's "parish council" remarks about devolution. In the sixth week a rogue poll by ICM for the *Guardian,* suggesting that the Labour lead was closing, also induced concern in the Labour camp. But these were minor upsets. In contrast, the Conservatives became deeply mired in divisions, arguing with each other and not addressing the public, as the splits over Europe burst open again. On 14 April the *Daily Mail* published a list of 183 Conservative candidates who had come out against EMU in their constituency leaflets, in contradiction to the official "wait and see" line. In response John Major tore up the election broadcast planned for 17 April, and instead broadcast an impromptu appeal to voters to trust him on Europe. But the Tories' internal row only intensified the following day with publication of a Conservative advertisement showing Blair as a puppet on Chancellor Kohl's lap. The advertisement incurred the wrath of Sir Edward Heath and Kenneth Clarke (as well as many Germans) and only highlighted Conservative splits. Other diversions included speculation about a leadership election to succeed Major and comments like Edwina Currie's prediction of a Conservative defeat in the campaign's twilight days. In short, the Conservative message of Britain's economic health was drowned out as much by internal conflicts, fuelled but not caused by the media, as by anything the Opposition did or said. The *Daily Mail* may have tossed the lighted match, but the row between Eurosceptics and Europhiles was a conflagration waiting to happen.

The shift towards the permanent campaign in Britain has still not gone as far as in the United States, in part because of Britain's longer electoral cycle.[22] Nevertheless, the way that the techniques for campaigning are becoming merged with the techniques of governing was symbolised by the way in which Tony Blair, once prime minister, announced monthly "meet the public" sessions, to attract popular support in addition to his appearances in the Commons, following the example of President Clinton's "town hall" meetings. Moreover, many of those who played a key role in controlling Labour's campaign communications were transferred to Number 10, with the aim of adopting the same techniques in government. New ministers, for example, were told that press briefings had to be cleared centrally with Peter Mandelson, Blair's new minister without portfolio. Whether these arrangements succeed or not remains an open question, but what they indicate is that, given a more complex communications environment, modern parties believe that they have to adapt to survive.[23]

Who Won the Battle of the Campaign Agenda?

Within this new environment, what were the contents of the media coverage of the 1997 campaign? In particular, did Labour win the battle of the campaign agenda as well as the election? Here we can turn to a content analysis of the national press provided by CARMA, which monitored 6,072 articles in the national daily and Sunday newspapers from the announcement of the election (18 March) until polling day (1 May). CARMA analysed whether the article featured the Conservative Party (4,827 articles), Labour (4,536), the Liberal Democrats (1,390), or the Referendum Party (319), and then, for each party, classified the major topic of these articles using 150 coding categories (such as inflation, education, and trade unions). CARMA counted the number of articles (although not the length) that mentioned each topic every day, as well as estimating the favourability or unfavourability of each.[24]

The CARMA analysis found that about a fifth of all the election coverage in the press (19 percent) focussed on campaigning, such as stories about party strategy and the prospects for marginal seats, with much speculation about the (in the event nonexistent) television debates. The minutiae of insider electioneering, such as the campaign battle buses (complete with colour layout maps), high-tech and wooden soapboxes, and the Blairforce One, were described in detail by journalists bored by listening to the leaders' stump speeches.

If we break the analysis down in more detail (see table 5.3), we find that one quarter of this coverage, but in total only 10 percent of all news stories, concerned opinion polls, far less than in other recent elections. The media commissioned fewer polls than in 1987 or 1992 and gave them less coverage. About a fifth of all front-page lead stories in the national press were devoted to the polls in 1987 (20 percent) and in 1992 (18 percent), compared with only 4 percent in 1997.[25] Coverage of the polls on television news dropped from 14 percent in 1992 to only 7 percent in 1997.[26] A number of factors contributed towards this trend. BBC coverage was influenced by new management guidelines restricting the use of polls. Newspapers gave them less attention because of the predictability of the race with perpetually large Labour leads. On the day the rogue ICM poll appeared in the *Guardian,* with the Labour lead apparently closing, the whole of Fleet Street, led by the *Guardian,* went berserk. The polls' lowered reputation following their 1992 debacle may also have led to fewer papers commissioning regular surveys. Overall there was relatively little difference in the amount of attention given to each party in terms of electioneering, although it is notable that more

TABLE 5.3

PRESS COVERAGE OF CAMPAIGNING, 1997

(IN PERCENTAGES)

	All	*Con.*	*Lab.*	*Lib. Dem.*
Electioneering	25.3	26.8	24.5	22.3
Opinion polls, pundits	23.2	19.9	24.2	31.1
Ads/PEBs	10.5	10.4	12.7	4.7
TV debate	10.1	8.7	10.9	12.4
Key marginal seats	8.8	7.9	8.8	11.7
Media party support	8.4	8.8	9.9	2.8
Voting behaviour	5.2	6.3	3.8	5.3
Leadership contests	3.2	6.7	0.2	0.1
Fund raising/donations	2.7	2.8	3.0	1.8
Tactical voters	2.7	1.7	2.0	7.8
Total	100.0	100.0	100.0	100.0

SOURCE: CARMA.

NOTE: Content analysis of 6,072 articles in national press, 17 March–1 May 1997.

stories about the Liberal Democrats focussed on tactical voting, such as the *Observer*'s detailed survey of marginal seats towards the end of the campaign (which may have influenced the high levels of tactical voting evident in the results).

Almost half of all the press coverage (45 percent) discussed policy issues (see table 5.4), with detailed sections in the broadsheets analysing the contents of each party's manifesto promises. About one-quarter of this coverage (27 percent) focussed on problems of domestic social policy, particularly education, the National Health Service, pensions, and crime. The priority given to education by Labour, and even more by the Liberal Democrats, seems to have paid dividends in the two parties' media coverage. The economy absorbed another quarter of the coverage, particularly taxation, trade unions (for Labour), unemployment, and privatisation. CARMA's analysis clearly reveals the extent of the Conservatives' failure to focus media attention on their positive achievements. There was remarkably little political coverage of Britain's low levels of inflation, its strong balance-of-payments figures, its healthy economic growth, and its low interest rates, not to speak of the booming stock market.[27]

Altogether, economic and social policy absorbed the majority (58 percent) of Labour's issue coverage, broadly reflecting its manifesto priorities, particularly the five specific policy pledges mentioned earlier. In terms of agenda setting, the only major topics given significantly more attention in the press than in Labour's manifesto were the issues of trade unions and privatisation. In contrast, despite John Major's strenuous attempts to trumpet the government's economic record at daily press conferences and in the Tories' "Britain Is Booming" slogan, only a fifth (22 percent) of their issue coverage in the press focussed on the economy. The Conservatives simply failed to set the media agenda: there was twice as much coverage of their record on unemployment as on inflation.

In most elections foreign policy rarely surfaces as a major issue, unless the country is at war or there is major international conflict. During the 1992 campaign, for example, although Labour's defence policy was highlighted by Tory posters, foreign affairs occupied a mere 1 percent of all front-page news.[28] Yet in 1997, despite an era of peace and prosperity, at a time when the West had won the Cold War, a remarkable 17 percent of all issue coverage in the press focussed on foreign policy, nearly all concerning Britain's role in the European Union.[29] As discussed earlier, the press headlined Conservative splits over Europe: almost a fifth of the coverage of Conservative issues (19 percent) focussed on Europe, with a peak in the fifth week of the campaign (see figure 5.2, p. 134).

The Conservatives' agenda was also sabotaged by the issue of stan-

TABLE 5.4
COVERAGE OF POLICY ISSUES, 1997
(IN PERCENTAGES)

	Major issues	Major issues, total by category	Con.	Lab.	Lib. Dem.
Domestic social issues		26.8			
Education	6.9		5.1	8.0	11.1
NHS	4.6		4.0	5.1	5.5
Law and order	2.8		2.7	2.6	3.8
Pensions	2.4		3.0	2.0	1.7
Social security	1.4		1.4	1.6	1.0
Youth issues	1.2		1.0	1.0	3.0
Housing	1.0		1.2	.8	.5
Local government	.8		.6	.9	2.2
Environment	.9		.7	.8	2.6
Technology	.8		.6	.8	1.1
Food safety	.8		1.2	.4	.2
Family values	.7		1.1	.4	.2
Other	2.6		2.3	2.9	3.4
Economic issues		25.5			
Taxation	7.2		6.5	7.4	10.4
Trade unions	3.9		1.9	6.3	.3
Unemployment	3.7		3.5	4.3	1.9
Privatisation	3.4		2.1	5.2	.2
Public spending	1.8		1.6	2.0	1.7
Inflation	1.3		1.8	1.0	.4
Minimum wage	1.1		.4	1.9	.2
Economic growth	.8		1.5	.3	.2
Other	2.3		2.3	2.6	1.8

Continued ...

dards in public life: 18 percent of their total press coverage concerned stories about sex and sleaze. This was also the number-one topic in editorials,[30] and the story dominated the early stages of the campaign (see figure 5.2). The extent to which the Conservatives lost the battle of the media agenda can be illustrated most clearly by this single issue. The first week of the campaign was dominated by the "cash for questions" row, when some of the evidence given to the Commons inquiry headed by Sir Gordon Downey was leaked to the *Guardian* on 21 March.

During the second week, the Tories started to mount a counteroffensive: both the *Daily Mail* and the *Daily Telegraph* led with a splash story about the "union threat" under Labour, with the *Mail* publishing a

TABLE 5.4 — *Continued*

	Major issues	Major issues, total by category	Con.	Lab.	Lib. Dem.
Foreign affairs		17.0			
Single currency	4.6		6.4	3.1	2.2
European Union	3.3		3.7	3.1	2.7
Eurosceptics	2.4		4.1	.9	.9
Social chapter	1.7		1.1	2.5	.3
Federalism	1.2		1.5	1.2	.8
EC directives/laws	1.2		1.3	1.2	.8
Referendum on EU	1.0		1.1	.8	1.3
Other	1.2		.6	1.8	1.0
Standards in public life		11.8			
Sleaze	8.5		13.6	3.2	10.5
Trust/confidence	1.8		1.3	2.4	1.0
Sex	1.5		3.1	.2	.3
General party policies	9.4				
Manifesto	4.8		3.9	5.5	5.1
Party policy, general	2.5		1.7	3.1	2.6
Government record	1.4		2.5	.5	.3
Local issues	.8		.7	.7	2.0
Constitutional issues		5.7			
Devolution	2.4		1.1	3.7	2.0
Constitutional reform	1.7		1.6	1.7	2.1
Northern Ireland	1.0		.8	1.3	.3
Electoral reform	.6		.2	.7	2.5
Miscellaneous	3.7	3.7	3.3	3.5	7.7

SOURCE: CARMA.

NOTE: Content analysis of 6,072 articles in national press, 17 March–1 May 1997.

"secret union hit list" of employers. Conservative Central Office tried to lead its press conference on this story, but before it could make any headway the trade unions were swept off the front pages by the resignation of Allan Stewart, an ex-minister and Conservative MP for Eastwood in Scotland, forced to stand down following allegations of an old affair that were published in the *Mail on Sunday.* On Thursday, 27 March, in a classic case of chequebook journalism, the *Sun* splashed with photos of the Conservative MP, Piers Merchant ("father of two"), caught embrac-

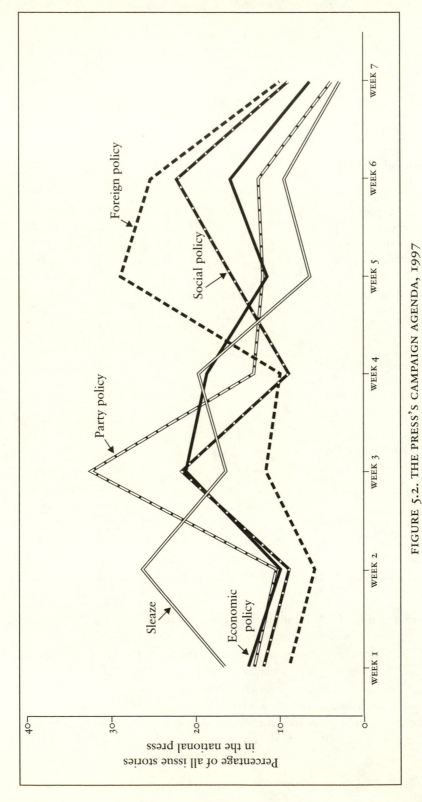

FIGURE 5.2. THE PRESS'S CAMPAIGN AGENDA, 1997

SOURCE: CARMA Content Analysis (*n* = 6,072 articles) 18 March–1 May 1997.

ing a "17-year-old blonde Soho nightclub hostess" while out canvassing in his Beckenham constituency ("Scandal of Tory MP's Mistress, 17," said the *Sun*). Even the pro-Conservative *Express* and *Mail* could not resist giving this set-up story front-page coverage, and it continued to rumble on in the press throughout the quieter Easter weekend.

As if this were not enough, that same day Tim Smith, Conservative MP for Beaconsfield, confessed to taking £25,000 from Harrods owner Mohamed al-Fayed, and he stood down from his candidacy. While the tabloids headlined sex, the broadsheets splashed corruption, with the crusade against Tim Smith led by the *Guardian* ("The Dishonourable Member") further renewing the pressure on Neil Hamilton in Tatton. The following week Sir Michael Hirst, chairman of the Scottish Conservative Party, and front-runner for the recently vacated Eastwood seat, had to resign because of allegations of past indiscretions in his private life. The story first broke in the Scottish press, but it was reputed to have been planned by malcontents from within the Scottish Conservative Party.

The start of April saw the launch of the official manifestos, and more traditional, issue-oriented coverage returned, but by then a third of the campaign period had been dominated by sleaze. Newspaper coverage reinforced the widespread sense that the government had run its course and had become disreputable as well as tired and divided. Moreover, the issue of sleaze failed to go away because Neil Hamilton, protesting his innocence, refused to stand down. John Major declined to intervene in Hamilton's Tatton constituency, although Heseltine indicated that Piers Merchant (guilty only of kissing a teenager) should consider his position. This was a curious choice of priorities concerning suitable standards in public life and one apparently not shared by the electorate.[31]

The "battle for Tatton" made headlines throughout the fourth week after Labour and the Liberal Democrats agreed to withdraw their candidates. This decision allowed the former BBC war correspondent, Martin Bell, to stand as an independent antisleaze campaigner. The soap opera of Tatton, with all the personal drama of Hamilton versus Bell, was just too good a story for any journalists, even those working for the Tory tabloids, to keep off their front pages. By dissolving Parliament six weeks before polling day, well before the traditional launch of the manifestos and the formal beginning of the campaign, Major had blundered into creating a yawning news hole into which, like the White Rabbit, the Conservative Party fell. Without policy conflict, something had to fill the political columns. Throughout the first two weeks, these stories reinforced the image of a discredited government under weak leadership, further nails in the Tories' coffin.

Overall CARMA estimated that, on balance, Conservative coverage was generally negative (44 percent rated unfavourable to only 18 percent favourable, with the rest neutral). CARMA confirmed that the papers most positive towards the Conservatives in their contents, reflecting their editorial preferences, were the *Daily Telegraph,* the *Daily Express,* and the *Daily Mail.*[32] If the ratings are weighted by the size of circulation of newspaper articles, the government's overall disadvantage in the press was even more marked. The Labour Party's and the Liberal Democrats' coverage was far more evenly balanced between positives and negatives.

Just over a third of all the press stories concerned party leadership and candidates (probably a substantial increase on previous campaigns).[33] Here, as shown in table 5.5, most of the coverage focussed on the two main leaders, with Blair enjoying a slight edge over Major, while Ashdown trailed far behind (with only 4 percent of the leadership stories). Within the Labour Party, Blair clearly dominated coverage (with 51 percent of the stories), followed by Gordon Brown, John Prescott, Peter Mandelson, and Robin Cook. Ashdown's dominance of the Liberal Democrats' coverage was even more pronounced, with almost no stories about any of his colleagues. In contrast, only a third of the Conservative stories focussed on Major. In second place within his party, Neil Hamilton attracted slightly more coverage than Margaret Thatcher, Kenneth Clarke, or Michael Heseltine. The list is overwhelmingly masculine, due in large part to the predominance of the three main party leaders, although women spokespersons were slightly more prominent on the Labour side. The content analysis also rated the favourability of the coverage of the leaders, and here coverage of all Conservative personalities was on balance classified as unfavourable, with particularly poor ratings for Tim Smith, Neil Hamilton, Stephen Dorrell, and Michael Forsyth. The equivalent coverage of the Labour leadership was generally neutral.

Public Evaluations of the Campaign Coverage

If political campaigns in Britain are moving towards the postmodern era, how did viewers react to the coverage on television? In particular, did they reach for their remotes to turn off or turn away from news and current affairs on television? And did viewers feel that the election coverage was interesting, informative, and fair? Here we can monitor viewership figures using data supplied by the Broadcasters' Audience Research Board (BARB), which provides the industry-standard measure of viewing behaviour from a panel sample of over 4,000 monitored households.

The evening news and current affairs programmes on British televi-

TABLE 5.5

COVERAGE OF MAJOR POLITICAL FIGURES, 1997

(IN PERCENTAGES)

	All	*Con.*	*Lab.*	*Lib. Dem.*
Conservatives				
John Major	17.7	32.9	.5	.1
Neil Hamilton	3.9	7.3	.5	.1
Margaret Thatcher	3.9	7.1	.2	.0
Kenneth Clarke	3.7	7.0	.0	.0
Michael Heseltine	3.4	6.4	.0	.0
Michael Howard	1.7	3.2	.1	.0
Brian Mawhinney	1.7	3.1	.0	.0
Michael Portillo	1.4	2.7	.0	.0
John Redwood	1.4	2.4	.3	.0
Peter Lilley	1.1	2.0	.0	.0
Tim Smith	1.1	2.0	.1	.0
Others	4.0	7.4	.1	.2
Labour				
Tony Blair	19.7	.5	51.3	.2
Gordon Brown	4.6	.0	12.0	.2
John Prescott	2.3	.1	5.8	.0
Peter Mandelson	1.7	.0	4.6	.2
Robin Cook	1.5	.0	4.0	.1
Cherie Booth	1.1	.1	2.9	.0
Neil Kinnock	1.0	.0	2.4	.5
Others	1.6	.0	4.1	.0
Liberal Democrats				
Paddy Ashdown	4.3	.0	.0	58.4
Lord Holme	.3	.0	.0	4.3
David Steel	.2	.0	.0	2.9
Simon Hughes	.2	.0	.0	2.3
Others	.3	.0	.0	3.6
Other candidates	13.5	13.7	11.0	26.8
"Celebrities"	2.8	1.9	4.0	3.4

SOURCE: CARMA.

NOTE: Content analysis of 6,072 articles in national press, 17 March–1 May 1997.

sion continue to reach a mass audience, but the availability of alternative channels has slightly eroded their market share. The BARB figures confirm that BBC1's *Nine O'Clock News* suffered a particularly sharp fall in viewership after it was specially extended to fifty minutes with campaign news after Easter. The programme lost one-third of its viewers, down from 5.8 million in the first week of April to 4 million thereafter (see figure 5.3). This figure was also well down from the equivalent during the 1992 campaign, when about 6.3 million viewers tuned into BBC's main evening news. But ITN's *News at Ten,* with its regular thirty-minute slot, also lost a part of its audience during the campaign, down from 6 million in the first week to 5.6 million in the last. *Channel 4 News* at 7.00 P.M. (with 0.6 million viewers), ITV's *Early Evening News* at 5.45 P.M. (with 4 million), and BBC1's 6.00 P.M. *News* (with 5.8 million) remained popular, with relatively stable audiences, subject only to the normal trendless fluctuations caused by the television schedules as a whole.

The Labour and Conservative parties showed five election broadcasts each, attracting an average audience of about 11.2 million across all channels, while the four Liberal Democrat broadcasts were seen by about 10.1 million. A few aroused minor controversy (such as a pro-life film featuring graphic footage of abortions and Labour's use of a bulldog, traditionally a symbol of the far right). None aroused anything like the discussion surrounding the "Jennifer's Ear" film in 1992 or "Kinnock the Movie" in 1987. The ratings were well down on 1992, when the party election broadcasts averaged about 13 million viewers.[34]

Yet viewing figures may provide a poor indication of interest, since the size of the audience for news and current affairs is strongly influenced by the placement of a programme in the schedule. For more information about viewers' reactions we can turn to data from the four-wave panel survey with viewers conducted before, during, and after the campaign by RSL for the Independent Television Commission.

The public were asked to evaluate television's coverage of the campaign. As shown in table 5.6 (p. 140), the results confirm that the public felt that there was far too much coverage of the general election, as many television reviewers suggested. This pattern may have important implications for future elections as British broadcasting moves into the digital media environment. A multiplicity of channels will make it easier for the apathetic to tune out from politics while political junkies will be able to watch continuously. In terms of coverage by different channels, contrary to the conventional wisdom, Sky News (with Adam Boulton's rolling live campaign) and ITV were most criticised for providing too much coverage, while the public seemed more satisfied with the BBC's scheduling. Despite the decline in coverage of opinion polls noted earlier, the public

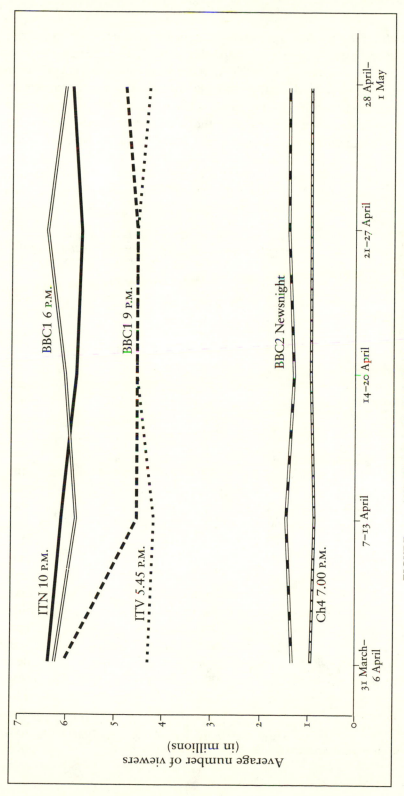

FIGURE 5.3. AUDIENCE FOR TELEVISION NEWS, APRIL 1997

SOURCE: BARB.

still felt that far too much attention was paid to the horse race on television. Outside pundits were also unpopular, and viewers seemed happier
with television's own correspondents. Reflecting the government's unpopularity in the polls, the public thought there was too much coverage
of the Conservative Party in the news while, in contrast, a fifth of all
viewers would have liked more about the Labour Party and such minor
parties as the Greens, who rarely featured in the news. As we have seen,

TABLE 5.6

PUBLIC EVALUATION OF TELEVISION COVERAGE
(IN PERCENTAGES)

Coverage of election	Far too much	Too much	About right	Too little	Far too little	PDI
Coverage by channel						
Sky News	72	21	7	0	0	92
ITV	57	19	19	5	0	71
Channel 4	35	35	26	2	1	66
BBC1	35	22	42	1	0	57
BBC2	25	26	45	4	1	46
Channel 5	7	14	67	10	2	10
Coverage of topics						
Opinion polls	41	36	22	1	0	76
By outside experts	63	15	18	4	1	73
Party leaders	12	53	34	1	0	64
Press conferences	31	28	28	3	1	56
By TV's correspondents	39	22	33	6	0	54
Party policies	23	30	42	3	2	48
Coverage of parties						
Conservatives	28	39	31	1	0	66
Liberal Democrats	41	13	33	7	6	41
Labour	22	39	17	22	0	38
Referendum	43	9	29	12	7	34
Green	37	14	27	11	9	31
Coverage of issues						
European issues	25	29	37	5	5	45
Economy	41	13	33	7	6	41
Foreign affairs	37	14	28	12	9	31
Social policy	43	9	39	12	7	34
Constitutional issues	17	22	45	10	6	24
Environment	15	20	42	13	10	13

SOURCE: ITC (n = 15,536).

NOTE: Q: "Thinking about television news during the campaign, what did you feel about
coverage of - - - - -." The percentage difference index (PDI) is the proportion who think
there is too much minus the proportion who think there is not enough.

Europe received extensive attention in the press, but the public felt that the amount of news about Europe was excessive.

Viewers were also asked to evaluate the quality of television news. Did it meet the requirements of public-service broadcasting by being accurate, informative, balanced, and interesting? Here they reacted largely positively (see table 5.7). *Channel 4 News* presented by Jon Snow came out particularly well, especially in terms of accuracy and balance, perhaps because the programme's longer duration allows more opportunity to present all points of view. The general picture that emerges confirms that British television news is regarded as providing a fairly impartial source of information across all the major channels.

Conclusions: Evaluating the Coverage

During the election many voices expressed disquiet about the media coverage. On the one hand, some observers claimed that television failed to provide serious, critical, and informed debate about policy issues.[35] As we have seen, the media agenda was taken over in the early stages by a feeding frenzy focussing on sleaze and later on the high drama of Conservative splits over Europe. The obsession with sensationalism may have obscured debate about many complex issues facing Briatin and hindered detailed scrutiny of many aspects of the new Blair agenda. On the other hand, other critics argued that, far from providing too little serious coverage of the election, television, particularly the BBC, provided far too much.[36] The media were charged with presenting a saturation diet of pol-

TABLE 5.7

PUBLIC EVALUATION OF QUALITY

OF TELEVISION NEWS

(IN PERCENTAGES OF POSITIVE RESPONSES)

	BBC1	*BBC2*	*ITV*	*Channel 4*	*Channel 5*
Accurate	56	73	51	87	64
Interesting	35	71	51	54	56
Informative	46	59	65	60	40
Balanced	31	48	49	89	41

SOURCE: ITC (*n* = 15,536).

NOTE: Q: "To what extent do you think that news programmes on - - - - - are - - - - -." Percentage positive represents those who responded "Just about always" or "Most of the time" (rather than "Some of the time" or "Hardly ever").

itics during the campaign, including BBC1's specially extended *Nine O'Clock News,* as well as the pages of campaign news in the broadsheet newspapers, and this, some suggest, may have turned off voters. At present, pending the analysis of more detailed survey evidence, we can only speculate about the full effects of the campaign on voters. What does seem clear, however, is the effects on parties. Little is certain in politics, but we can take a fairly safe bet that the techniques learnt by the Blair team for staying on-message in a more complex and diverse media environment during the permanent campaign are going to be emulated by their opponents. Indeed, shortly after assuming the Tory leadership, William Hague announced that Conservative Central Office would give the highest priority to improving its communication strategy and organisation. In this regard the 1997 election did represent a watershed, not just in terms of the outcome, but also for the process of British election campaigning.

Acknowledgements

The author would like to thank Bill Meredith at the Broadcasters' Audience Research Board (BARB) for releasing reports of television audiences during the campaign. Peter Christopherson at CARMA kindly provided content analysis of the national press during April 1997. Jane Sancho-Aldrich and Bob Towler at the Independent Television Commission generously released advanced data from the ITC 1997 four-wave campaign survey *Television: The Public View.* Lastly, Colin Seymour-Ure is to be thanked for providing information on national press circulation and partisanship.

Notes

1. One content analysis found that during April the election absorbed 46 percent of television news. Peter Golding, David Deacon, and Michael Billig, *1997 Election Study for the Guardian,* Report No. 5 (Loughborough: University of Loughborough, 2 May 1997).

2. David L. Swanson and Paolo Mancini, *Politics, Media and Modern Democracy* (Westport, Conn.: Praeger, 1997).

3. For a more detailed discussion, see Pippa Norris, *Electoral Change since 1945* (Oxford: Blackwell, 1997).

4. See Colin Seymour-Ure, *The British Press and Broadcasting since 1945* (Oxford: Blackwell, 1996).

5. For a discussion of the ethos of election broadcasting, see Jay G. Blumler

and Michael Gurevitch, *The Crisis of Public Communication* (London: Routledge, 1995).

6. For accounts of these developments up until the 1992 election, see Dennis Kavanagh, *Election Campaigning* (Oxford: Blackwell, 1995); see also Margaret Scammell, *Designer Politics* (New York: St. Martin's Press, 1995).

7. For an insider account of government-press relations in these years, see Bernard Ingham, *Kill the Messenger* (London: HarperCollins, 1994).

8. Alan Watkins, *A Conservative Coup: The Fall of Margaret Thatcher* (London: Duckworth, 1991).

9. Martin Harrop and Margaret Scammell, "A Tabloid War," in David Butler and Dennis Kavanagh, *The British General Election of 1992* (London: Macmillan, 1992).

10. For a discussion of press partisanship during the 1992–97 period, see Colin Seymour-Ure, "Newspapers: Editorial Opinion and the National Press," *Parliamentary Affairs* 50, no. 4 (1997).

11. See Andrew Neil, "Why Blair's Honeymoon with Murdoch Is Going to End in Tears," *Daily Mail,* 19 March 1997.

12. It is remarkable, though, that immediately after Blair's victory Lord Rothermere announced that he was defecting from the Conservatives and would henceforth take the Labour whip in the Lords.

13. See Brian McNair, *News and Journalism in the UK* (London: Routledge, 1994); see also Jeremy Tunstall, *Newspaper Power: The New National Press in Britain* (Oxford: Clarendon Press, 1996).

14. *Social Trends* 27 (London: The Stationery Office, 1997), table 13.10.

15. Lord Rothermere, quoted in *The Times,* 24 May 1997. For an analysis of the trends in voting support among different groups of readers, see Martin Linton, "Was It the *Sun* Wot Won It?" Seventh Guardian Lecture, Oxford: Nuffield College, October 1995.

16. See Swanson and Mancini, *Politics,* 15.

17. See, for example, Nicholas Jones, *Soundbites and Spin Doctors* (London: Cassell, 1995).

18. See Dennis Kavanagh, "The Labour Campaign," *Parliamentary Affairs* 50, no. 4 (1997). For journalistic accounts of the Labour campaign, see Sidney Blumenthal, "All the Prime Minister's Men," *The Times,* 3 May 1997; Robert Harris, "Behind Closed Doors," *Sunday Times,* 4 May 1997; Paul Vallely et al., "Blair's Long Trek to Victory," *Independent,* 3 May 1997.

19. It should be noted that this figure still remains below estimated individual Labour Party membership in 1979. See David Butler and Gareth Butler, *British Political Facts 1900–1994* (London: Macmillan, 1994).

20. Peter Riddell, "Conservative Membership Falls by Half in Five Years," *The Times,* 6 June 1997.

21. See Paul Whiteley, "The Conservative Campaign," *Parliamentary Affairs* 50, no. 4 (1997); Tom Baldwin, "How They Designed a Disaster," *Sunday Telegraph,* 4 May 1997.

22. See Anthony King, *Running Scared* (New York: Free Press, 1997).

23. For this debate, see Dennis Kavanagh, "New Campaign Communications: Consequences for British Political Parties," *Harvard International Journal*

of Press/Politics 1, no. 3 (Summer 1996); Bob Franklin, *Packaging Politics* (London: Edward Elgar, 1994); Ralph Negrine and Stylianos Papathanassopoulos, "The Americanization of Political Communications: A Critique," *Harvard International Journal of Press/Politics* 1, no. 2 (Spring 1996).

24. CARMA stands for Computer-Aided Research and Media Analysis. The newspapers analysed by CARMA comprised the *Daily/Sunday Telegraph, The Times/Sunday Times,* the *Independent/Independent on Sunday,* the *Guardian/Observer,* the *Financial Times,* the *Daily Mail/Mail on Sunday,* the *Express/Express on Sunday,* the *Sun/News of the World,* the *Mirror/Sunday Mirror,* the *Daily Star,* and the *People.* Articles relevant to the general election were selected from all major sections of the paper, excluding cartoons and events listings.

25. Ivor Crewe, "The Opinion Polls: Confidence Restored?" *Parliamentary Affairs* 50, no. 4 (1997).

26. Golding, Deacon, and Billig, *1997 Election Study.*

27. For an analysis of television's coverage of the economy, see Neil Gavin and David Sanders, "The Economy and Voting," *Parliamentary Affairs* 50, no. 4 (1997).

28. See Holli Semetko, Margaret Scammell, and Tom Nossiter, "The Media's Coverage of the Campaign," in *Labour's Last Chance?* edited by Anthony Heath, Roger Jowell, and John Curtice (Aldershot: Dartmouth, 1994).

29. Another content analysis confirmed that Europe was the most important topic on broadcast news during April, after coverage of the conduct of the election itself. See Golding, Deacon, and Billig, *1997 Election Study.*

30. Colin Seymour-Ure, "Editorial Opinion in the National Press," *Parliamentary Affairs* 50, no. 4 (1997).

31. While all the Conservative MPs who entered the election with a cloud hanging over them suffered slightly higher than the average swings against them, Piers Merchant was (just) returned to the depleted Tory backbenches, whereas Neil Hamilton was roundly defeated. See Pippa Norris, "Anatomy of a Labour Landslide," *Parliamentary Affairs* 50, no. 4 (1997).

32. Another content analysis of the press confirmed that the papers most favourable to the Conservatives were the *Mail* and *Express,* with the pro-Conservative bias slightly less marked in the *Telegraph.* See Golding, Deacon, and Billig, *1997 Election Study.*

33. For a comparison with 1992, see Semetko, Scammell, and Nossiter, "Media's Coverage."

34. Margaret Scammell and Holli A. Semetko, "Political Advertising on Television: The British Experience," in *Political Advertising in Western Democracies,* edited by Lynda Lee Kaid and Christina Holtz-Bacha (Thousand Oaks, Calif.: Sage, 1995).

35. See Peter Golding and David Deacon, "The Media Election: Campaign Fails to Hold Front Page," *Guardian,* 14 April 1997.

36. See Holli Semetko, Margaret Scammell, and Peter Goddard, "Television," *Parliamentary Affairs* 50, no. 4 (1997).

6

The Semi-detached Election: Scotland

Iain McLean

And it is hereby statute and ordained that this Act of Parliament with the Establishment therein contained shall be held and observed in all time coming as a Fundamental and Essential Condition of any Treaty or Union to be concluded betwixt the two Kingdoms without any Alteration thereof or Derogation thereto in any sort for ever.

> The Act of Union, 6 Anne c. 11, Art. XXV

We're bought and sold for English gold —
Such a parcel of rogues in a nation!

> Jacobite song

290 Years of Union

The 1997 election was held on the 290th anniversary of the day the Union of 1707 came into being.[1] The United Kingdom of Great Britain was formed by the dissolution of the previously separate legislatures of England and Scotland, which had had a common executive (i.e., king) since 1603. The Conservative Party, which had inserted *and Unionist* into its title in the 1880s to signify its devotion to the integrity of the United Kingdom, fought the 1997 election on a platform of preserving the Union. It lost all 11 of the seats it was defending in Scotland and all 6 in Wales. It holds none in Northern Ireland. The Conservative (and Unionist) Party therefore holds seats in only one of the four parts of the Union. Was 1 May 1997, then, the beginning of the end of the Union?

To answer this, we need to look at both the politics and the administration of union since 1707. The Act of 1707 gave Scotland 45 members of the united House of Commons and 16 representative Lords. It had been a hard bargain; the Scots had requested 50 Commons seats and the English had offered 38. The agreed 45, out of a Parliament of 558 members, represented less than half Scotland's population proportion at the time. Although some aspects of the Union remained controversial in the eighteenth century, this one did not. Representation at the time was regarded as due to property, not to people. Scotland certainly contained less than 45/558ths of the capital of the UK.[2]

For 180 years, Scotland as such played no distinctive role in the government of the UK. In the eighteenth century, the Scottish MPs were managed as a bloc by government business managers. In the nineteenth century, this broke down, but there were no distinctive Scottish political institutions before the 1880s. The Act of Union purports to entrench Scots law, Scottish representation, and the government of the Scottish established church. As the extract from the act in the heading to this chapter shows, these are supposed to be guaranteed, and untouchable by subsequent legislation, contrary to the convention of parliamentary sovereignty. According to that convention, Parliament may do anything except bind its successor. Therefore, guarantees included in a constitutional act have no special force.

On the whole, however, the special status of the Act of Union has been accepted. In particular, the Scottish legal system remains distinctive, being oriented less towards common law and more towards Roman law than is the English. But Scots law has never been well understood in England. Some legislation specifically for Scotland has been passed, especially in matters covered by Scots private law. But, especially with the growth of government in the twentieth century, statutes drafted for, and by, the English were applied to Scotland by "the abominable habits of the 'application to Scotland clause.'"[3] One tempting (but oversimple) answer to the question *What powers should be delegated to a Scottish Parliament?* is *The making and amending of Scots law.* Unfortunately, Scots law covers many subjects that Westminster might be reluctant to devolve, such as commercial and industrial regulation.

100 Years of Devolution

Scottish government changed in the 1880s as an indirect consequence of agitation for Home Rule in Ireland. An Irish Act of Union in 1800 had incorporated Ireland on similar terms to Scotland. The 1800 act was bitterly unpopular in Ireland, as was 1707 in Scotland. After Union, Scotland was speedily reconciled; Ireland was not. The campaign for the repeal of the Irish Union began in earnest in 1828. By the general election of 1880, over 80 of the 105 parliamentary seats in Ireland were held by the Irish Party, which took no part in government at Westminster except to demand Home Rule—as we would now say, devolution—for Ireland. Most of the rest of the Irish seats were in Ulster, held by Protestant Unionists who bitterly opposed Home Rule. They feared that in any devolved government, representatives of the Catholic majority would persecute the Protestant minority. They knew, but could not say, that the Protestant minority had persecuted the Catholic majority on and off for nearly three centuries. In Catholic Ireland, the famine of the 1840s caused over a million deaths and massive migration, but grinding poverty persisted, especially in the west, where acts of violence against landlords were growing. A government, of either party, holding no seats in Catholic Ireland could not maintain public order there.

In December 1885, the Liberal leader, W.E. Gladstone, decided that the loss of government legitimacy in Ireland could be cured only by Home Rule. He failed to obtain it; his Home Rule bills of 1886 and 1893 were defeated. In 1914 Home Rule was enacted, but its operation was suspended by the First World War. The only devolution successfully granted was by the Government of Ireland Act 1920. This envisaged devolved Parliaments in southern and northern Ireland. But the southern Irish were by then fighting for independence, which they won in 1921. Hence the only part of the UK to get devolved government was Northern Ireland, whose Unionist leaders had specifically rejected the idea. Once they had it, however, they found that "a Protestant Parliament for a Protestant people," as an early Unionist prime minister of Northern Ireland called it, was a congenial institution—for them. Its illegitimacy among Northern Ireland Catholics led to civil disobedience and violence in the late 1960s, and the ending of the devolved Northern Ireland Parliament in 1972.

In the 1880s, with growing awareness of the separateness of non-England, the first moves for Scottish devolution also occurred. The Scottish Office was set up in 1885 to unite the civil service departments managing Scottish affairs. This changed nothing as to *how* Scotland was run, but did change *where* it was run from. In the same year, the number of Scottish MPs in the House of Commons rose to become proportionate to population for the first time. The post of secretary (later secretary of state) for Scotland became a cabinet post in 1892. Its modern role was defined by Tom Johnston, a forceful Labour MP who was secretary of state during the Second World War. His cabinet colleague Herbert Morrison described him as "one of the most able men in the technique of getting his own way at cabinet committees. . . . He would impress on the committee that there was a strong nationalist movement in Scotland and it could be a potential danger if it grew through lack of attention to Scottish interests."[4]

Every secretary of state since then, regardless of party, has used the Johnston gambit. Michael Forsyth (Conservative, 1995 to 1997) was one of the most successful. The Scots and Welsh members of a 1944 Speaker's conference on parliamentary boundaries also used the Johnston gambit to ensure that Scotland and Wales were overrepresented at Westminster and that the overrepresentation would be built in by means of a separate Boundary Commission and statutory minimum number of seats for each country.[5] Since 1944 Scotland has been guaranteed at least 71 seats in the House of Commons, and Wales 35, irrespective of their population shares, although the House size is supposed to be "not substantially" above 630. The current numbers are 72 seats for Scotland, 40 for Wales, and 659 overall. Representation proportionate to population, with an allowance for thinly populated areas, would give Scotland perhaps 60 seats.

The administrative devolution to Scotland is almost complete. The Scottish Office runs virtually every aspect of domestic government in Scotland, apart from the tax and benefit systems. The Johnston gambit has helped to ensure that Scotland does very well in the regional distribution of UK public spending. On various measures, Scottish public spending per head has been calculated as being anything from 15 percent to 30 percent above that for England. We return to this later in this chapter.

Fifty Years of Nationalism

To be credible, the Johnston gambit required there to be some real evidence of nationalism. The Scottish National Party (SNP), in its modern form, dates to 1934.[6] It tapped a vein of romantic cultural nationalism and won its first parliamentary seat in a wartime by-election in 1945. It quickly lost it again when normal party politics resumed at the 1945 general election. Its next good by-election performance was at West Lothian in 1962. It has been represented at Westminster continuously since 1967. Its best election to date was that of October 1974, when it won 11 seats and 31 percent of the Scottish vote (and the Conservatives won 16 seats on 25 percent of the vote; the contrast with 1997 is discussed later in this chapter). Since 1974, the SNP has been a predominantly social democratic party, claiming that an independent Scotland would greatly increase welfare expenditure out of the income that, it alleges, England currently siphons away from the Scots. Its electoral base, however, is strongest in rural and small-town Scotland.[7]

The upsurge of SNP support was already evident in the first (February) 1974 general election. It flowed on a tide of oil. Commercially exploitable oil fields in the North Sea were proven in 1970; the first oil was landed in 1975. This gave the SNP its electoral breakthrough. It ran a series of posters depicting poverty-stricken Scots with the slogan "It's his/her/their oil." The most forceful showed a haggard elderly lady with the slogan "It's her oil—so why do 50,000 people a year in Scotland die of hypothermia?" The other parties challenged the SNP's statistics but could not blunt their effect. Labour narrowly won the February 1974 election but became extremely worried at the prospect of losing its massive majority of parliamentary seats in Scotland. The plurality electoral system was rewarding Labour with overrepresentation and punishing the SNP. But if the SNP share of the vote should rise to around 35 percent, the effect of the system would swing as sharply the other way. Labour would be decimated and the SNP might win the majority of Scottish seats. In the summer of 1974, however, the Scottish executive of the Labour Party rejected devolution. The national party therefore brusquely converted its own Scottish executive to a position in support of devolution. The irony was lost on nobody at the time. The Labour Party, alone of the four main parties operating in Scotland, has a unified Britain-wide command-and-control structure. Unlike any of the other parties, it could and did simply overrule its Scottish executive, forcing it to favour devolution of power (of a sort that would have made its own manœuvre impossible).

This gave the devolution legislation of the 1974–79 Labour governments an unfortunate start. For five long years, it was clear that Labour proposed devolution for Scotland and Wales, not because the government believed in it, but because the governing party needed to save its seats. It succeeded, but at a price. It saved its Scottish seats but lost the ensuing general election.[8]

The government's first move was a Scotland and Wales Bill, proposing devolution to both countries (more extensive for Scotland than for Wales). That bill fell in February 1977 to an unprecedented mutiny led by the hitherto loyal Northern Group of Labour MPs. "Northern" here refers to the northeast of England, whose MPs could not tolerate that their area was getting less from a Labour government in return for voting Labour than was Scotland in return for voting SNP. The Northern Group built up a network of disaffected Labour MPs from other deprived areas of England, notably Merseyside. The prime minister, Jim Callaghan, attempted to buy them off by two gestures typical of a cornered politician. One was a visit by the newly installed U.S. president, Jimmy Carter, to Newcastle, where he opened his speech with a carefully prepared (but unconvincing) chant of "Ha'way the lads." (Carter's Geordie was no more convincing than JFK's German.) The other was an order for power station equipment that the Central Electricity Generating Board did not want. The government overruled it and placed the order with the Newcastle firm Reyrolle Parsons. Neither gesture succeeded.[9]

The government then detached Scotland from Wales and presented two separate bills. Further backbench rebellions imposed first a referendum and then stringent conditions for its acceptance. According to the version finally enacted (the Scotland Act 1978), the devolved Parliament it introduced would not go ahead unless it was approved in a referendum in which at least 40 percent of the registered electorate had voted yes. The 40 percent rule was imposed in a rebellion led by an expatriate Scots Labour MP, George Cunningham. The Cunningham amendment was a pure wrecking move. No UK government since 1945 has had the support of as much as 40 percent of the electorate.[10] The Cunningham amendment turned out to wreck not only devolution but the Labour government.

The required referendums took place in Scotland and Wales on 1 March 1979. The Scots voted yes to devolution by 51.6 percent to 48.4 percent. But a turnout of 63.6 percent meant that only 32.9 percent of the registered electorate voted yes. In Wales, the no's won by a crushing 80-to-20 majority. The government could not implement the Scotland Act. The Scottish Nationalists therefore tabled a vote of no confidence in it. As their poll standing had slumped, "Mr Callaghan likened their action to that of turkeys voting for an early Christmas."[11] The Scottish (but not the Welsh) Nationalists joined with the Conservatives and most of the other minor parties in the confidence vote, which resulted in the defeat of the government by one vote—311 to 310—on 28 March 1979. In the ensuing general election, Labour lost heavily, and Margaret Thatcher came to power, inaugurating the Conservative hegemony that was to last until 1997. Without the devolution debacle, Labour would probably still have lost, but more gracefully and in its own time.

Twenty Years of Illegitimate Government

There was an eerie silence in Scotland after the general election of 1979. The whole life of political elites had centred on devolution for five years. The magnificent Greek Revival Royal High School in Edinburgh (where both Robin Cook MP and I learned Greek) had been converted into a home for the Scottish Parliament. Margaret Thatcher came to power with a comfortable majority overall but with only 22 of the 71 Scottish seats and 31.4 percent of the popular vote (Labour got 41.5 percent of the vote and 44 seats). The Conservative government was therefore in a minority in Scotland, and remained so, as table 6.1 shows.

Immediately on coming to power, Thatcher announced that the Conservatives would not proceed with devolution. They maintained an uncompromisingly Unionist stance right through to the 1997 election campaign. During the Conservative years, the government proceeded with other policies that were deeply unpopular in Scotland. For instance, the poll tax (community charge) was introduced a year earlier in Scotland than in England and Wales.[12] Therefore, from 1979 until 1997 the Conservatives governed Scotland in the same way as both British parties had governed Ireland from 1800 until 1921: without a majority and with uncertain legitimacy.

Two straws in the wind suggest that Scots' commitment to devolution may have been broad but not deep in those years. One is the very silence of the Scottish lambs at its abandonment in 1979. The abandonment raised obvious questions of legitimacy, since the government that did it did not have a majority in Scotland; yet there was very little protest. Perhaps the Scots had become bored with devolution. Political commentators who had talked of little else for five years were so shocked and disillusioned that they packed their tents and disappeared. The poll tax occasioned much greater protest, although that of course was not confined to Scotland.

The other straw in the wind was the slight upturn of the Conservative vote in 1992, against the trend in the rest of the country. Shortly before polling day, the Conservative leader John Major warned: "If I could

TABLE 6.1
CONSERVATIVE VOTE AND SEAT SHARES 1979–92:
SCOTLAND VS. UK
(IN PERCENTAGES)

	Scotland		United Kingdom	
Year	Seat share	Vote share	Seat share	Vote share
1979	31.0	31.4	53.4	43.9
1983	29.2	28.4	61.1	42.4
1987	13.9	24.0	57.7	42.2
1992	15.3	25.7	51.6	41.9

SOURCE: David Butler and Dennis Kavanagh, *The British General Election of 1979/1983/ 1987/1992* (London: Macmillan), Appendix 1 in each volume.

summon up all the authority of this office, I would put it into this single warning—the United Kingdom is in danger. Wake up, my fellow countrymen! Wake up now before it is too late!"[13]

The English did not wake up (or, if they did, more of them fell asleep at the same time): the Conservatives in England lost ground. But in Scotland the Conservative vote and seat shares both inched up. The only Conservative seat gain in the whole UK, other than recoveries of by-election losses, was in Scotland. After 1992, the Conservatives analysed their relative success there and put it down to their niche marketing of themselves as the only Unionist party. This same niche marketing failed to save them in 1997.

How fair is it to regard Scotland during the years of Conservative government as a colony? On the one hand, the country was governed by a party whose minority of votes and seats did not inhibit it from radical and unpopular policy. Partly for this reason, politically aware Scots tend to be impatient with the West Lothian Question (WLQ). Because the question will be discussed extensively in this chapter, here is a statement of it:

> In its present form the Question has apparently boiled down to the issue of whether and why "Scottish" MPs should be entitled to sit and vote at Westminster on "English" matters, while "English" MPs would not be able to participate on equivalent matters transferred to a Scottish Parliament.[14]

The West Lothian Question is so called because in the 1970s it was constantly posed by Tam Dalyell, Labour MP for West Lothian, and the most articulate opponent of his own government's devolution plans.[15] But, argue proponents of devolution, "It is ironic that those who are preoccupied with this so-called West Lothian question appear unconcerned by the converse Westminster question. Why is it that 560 non-Scottish MPs decide legislation which will be implemented only in Scotland? This is surely a much greater anomaly and democratic affront than the position of Scottish MPs at Westminster."[16] The WLQ is often viewed as a mere rhetorical device: "As ... Professor Bill Miller of Glasgow University ... remarked, the West Lothian question is not really a *question* at all because 'no matter how often it is answered, Tam simply waits a while and then asks again.' "[17]

All of this might lead one to expect the Scots to have a systematically different political and social outlook to the English. But Miller has conducted a large survey that reveals remarkably slight differences. The Scots were slightly more egalitarian, and also slightly more libertarian, than the British public as a whole in response to a battery of questions on economic and social rights, "but these were differences of opinion within the same political culture, not proof of a fundamental difference of culture." Furthermore, non-Scots favoured Scottish self-government by two percentage points more than Scots did.[18] Although, as we argue in the next two sections, Scottish culture differs profoundly from English in popular perceptions of the past, this does not particularly affect social attitudes. Therefore, although what the Scottish Labour Party calls the "Westminster Question" is a good one, it did not lead the Scots into such profound disillusion with Westminster as it had led the Irish a century earlier.

Furthermore, the Westminster Question no more answers the West Lothian Question than two wrongs make a right. Indeed, if the answer to the rhetorically posed Westminster Question is that 560 non-Scottish MPs have no right to decide legislation that will be implemented only in Scotland, then the answer to the rhetorically posed West Lothian Question must, in consistency, be that 72 Scottish MPs have no right to decide legislation that will be implemented only in England and Wales. So the WLQ will not go away.

Devolution and Scottish Public Opinion

Devolution has never been the top issue on the Scots electorate's agenda. Miller's survey reinforces twenty years' worth of evidence on the same point, going back to the Kilbrandon Commission on the Constitution, which reported in 1973. In one of its supporting research studies, Kilbrandon reported the embarrassing fact that support for devolution was not much greater in Scotland than in the northwestern and central-southern regions of England.[19] This did not alter the path of devolution policy, which, like some unwieldy supertanker, could not turn for six years after Kilbrandon. The nonsalience of devolution has been confirmed by every opinion survey since then. One snapshot was taken by Gallup in May 1996, when the constitution writing shortly to be described had been under way for seven years. It showed that support for devolution and independence combined had fallen from 80 percent to 69 percent since 1986. When asked "If independence or a separate Parliament were to mean higher taxes for Scotland, which option would you then prefer for running Scotland?" the proportion supporting independence or devolution dropped again to 56 percent. Only 7 percent of the sample spontaneously mentioned independence or devolution as one of the main election issues, and only 14 percent did so even when prompted.

The commentary concluded, "The Conservative Party seems to have little to lose—and possibly a good deal to gain—by warning Scottish voters of devolution's adverse effect on both their country's future and the amount of tax they pay."[20] The Conservatives took this advice to heart.

Trends in opinion on devolution, and in party support in Scotland from 1985 to 1997, are shown in figures 6.1 and 6.2. Figure 6.1 tracks support for each of the following options:

- "A completely independent Scottish Parliament separate from England" (changed to "A completely independent Scotland" in 1996). Shown as *Independence* on figure 6.1.
- "A Scottish Parliament with substantial powers, but within the framework of British government." Shown as *Devolution* on figure 6.1.
- No change from the present system.
- Don't know.

The years of the Constitutional Convention (1989 to 1995) seem to show a slight rise in the popularity of devolution at the expense of independence, but the trend is sharply reversed during 1996. Opinion against any change is roughly constant and not much higher than the level of Conservative support in 1997. The movements are not great and should not be overinterpreted.

Figure 6.2 tracks the answer to the voting intention question asked every month by System 3, one of the two polling organisations that run a monthly Scottish opinion survey. It is quite consistent with the equivalent picture for the UK as a whole, except that Labour starts from a higher base and the Conservatives from a lower one. At the start of the period, the Conservatives lie a rather distant second from Labour, with the SNP in third place. The SNP temporarily rises to second place just before the 1992 general election (but did not attain second place in the election itself). In Scotland, as in the UK as a whole, September 1992 seems to be the pivotal month. In that month, the Conservatives lost their reputation for economic competence at a stroke, with the ignominious exit of the pound sterling from the ERM. Although the objective economy recovered, people's perceptions of the Conservatives' competence did not. At no time after September 1992 do the Conservatives come second in the series, and in their worst months they fall to fourth behind the Liberal Democrats as well as the SNP. That wise commentator Anon first said in the 1970s, "Politicians think the Scots want devolution when all they want is more."

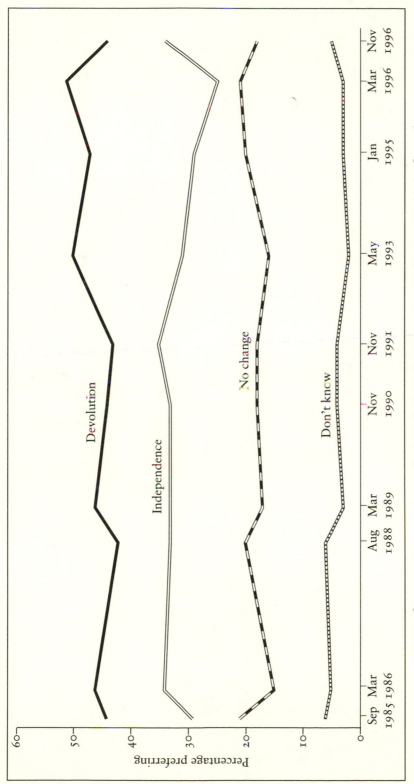

FIGURE 6.1. SCOTTISH PUBLIC OPINION ON INDEPENDENCE AND DEVOLUTION, 1985–96

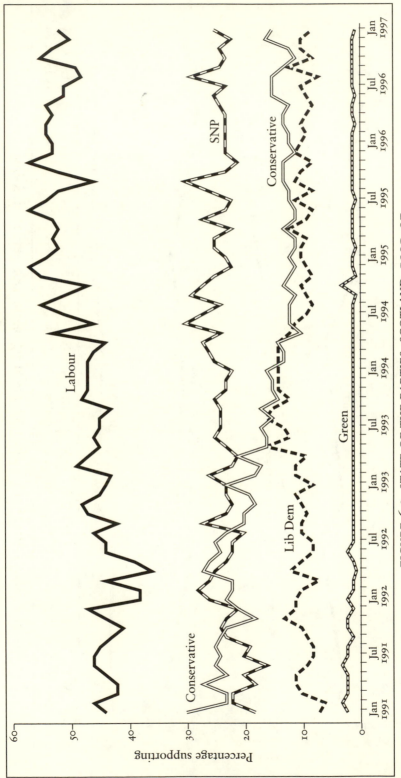

FIGURE 6.2. STATE OF THE PARTIES, SCOTLAND, 1991–97

SOURCE: System 3 monthly polls.

Ten Years of Constitution Writing

The Abolition of Domestic Rates (etc.) Scotland Bill received its second reading in December 1986. The *(etc.)* in the bill title stood for *(and substitution of a poll tax)*. It was enacted just before the 1987 general election, at which all the Scottish Conservatives who had piloted it through Parliament or spoken in favour of it lost their seats. In the election campaign itself, "the poll tax proved to be a nonissue,"[21] and it did not erupt in Scotland until the turn of 1988–89, when the first poll tax bills were set and it became clear that the rate would be much higher than government spokesmen had predicted. By then the Opposition parties had decided to draw attention to the Conservatives' lack of legitimacy, even at the expense of advertising their own impotence. A sonorous "Claim of Right for Scotland" was published in 1988, to be followed the next year by the creation of a Scottish Constitutional Convention.

The Claim of Right went unnoticed outside Scotland. As adopted at the first meeting of the Constitutional Convention, it begins: "We, gathered as the Scottish Constitutional Convention, do hereby acknowledge the sovereign right of the Scottish people to determine the form of Government best suited to their needs, and do hereby declare and pledge that in all our actions and deliberations their interests shall be paramount." It goes on to pledge its signatories to agree to a scheme for a Scottish assembly or Parliament, to mobilise Scottish public opinion in its favour, and "to assert the right of the Scottish people to secure the implementation of that scheme." The Convention calls the Claim of Right "the third in Scotland's history." It was signed in the General Assembly Hall of the Church of Scotland.[22] This string of symbols requires a little postmodernist deconstruction.

By the two predecessors of the Claim of Right, the Convention must mean two out of the following: the Declaration of Arbroath, 1320; the National Covenant, 1638; and the Solemn League and Covenant, 1643. The first was a document produced by Scottish clergy and barons to dissuade the Pope from ceasing to recognise King Robert the Bruce, who had defeated an English invasion at Bannockburn in 1314. It states: "For so long as there shall but one hundred of us remain alive, we will never consent to subject ourselves to the dominion of the English." Framed copies of the Declaration of Arbroath frequently adorn SNP campaign offices. The 1638 National Covenant was an agreement "to be made and subscribed by his Majesty's subjects of all ranks" to the effect that "innovations" in religion would be the "subversion and ruine of the true Reformed Religion and of our Libertie, Law, and Estates." The occasion was an attempt by King Charles I, monarch (separately) of Scotland and

of England, to introduce a new church liturgy in Scotland. A legendary
figure in Scottish history, Jenny Geddes, is supposed to have hurled a
stool at the minister of St Giles' Church in Edinburgh in protest. Rosalind Mitchison, in her standard *History of Scotland,* says of the National
Covenant, "Through it all ran the Old Testament analogy, the concept of
a nation binding itself in a special relationship to God." The ensuing
Scots-English war (the Bishops' War) began well for the Scots, whose decision-making body was the General Assembly of the Scottish Church.
This led them to promulgate the Solemn League and Covenant, what
Mitchison calls a "preposterous undertaking" to export Scots Presbyterian church government to England and Ireland. It failed, but produced
the Westminster Confession, which governs the Church of Scotland, and
the metrical psalms that have "lain like a wet blanket on Scottish poeti-
cal talent ever since."[23]

The language of covenanting has pervaded Scotland—or at least
Protestant Scotland—ever since 1638. The covenanting tradition is simultaneously nationalist and puritanical. It emerges at times and places that
are ostensibly unconnected with religion. The Ulster Protestant rebels of
1912, many of them of Scots descent, signed another Solemn League and
Covenant in protest against Home Rule for Ireland. When Labour won
10 out of 15 seats in Glasgow at the 1922 general election, their MPs
signed a declaration described as "breathing the noble spirit of the Covenant." One of them wrote: "We were all Puritans. We were all abstain-
ers. Most of us did not smoke. We were the stuff of which reform was
made." They fortified themselves not with a Labour or socialist song but
with Psalm 124, "Scotland's psalm of deliverance," in a metrical version
composed by the Covenanters to tell the world that God was on their
side.[24]

The covenanting version of Scottish history was codified by Sir Walter Scott, and every non-Catholic Scottish school child has been imbued
with it ever since. It has always sat uneasily with another, romantic
strand that equally derives from seventeenth- and eighteenth-century
Scotland—that of Episcopalian or Catholic royalism, which culminated
in the Jacobite Risings of 1715 and 1745. If a real Covenanter had met a
real Jacobite, only one of them would have emerged alive from the encounter, but in the fictive past created by Walter Scott and many since
him, they are equally powerful nationalist symbols. Jenny Geddes "stood
for" Scottish nationalism in the seventeenth century; the Jacobites
"stood for" it in the eighteenth. Robert Burns, who was well aware of
the differences between Covenanters and Jacobites, collected Jacobite
songs from oral tradition in his *Scots Musical Museum.* "Such a Parcel of
Rogues in a Nation," with its arresting melody, is one of them. The En-

glish, quite unaware of either the real or the fictional history of Scotland, did not notice the 1988 Claim of Right.

The main players in the Constitutional Convention were the Labour and Liberal Democrat parties and the churches. Most Scottish trade unions and a few business bodies were also represented. The Conservatives had no hesitation in keeping out; the Scottish Nationalists hesitated, but also stayed out. The Convention appointed a Constitutional Commission to draft arrangements for a Scottish Parliament (including "electoral system[s] and gender balance provisions") and for post-devolution relations between Scotland and Westminster ("including entrenchment and Scottish representation in the Westminster Parliament").[25] It reported on 30 November 1995 (St Andrew's Day), its report once again unnoticed outside Scotland. It proposed a Scottish Parliament of 129 members, elected on the German "additional member" system, which would preserve single-member districts but make the overall composition of the Parliament depend on the party distribution of second votes. Labour and the Liberal Democrats signed a supplementary agreement to "select and field an equal number of male and female candidates for election."[26]

On finance, the report states:

> The principle of equalisation will continue. This means [that] resources will be pooled on a UK basis and distributed on the basis of relative need. The establishing Act will embody the principle of equalisation—which has provided a stable, long-term foundation for government expenditure in Scotland for many years, receives the support of all the UK parties, and has served Scotland and the UK well. Thus, Scotland will continue to be guaranteed her fair share of UK resources, as of right.
>
> The current formula for the calculation of government expenditure in Scotland—the Barnett/Goschen formula—will continue to be used as the basis for the allocation of Scotland's fair share of UK resources.[27]

These two paragraphs are problematic—indeed, arguably, contradictory. The regional distribution of public spending was the problem that killed the 1974 devolution plan, and its solution after 1997 will not be as simple as these paragraphs imply. The Barnett/Goschen formula is analysed later in the chapter.

The report went on to propose that Scotland's Parliament should have the power to vary the rate of income tax from the UK level by three pence in the pound either way: "The power of variation of income tax will be distinct from the formula for equalisation."[28] On Scottish representation and powers at Westminster, the report is completely silent, apart from a section stating that, despite the tradition of parliamentary sovereignty, "there could, and should, be some way of formally embedding the powers and position of Scotland's Parliament." It calls for a "solemn declaration of intent of the Parliament of the United Kingdom" that "a democratic institution like Scotland's Parliament would not be unilaterally weakened or abolished by Westminster."[29] Reinforcing the solemnity of it all, the Convention's chairman, a clergyman, later described the report's proposals as "the ten commitments brought down from the Mound."[30]

The Conservatives immediately launched an attack on the tax-varying power, which they called the "tartan tax." This caught Labour off balance. On acceding to the Labour leadership in 1994, Tony Blair decided that Labour must never again be vulnerable to attack as a "tax and spend" party. As the "tartan tax" arrows began to hurt, Blair and his Scottish shadow secretary, George Robertson, suddenly changed tack. On 26 June 1996 they announced that, if elected at the general election, Labour would propose a two-question referendum before going ahead with a Scottish assembly. Voters would be asked, first, whether they approved the proposed Scottish Parliament and, second, whether it should have tax-raising powers. Although some journalists said that this policy change had been brewing for months,[31] it surprised and annoyed the Scottish Labour Party. One of Blair's Scottish spokesmen resigned, and the troublesome Scottish executive looked set to reject the leader's devolution plans—as in 1974, although for different reasons. But the outcome was the same as in 1974. For a while, a third referendum question hovered over Scotland: the Scottish Parliament was to have its own referendum on using the tax powers if they had been granted by the earlier referendum. This third question carried a resentful Scottish executive,[32] but it was soon laughed out of court and Labour's proposal reverted to two referendum questions. Once again, national Labour had imposed a Scottish devolution policy on its own nondevolved Scottish executive.

The parties thus entered the 1997 election campaign with the following policies on devolution. The SNP had held aloof from the Constitutional Convention and in theory wanted to have nothing to do with devolution. Nevertheless, an internal reorganisation since the 1992 general election had brought to power people who felt that the party's 1992 campaign (slogan: *Scotland Free in '93*) had been incompetent and unrealistic. This time they decided to accept devolution as a temporarily sticky place on the slippery slope to independence. Nationalists and Unionists share a "slippery slope" perspective. In 1997, as in 1974, it was common ground between them that devolution, as proposed by Labour and the Liberal Democrats, was an unstable option and that, as its internal contradictions were revealed, Scotland might slide into full independence. The difference between Nationalists and Unionists was the use they made of this common perspective. In 1997 the SNP leadership was content to sit tight, quietly intending to advise its supporters to vote *yes* in the first referendum question (i.e., whether there should be a Scottish Parliament). They were uncertain about the second (whether it should have taxing powers). It was tempting to recommend SNP supporters to vote *no* to that, in order to show what a pointless Parliament it would be, but the advice might be too cynical to be widely followed and would be difficult to justify in public.

The Conservatives had been trying to make Scottish voters' flesh creep with threats of a tartan tax and a slippery slope. Their campaign was run very effectively by Michael Forsyth, the Scottish secretary. He added what economists call the "cheap talk" gesture of repatriating the Stone of Scone, on which Scottish kings were believed to have been crowned (and Jacob was believed, by some, to have slept). Carted to Westminster by King Edward I during the Anglo-Scottish war that ended with the Scots victory at Bannockburn, the Stone was briefly captured by some nationalist Scots undergraduates in 1950. The evident dismay of the Westminster Abbey authorities at Forsyth's second capture of the Stone made his gesture all the more effective.

The Conservatives eagerly accepted Labour's claim that, once done, devolution could not be undone. This claim was needed to grease the slippery slope. When the health secretary, Stephen Dorrell, who had been given a roving brief on devolution, roved into Michael Forsyth's field in February 1997, he was promptly ejected. Dorrell said that if a devolved Scottish Parliament failed to address the West Lothian Question it would be "absolutely" right for a future Conservative government to get rid of it. The following day, his role as devolution spokesman was as if it had never been.[33] John Major's foreword to the 1997 Conservative manifesto for Scotland states:

> The menace of separatism—introduced through the Trojan Horse of devolution—would blight the lives of Scots for generations to come. The failure of the Labour and Liberal Democrat parties to answer the West Lothian Question after twenty years and the prospect of Scottish MPs being excluded from English and Welsh legislation are chilling portents of disintegration.[34]

The denunciation is somewhat inconsistent. As the most obvious solution to the West Lothian Question is precisely the exclusion of Scottish MPs from English and Welsh legislation, it seems that Major was damning both his opponents' failure to answer and the answer they should have given. At least it prepared him for any surprise Labour moves during the campaign.

Labour and the Liberal Democrats had almost identical policies. They had cooperated closely during the whole life of the Constitutional Convention and both stood by its recommendations, pledging to introduce the 129-member Parliament it proposed, with proportionality guaranteed by the 56 additional members. The main difference between the parties was that the Liberal Democrats were prepared to recognise that the West Lothian Question needed an answer. They proposed to cut the number of Westminster MPs from Scotland, a proposal that Labour was able to turn against them in the main marginal seat where they competed head-to-head (Inverness East, Nairn, and Lochaber—the second-largest constituency, by land area, in the UK).[35] At hustings in the constituency, Labour was able to taunt the Liberals that they intended to make it even bigger. Labour won.

Forty Days of Campaigning

The 1997 general election may turn out to be the most crucial for the government of Scotland since 1707. But it was not won or lost on devolution. Devolution was prominent in politicians' thinking, but, apart from the Conservatives, they all had reasons for publicly downplaying it. Labour did not want to answer awkward questions about the West Lothian Question or the Barnett/Goschen formula for allocating public spending. George Robertson's mission was to keep the campaign as low-key as possible. Apart from a few incidents discussed later, the campaign was therefore thoroughly boring, as Labour wished it to be. The Liberals did not want to draw attention to their proposed solution to the WLQ. For the SNP, devolution was an irrelevance, at least in public. The West Lothian Question was put on the agenda, but by the *Scotsman* newspaper as much as by politicians. The other constitutional issue was the SNP's budget for Scotland.

In March, in the words of Andrew Marr, editor of the *Independent* (another expatriate, who described himself as a former "spear-carrier" on the *Scotsman*):

> The Scotsman has just lobbed a small hand-grenade into the Labour establishment by arguing that for home rule to work, Scottish MPs must now lose the right to vote on English affairs at Westminster. . . . [I]t is a

very painful kick up the Scottish leftish establishment's fundamental principle from a once-dependable ally.[36]

The *Scotsman* leader had boomed:

> If it believes anything, this newspaper believes in home rule for Scot-
> land.... But what of Labour's intentions for the Parliament, if it is ap-
> proved? The frustrations of Scots have tended to make us uncritical of the
> scheme. Desperate to see the Tory government removed, and keen (though
> rarely as a first priority) to win home rule, the majority of us have given
> tacit approval to Labour's plans for no better reason than that they are the
> only plans realistically on offer. It has been a kind of intellectual blank
> cheque, a compromise with party politics.... We say, bluntly, that La-
> bour's scheme is grievously wounded by its refusal to confront the funda-
> mental issue of the West Lothian question.... [T]he answer open to Mr
> Blair is the one he refuses, for party political reasons, to give. The answer
> to the West Lothian question, we believe, can be simply put. If devolution
> is to proceed legislation must be enacted to ensure that Scottish MPs have
> no vote on purely English matters. Problems of definition are not insuper-
> able. The work of the Scottish Parliament would not be impeded. Democ-
> racy would be secured.... The party that once claimed a Scottish Parlia-
> ment would be an irrelevance without taxation powers now tells us,
> scarcely blushing, that such powers would be forsworn for years after the
> Parliament's creation. Such intellectual elasticity might be thought admi-
> rable to some. It causes us merely to wonder why Labour will not give the
> right answer to the West Lothian question now.[37]

The paper was very proud of this leader. Andrew Neil, its editor in chief,
went on the BBC Radio *Today* programme—the forum in which the
British chattering classes chatter to one another—on the day it appeared
to announce that for the first time the *Scotsman* was going on general
sale in London. For the whole duration of the election campaign, the paper kept this leader on the daily news summary in its Web pages, with a
hot link to a feature entitled "Can Blair Finish What Gladstone
Started?"[38] It was championing Gladstone's "in and out" solution to the
WLQ. The Government of Ireland Bill 1893, clause 9, provided that Irish
MPs (to be reduced from 105 to 80, which would have been proportionate to population in 1893) would be unable to vote on, inter alia, any
proposal whose operation would be "confined to Great Britain or some
part thereof." Decisions on which matters were "in" and which were
"out" were to be left to the authorities of each House. These provisions
were dropped during the passage of the bill through the Commons.

Gladstone's bill nevertheless failed even after dropping the in-and-out solution.

The *Scotsman* ignored both this melancholy history and the fact that the in-and-out solution would hit serious trouble if ever Labour held a majority of UK seats narrower than its majority in Scotland. In that case, "in and out" would leave the UK government without a majority at Westminster for its English domestic business, and hence to devolution for England, even if that was never intended.

Andrew Marr's theory was that Neil, as a radical Unionist in charge of a paper that had favoured Home Rule for over a century, was using the only weapon he had to attack Labour. Unable to attack Home Rule head on, he sought instead to embarrass Labour with its inconsistency.[39] Others disagree. Whether or not the leader was part of a deep-laid Unionist scheme, it failed to embarrass Labour or to ignite the electorate.

The SNP budget attracted more attention than the WLQ. Led by a professional economist, the SNP produced very professional-looking economic documents. A series of SNP parliamentary questions prior to the campaign had elicited the Treasury admission that "over the last 18 years we have contributed over £27,000,000,000 more in taxes than we have received in public expenditure." The SNP calculated that Scotland's fiscal surplus with the rest of the UK would be £1.1 billion in 1997–98, rising to £5.4 billion in 2000–2001. Out of this surplus, the party proposed to spend extra sums ranging from £0.9 billion in 1997–98 to £2.1 billion in 2000–2001 on education, social services, and services to business.[40]

Neutral (or hostile) economists accepted the SNP's history but rejected its future. Scotland did indeed have a fiscal surplus with the rest of the UK over the 1979–97 period. But this was solely attributable to a huge flow of oil tax revenue during the peak of North Sea oil production between 1983 and 1986. Before and after the peak, Scotland was in fiscal deficit with the rest of the UK. Some claimed that the years 1983 to 1986 were the only years since 1707 when the net flow of public funds was from Scotland to England. "The oil supported fiscal surpluses of the 1980s have been absorbed into the UK Treasury and used to support welfare spending. Outside the UK, these are a sunk cost to having belonged to the Union in that period."[41] The SNP analysis was vulnerable on three main grounds, in ascending order of importance:

1. It overestimated both North Sea oil revenues and an independent Scotland's likely share of them.
2. It was unrealistically optimistic about unquantifiable gains from independence.
3. It "disinvents the fact that Scotland has a structural deficit."[42]

The SNP claims that an independent Scotland would be entitled to 90 percent of UK oil revenue. This claim is based on the 1968 Continental Shelf Jurisdictional Order,[43] which states that offshore installations north of latitude 55°50′ N are within the jurisdiction of Scots law. Latitude 55°50′ N is the latitude of the English-Scots border where it meets the North Sea, near Berwick-upon-Tweed, where an attractive wrought-iron notice on the main East Coast railway marks the spot. But in any arbitration between an independent Scotland and England on their international boundary in the North Sea, the arbitrated frontier would run northeast, or NNE, from Berwick.[44] So the SNP claim to 90 percent of UK oil revenue is almost certainly untenable. In any case, oil revenue is rapidly declining.

On the gains from independence, "the structural equations underlying this model are not shown by the SNP but it would be useful to be able to inspect them. . . . A very large boost to demand is shown to produce rapid output growth without adverse impacts on inflation or, apparently, the Balance of Payments."[45] The SNP might retort that the staggering success of the Irish economy since 1987 bolsters their claims. On one measure, Ireland has moved from under 70 percent of EU average gross domestic product per head to over 95 percent, overtaking Britain en route; one possible explanation is the attractiveness of an alternative English-speaking investment destination in the EU.[46]

But the most subtle issue is the calculation of Scotland's structural deficit or surplus. The SNP's method was to take the Scottish share of UK government debt at a particular date (17.1 percent in 1994–5), to assume that that would be a fixed proportion and to derive a Scottish government debt/surplus from Treasury projections of UK debt/surplus. At the time of the election, the Treasury Red Book projected a decline in the UK's net borrowing requirement to zero by 2001. Both major parties had lashed themselves to the mast of the Red Book's projections. Therefore, as 17.1 percent of zero is zero, the SNP argued that an independent Scotland would inherit zero government debt. Its critics said that the assumption of a fixed proportion was wrong. Scotland had a structural deficit because public expenditure comfortably exceeded non-oil tax revenue. In consequence of this structural deficit, Scotland's proportion of the UK's general government borrowing requirement (GGBR) would increase the lower the UK debt fell. If non-Scottish UK GGBR fell to zero, Scotland's share would thus be 100 percent.

These fine details had no effect on the electoral debate. They are crucial, however, for evaluating the great hidden issue of the Barnett formula, to which we return below. The sums involved in this argument are so large that they utterly swamp the impact of the proposed "tartan tax," about which there was a great deal of argument during the election campaign. A three pence in the pound Scottish income tax surcharge (the upper limit of the "tartan tax") would bring in about £450 million in a full year, the equivalent of "less than 3 percent of the present Scottish Office budget."[47] The Scottish structural fiscal deficit has been calculated at £6.1 billion in 1994–95, even after crediting oil revenue[48]—that is, some 13.5 times the maximum that could be raised by the "tartan tax." Politicians strained at the gnat and ignored the camel.

During the election campaign, the *Scotsman* claimed its second scalp, to mount beside Stephen Dorrell's on the panelled walls of its baronial palace above Waverley Station. On 4 April 1997, the paper published an interview with Tony Blair in which he was quoted as saying that

"sovereignty rests with me as an English MP and that's the way it will stay." Mr Blair also ruled out the use of a Scottish Parliament's tax varying powers, which he likened to those of an English parish council, in the first term of a Labour government by saying [that] his five-year pledge of no rise in the basic and standard rates of tax applied to "Scotland as well as England."[49]

For the only time in the election campaign, these remarks put Scotland on the front pages in England. The English press accompanying Blair were reportedly shocked at the ferocity of the Scottish journalists' questions about this interview, which was generally described as "Blair's first gaffe." Alex Salmond, the SNP leader, was quoted as saying that Blair had "shown his contempt and derision for Scotland and Scotland's people, and even for his own party members here" and had "buried the Claim of Right."[50] He seemed to have a point. If the Scottish Parliament was to have no more tax powers than an English parish council, what was the point of it? If Blair was going to mandate Labour members of the Scottish Parliament to vote even against a parish-council tax, then, doubly, what was the point? How could he issue such an instruction unless Labour members of the Scottish Parliament were directly controlled by a nondevolved Labour Party headquarters in London? And, in any case, had Blair forgotten that thanks to the PR pledge from the Constitutional Convention Labour would not have a majority of seats in the Scottish Parliament unless, contrary to all precedent, they obtained more than 50 percent of the vote? Was "Trust me—I'm an English MP" a good slogan in a land suffused with Anglophobia? It seemed that the Blairite Scottish Parliament would resemble a design of ski boots in vogue in the late 1970s that were provided with a heel hinge, which was then welded shut. This was alleged to improve the performance of the boots.

After a few days, however, it was less clear that Blair's remarks were a gaffe. Their presentation as one in the London media was a twenty-four-hour wonder, to be blown away by the next day's crop of gaffes. Sources suggested that the parish-council analogy was deliberately chosen. Maybe Blair's strategy was to assume that Scotland was in the bag and to set about reassuring that famous place Middle England that Scottish devolution would not mean anything terrible for it. Whether deliberately or not, there was no discussion of the Scottish play in English public debate on any other day of the election campaign. The West Lothian Question was scarcely discussed in Scotland for the reasons analysed earlier; it was not discussed at all in England. The Scottish polling organisations detected neither a blip nor a permanent drop in Labour voting intentions after the "parish council" and "Trust me—I'm an English MP" remarks.

Of all the Scottish media, the *Scotsman* seemed the least sympathetic to the Lib-Lab devolution proposals. The other heavy broadsheet, the (formerly *Glasgow*) *Herald,* was prodevolution but much blander in its coverage. The Aberdeen and Dundee broadsheet papers stuck with their parish-pump agendas. Radio and television were constrained by statutory or quasi-statutory injunctions to avoid bias. The tabloids struck predictable poses. In Scotland, as in England, the *Sun* backed Labour—on proprietorial diktat, it was widely alleged. In 1992 the Scottish edition of the *Sun* had backed the SNP, and it rationalised its conversion thus:

> We believe that, once it is up and running, the new home rule Parliament will lead on to complete freedom. That, above all, is why we are backing Mr Blair tomorrow. Not because he shares our vision of a fully independent Scotland—he doesn't. Not because devolution is the perfect solution—it isn't. *But because his home rule scheme will be the key that unlocks the door to independence.*[51]

The *Sun* also obtained perhaps the most entertaining Scottish election coverage by sending a reporter to shadow Jacob Rees-Mogg, the Conservative candidate for Central Fife, and an Old Etonian son of a former editor of *The Times*. The seat, which was held by the Communists from 1935 to 1950, resisted the charms not only of Rees-Mogg but also of his nanny, who campaigned for him.[52]

The West Lothian Question and
the Barnett Formula

The result of the 1997 general election settled some questions and gave new life to others. Labour did not suffer from its alleged gaffes. The Conservatives' niche marketing failed. Tactical voting ensured that party shares of the vote and of seats were wide apart, as table 6.2 shows.

TABLE 6.2

VOTE AND SEAT SHARES IN SCOTLAND, 1997
(IN PERCENTAGES)

Party	Share of vote	Share of seats
Labour	45.6%	77.8%
SNP	22.0	8.3
Conservative	17.5	0.0
Liberal Democrat	13.0	13.9
Others	1.9	0.0

Tactical voting combined with the known properties of the plurality electoral system to deliver a very different result from previous four-way contests, especially those of 1974. Recall that in October 1974 the SNP also beat the Conservatives into third place in the popular vote. But then there was somewhat less tactical voting than in 1997; and the Conservative vote share in 1974 was above the precipice down which parties with an evenly distributed vote are doomed to plunge. In 1997 the Scottish Conservatives plunged down it even more surely than their Canadian counterparts when they were reduced to two seats in 1993. The Scots and Canadian Conservatives had obtained the same vote share of 17 percent. The Liberal Democrats achieved proportionate representation because their vote was efficiently distributed, whereas the Conservatives' was distributed more evenly. At 35 percent of the vote and above, even distribution pushes a party above its proportionate share of seats (note Labour's 78 percent of seats on less than half of the Scottish vote); below that, it punishes parties, sometimes catastrophically.

Most commentators think that the Labour landslide makes the West Lothian Question more tractable than it appeared before 1 May 1997. There are low reasons of party discipline for saying this. The draconian discipline code that now binds the parliamentary Labour Party could lead to the suspension or expulsion of any anti-devolution rebel, including Tam Dalyell, the original author of the WLQ. He still sits for West Lothian, now renamed Linlithgow. A Geordie revolt is less likely than in 1977 and, if it did happen, would be of no consequence.

But the Labour landslide also makes the WLQ more tractable for more elevated reasons. In 1974–79, Labour could not propose reduction in the number of Scottish seats at Westminster. It had then embarked on devolution solely for reasons of self-preservation, and in those Parliaments its UK majority was smaller than its Scottish majority. Therefore, removing the overrepresentation of Scotland would have destroyed the point of the whole exercise. Somewhat surprisingly, Scottish overrepresentation was not tackled between 1979 and 1997, although it would apparently have been in the Conservatives' partisan interest to do so. The Labour government can safely tackle it now. It has no partisan interest in maintaining Scottish overrepresentation. True, ending Scottish overrepresentation will lead to some Labour MPs being left without seats when the music stops. But at least they will have the Scottish Parliament to retire to.

Whatever solution the Blair government adopts, it cannot avoid some large constitutional questions. Every relevant expert has warned it that the form of the Scotland Act 1978 would have been unworkable if it had ever been tested. The 1978 act sought to define the powers of the Scottish Parliament by an exhaustive list. This led to months of civil service and ministerial time being spent on fighting turf wars during the drafting process. The act also failed to specify any forum for settling the future turf wars that would erupt whenever one Parliament passed an act or took an executive action that the other thought was outside its powers. Informed advice to the Blair government[53] favours reversing the onus of proof. The Government of Ireland Act 1920 specified, not the powers devolved to Stormont, but the powers reserved to Westminster. Although there would still be turf wars before and after drafting the next Scotland bill, they would be fewer.

Furthermore, a bill modelled on the 1920 Government of Ireland Act provides the most compelling available answer to the WLQ. During the passage of the Government of Scotland Act 2000, Parliament will vote to reserve certain powers. By voting not to reserve others, it will be voting away its right to intervene in those matters, at least on a day-to-day basis. By choosing not to pass a Government of England Act at the same time, it will have legitimised the West Lothian anomaly whereby its own Scottish members may vote on English affairs but not on Scottish affairs.[54]

But legislation in the 1920 framework radically alters the balance of power between the sovereign and the devolved legislature. It would force the Westminster government to think harder than any British government has had to do since 1920: *what are the core functions of government, not to be devolved?* The 1920 list offers a start. So indeed does the

Constitution of the United States in the equivalent clause which specifies what powers are reserved to the federal government.[55] Both the American and the Irish lists, though, contain reservations that now seem merely quaint (piracy and letters of marque and reprisal for the U.S. Congress; treason, submarine cables, lighthouses, buoys, and beacons for Westminster). Neither covers many of the most contested areas of modern government. The Labour Party promised before the 1997 election that it would devolve power. Will it actually do so? One body to whom it would necessarily delegate power would be the court that will have to adjudicate on disputes over the respective powers of the parliaments. It is true that no such court was needed for Northern Ireland between 1920 and 1972; the powers were policed by the speakers and clerks of the two parliaments. But it is universally agreed that that is too heavy a burden to lay on the Westminster and Edinburgh speakers. The constitutional court will have to be either the Judicial Committee of the Privy Council or the Appellate Committee of the House of Lords. The Constitution Unit favours the latter.[56] Into such deep waters the Blair government must be drawn. As this chapter goes to press, an ominous silence envelops the Labour government's devolution proposals. It has reneged on a proposal to put them into a White Paper to be published before the autumn 1997 referendum. There are rumours that the bill, whether on the 1978 or the 1920 model, is proving unexpectedly difficult to draft. The 1970s may be closer than they seem.

Finally, we must consider the biggest issue of all: the financial arrangements for devolved government. The first attempt to apportion spending to Scotland was made by George Goschen, chancellor of the exchequer in the Unionist government that succeeded Gladstone's in 1886. The Goschen formula apportioned spending to Scotland in proportion to Scotland's share of UK population.[57] The question was not revisited by central government until the 1970s. Then, pressure both for devolution to Scotland and for equitable treatment of the poorer regions of England generated data and proposals. The pattern of higher public spending per head in Scotland turned out to be long standing and deep rooted.[58] It surely resulted from successive applications of the Johnston gambit since 1941—probably since long before then. As part of the devolution process, the then chief secretary to the Treasury, Joel Barnett, proposed a formula for distributing territorial expenditure more equitably. (Recall that it was a Geordie revolt over the "unfair" share of public spending going to Scotland that killed the first devolution bill in 1977). The Barnett formula "allocated increases or decreases in public expenditure in Scotland, Wales, and England in the ratio 10:5:85, the rounded share of GB population for the three nations concerned in

1976. . . . For every £85 *change* in planned expenditure on comparable English services, Wales would receive £5 and Scotland £10."[59] The relatively higher spending on Scotland (relative not only to England but to the deprived regions of England) could not be abolished at a stroke. The Barnett formula was designed to achieve convergence over time. It has not done so, for various reasons.

1. The population proportions were from the outset too favourable to Scotland. (The Scottish share of GB population was 9.57 percent in 1976, when the Barnett formula was calibrated.)

2. Scotland's relative population decline has been continuous, but the population shares have only been rebased once (by Michael Portillo, chief secretary in 1991). As Scotland's population share continues to decline, even the rebased Portillo formula is too favourable to Scotland and will become increasingly more so until the next rebasing.

3. There has been no needs assessment since 1979. In the 1970s Scottish gross domestic product per head was some 85 percent of the UK average; now it is around 100 percent. While this change improves the Scottish revenue base, it weakens the case for differential public spending.

4. Secretaries of state have become, if anything, more blatant in their playing of the Johnston gambit. In particular, the last two Conservative Scottish secretaries, Ian Lang (1990–95) and Michael Forsyth (1995–97), openly boasted about the differential, in documents that they must have hoped were seen only in Scotland.[60] Their threat was that devolution would destroy the Scottish advantage because bringing it into the open would show that it was unsustainable in the long run. Maintaining, and even enhancing, the Scottish differential was thus (rather unexpectedly) Conservative policy.

It is this relativity that gives rise to Scotland's huge structural deficit, which we visited earlier in connection with the SNP budget. This deficit is a problem for devolution, just as it would be a problem for independence. If it is not addressed, the English—and particularly English MPs representing relatively poor areas of England—have a grievance that is justifiable as it was in 1977. The fact that Scottish GDP now equals the UK average makes the disproportion even harder to justify on egalitarian grounds (socialist grounds are presumably now irrelevant). Although the legislation is unlikely to encounter the fatal damage suffered in 1977, most MPs who vote for it will be voting against the material interest of their constituents. If the public spending relativities are dragged into the open, English voters and politicians may come to feel that "there does not seem any overwhelming need, other than sentiment, for the English to retain the Union."[61]

If, however, the deficit is addressed, the Scots will be severely disappointed. Despite Michael Forsyth's efforts, very few Scots know how favourably the UK state treats them. The Blair government is the first for many years that is strong enough to reduce the disparities. But that is not what Scots thought they were voting for when they voted for the devolutionist parties in 1997. For many years the Scots have been bought and sold (mostly bought) for English gold. That does not make them a parcel of rogues in a nation. It does, however, provide devolution with its greatest challenge.

Notes

1. Or so politicians claimed in 1997. Actually, they had forgotten about the change of calendar in 1752. From 1 May 1707 to 1 May 1997 was 13 days short of 290 years.
2. W.A. Speck, *The Birth of Britain: A New Nation 1700–1710* (Oxford: Blackwell, 1994), 106–118; R. Sutherland, "Aspects of the Scottish Constitution prior to 1707," in *Independence and Devolution: The Legal Implications for Scotland,* edited by J.P. Grant (Edinburgh: W. Green & Son 1976), 15–44; Iain McLean, "Are Scotland and Wales Overrepresented in the House of Commons?" *Political Quarterly* 66 (1995): 250–68.
3. Professor D.M. Walker cited in Grant, *Independence and Devolution,* xiii.
4. Lord Morrison of Lambeth, *Herbert Morrison: An Autobiography* (London: Odhams Press 1960), 199. See also G. Walker, *Thomas Johnston* (Manchester: Manchester University Press, 1988), chaps. 5–6.
5. "It was pointed out that a strict application of the quota for the whole of Great Britain would result in a considerable decrease in the existing number of Scottish and Welsh seats, but that in practice, in view of the proposal that the Boundary Commissioners should be permitted to pay special consideration to geographical considerations [*sic*], it was ... unlikely that there would be any substantial reduction. It was strongly urged that ... it would be very desirable, on political grounds, to state from the outset quite clearly that the number of Scottish and Welsh seats should not be diminished. The absence of any such assurance might give rise to a good deal of political feeling and would lend support to the separatist movements in both countries." House of Lords Record Office, CH/5/5. Speaker's Conference 1944, Minute of Meeting no. 9. Scottish and Welsh parliamentarians were overrepresented in the conference itself. For the contradictory rule that the following meeting adopted for England, see McLean, "Are Scotland and Wales Overrepresented?"
6. See Iain McLean, "Scottish Nationalism: Its Growth and Development, with Particular Reference to the Period since 1961," B. Phil. thesis, Oxford

University, 1969; H.J. Hanham, *Scottish Nationalism* (London: Faber and Faber, 1969); Jack Brand, *The National Movement in Scotland* (London: Routledge, 1978).

7. After its defeat in 1979, the SNP wobbled to the right and expelled some of its more socialist or social-democratic members. They subsequently regained control.

8. The story has been told in detail elsewhere. A useful summary is W.L. Miller, "The Scottish Dimension," in *The British General Election of 1979*, edited by David Butler and Dennis Kavanagh (London: Macmillan, 1980), 98–118. See also Grant, *Independence and Devolution;* Vernon Bogdanor, *Devolution* (Oxford: Oxford University Press, 1979); Tam Dalyell, *Devolution, the End of Britain?* (London: Jonathan Cape, 1977); David Heald, *Financing Devolution within the United Kingdom: A Study of the Lessons from Failure* (Canberra: Centre for Research on Federal Financial Relations, Australian National University, 1980); Iain McLean and Roger Guthrie, "Another Part of the Periphery: Reactions to Devolution in an English Development Area," *Parliamentary Affairs* 31 (1978):190–200.

9. McLean and Guthrie, "Another Part of the Periphery." The author was an active participant in these events, being at the time chairman of the Economic Development Committee of Tyne and Wear County Council. Facts not otherwise supported by citations are from memory.

10. The Labour Party, however, in 1951 obtained the votes of 40.25 percent of the electorate. They lost that election to the Conservatives, who won more seats with fewer votes.

11. Butler and Kavanagh, *British General Election of 1979,* 125.

12. See David Butler, Andrew Adonis, and Tony Travers, *Failure in British Government: The Politics of the Poll Tax* (Oxford: Oxford University Press, 1994).

13. 5 April 1992, quoted by David Butler and Dennis Kavanagh, *The British General Election of 1992* (London: Macmillan 1992), 130.

14. Barry Winetrobe, *The West Lothian Question,* House of Commons Library Research Paper 95/58, 1995, i.

15. Dalyell, *Devolution,* passim.

16. Labour Party, *A Parliament for Scotland: Labour's Plan 1995,* quoted by Winetrobe, *West Lothian Question,* 4.

17. W.L. Miller, quoted in Constitution Unit, *Scotland's Parliament: Fundamentals for a New Scotland Act* (London: Constitution Unit, 1996), 109.

18. W.L. Miller, A.M. Timpson, and M. Lessnoff, *Political Culture in Contemporary Britain* (Oxford: Clarendon Press, 1996), 370. The data are in table 11.1, p. 371 (cultural matters); table 6.3, p. 190 (devolution).

19. *Report of the Royal Commission on the Constitution,* chairman Lord Kilbrandon (Cmnd. 5460/1973), Research Paper 7, *Devolution and Other Aspects of Government,* table 45.

20. Anthony King, "Fear Factor Hits Support for Home Rule," *Daily Telegraph,* 9 May 1996.

21. Butler, Adonis, and Travers, *Failure in British Government,* 104.

22. Scottish Constitutional Convention, *Scotland's Parliament. Scotland's*

Right (Edinburgh: Scottish Constitutional Convention, 1995), 10.

23. All facts and quotations in this paragraph (except Jenny Geddes) are from Rosalind Mitchison, *A History of Scotland* (London: Methuen, 1970), 49–50 and 195–222.

24. Iain McLean, *The Legend of Red Clydeside* (Edinburgh: John Donald 1983), 98–99. The metrical Psalm 124 ("Now Israel may say, and that truly") should have escaped Mitchison's censure. It is much better verse than most of the others: poetry, even.

25. *Scotland's Parliament. Scotland's Right,* 36.

26. Ibid., 23.

27. Ibid., 27.

28. Ibid., 28.

29. Ibid., 19.

30. Canon Kenyon Wright, quoted in R. Dinwoodie, "Devolution 'Lies' Attacked," *Herald,* 24 April 1997. The Mound is the steep Edinburgh street with the Church of Scotland Assembly Hall at its head.

31. For example, "The Tug for the Flag," *The Economist,* 29 June 1996, 29.

32. "A vote too far," *The Economist,* 7 September 1996, 22.

33. A. Parker, "Dorrell in Devolution Warning," *Scotsman,* 10 February 1997; A. Parker, J. Penman, and P. MacMahon, "Rift Deepens on Home Rule," *Scotsman,* 11 February 1997; "Major Stakes Out His Scapegoat," *Scotsman,* 11 February 1997.

34. Scottish Conservative and Unionist Party, *Fighting for Scotland: the Scottish Conservative and Unionist Manifesto 1997* (Leith: Scottish Conservative and Unionist Party, 1997), 2.

35. Information in this paragraph and in the next section, where not otherwise acknowledged, is from interviews with party figures, April 1997. On the earlier travels of the Stone of Scone, see Brand, *National Movement in Scotland,* 118–19, 132, 234.

36. A. Marr, "The Scotsman's Home Rule Hand-Grenade," *Independent,* 19 March 1997.

37. "Labour Must Answer the Question Now," *Scotsman,* 18 March 1997.

38. http://www.scotsman.com/public/news/neo1ed858582006.7.html.

39. Marr, "The Scotsman's Home Rule Hand-Grenade."

40. Scottish National Party, *Yes We Can Win the Best for Scotland: The SNP General Election Budget 1997* (Edinburgh: SNP, 1997), p. iii and table 1. Emphasis in original.

41. Jim Stevens, "The SNP Budget for Scotland: A Comment," ms., Fraser of Allander Institute, Strathclyde University, 1997; confirming C.H. Lee, *Scotland and the United Kingdom: The Economy and the Union in the Twentieth Century* (Manchester University Press, 1995), 151.

42. Jim Stevens, "Scotland's Budget: SNP's Fantasy Fiscal Bonanza" (letter), *Scotsman,* 8 April 1997.

43. *Yes We Can Win the Best for Scotland,* 18. The Order is SI 1968/892.

44. J.P. Grant, "Oil and Gas," in Grant, *Independence and Devolution,* 86–99.

45. Peter Wood, "The Scottish National Party's Election Budget: An Analysis," ms., Edinburgh: Pieda plc, 1997.

46. "Europe's Tiger Economy," *The Economist,* 17 May 1997, 25–28.
47. Constitution Unit, *Scotland's Parliament: Fundamentals for a New Scotland Act* (London: Constitution Unit, 1996), 82.
48. Stevens, "The SNP Budget for Scotland: A Comment," table A5.
49. J. Penman, "Real Power Will Stay with MPs in England, Blair tells Scotland," *Scotsman,* 4 April 1997.
50. J. Penman and P. MacMahon, "24 Hours Show Blair What a Difference a Day Makes," *Scotsman,* 5 April 1997.
51. "The *Sun* Says We Can Trust Tony to Deliver," *Sun* (Scottish edition), 30 April 1997. Emphasis in original.
52. M. Bendoris, "I'm No Loony, says Jacob," *Sun* (Scottish edition), 25 April 1997.
53. For example, from the Constitution Unit. See *Scotland's Parliament: Fundamentals for a New Scotland Act,* 34–42.
54. The Government of Scotland Act 2000 will probably have a clause modelled on the notorious s.75 of the 1920 Act, which states, "the supreme authority of the Parliament of the United Kingdom shall remain unaffected and undiminished over all persons, matters, and things in Ireland and every part thereof." The history of that act suggests that s.75 is empty. When things got to such a pass that it was invoked, in 1972, this was followed shortly by the abolition of the parliament of Northern Ireland.
55. Constitution of the United States of America, Article I, Sec. 8. By the Tenth Amendment, "The powers not delegated to the United States by the Constitution, nor prohibited by it to the States, are reserved to the States respectively, or to the people."
56. *Scotland's Parliament: Fundamentals for a New Scotland Act,* 48–49.
57. Ibid., 172.
58. Heald, *Financing Devolution within the United Kingdom,* 17–45.
59. *Scotland's Parliament: Fundamentals for a New Scotland Act,* 66.
60. See D. Heald and N. Geaughan, "Financing a Scottish Parliament," in *The State and the Nations: The Politics of Devolution,* edited by S. Tindale (London: Institute for Public Policy Research, 1996), 167–83.
61. Lee, *Scotland and the United Kingdom,* 225.

7

Why Labour Won — At Last

Anthony King

By the time John Major finally got around to calling the 1997 election, almost everyone knew Labour was going to win. The only question was by how much. The Tories had lost every by-election fought during the 1992 Parliament. They had been hammered in local elections and the Euroelections. They had been behind, usually far behind, in every opinion poll conducted since the autumn of 1992. Only memories of the polls' debacle in April 1992 provoked the occasional frisson of doubt.

But the fact that a Labour victory had come to seem inevitable by the time the 1997 election was called should not be allowed to obscure the fact that such a victory had seemed anything but inevitable only five years before. In the aftermath of Labour's defeat in 1992—its fourth electoral defeat in succession—one normally reliable commentator on British politics wrote: "Britain no longer has two major political parties. It has one major party, the Conservatives, one minor party, Labour, and one peripheral party, the Liberal Democrats." He went on to speculate that the Conservative Party might remain in power well into the next millennium.[1] Anyone who had predicted in 1992 that the Labour Party would win the next general election with an overall parliamentary majority of 179 would have been thought to be mad. The astonishing should never cease to astonish merely because, in retrospect, it has come to seem commonplace. What happened between 1992 and 1997 constituted, in fact, one of the greatest reversals of political fortune in the history of any democratic country. What brought it about?

This chapter seeks to answer that question. It is hard to weigh with any degree of precision the relative importance of the various individual factors, but it should be possible to identify what those factors were.

Three Unsatisfactory Theories

We begin, however, by dismissing out of hand three theories that could be advanced to explain the election outcome—three theories that may (or may not) sound plausible on the face of it but that can easily be shown to be false.

One of the three might be dubbed the "time-lapse" theory. This theory was advanced on election night television by Lord Parkinson who, as Cecil Parkinson, had served in the cabinet under Margaret Thatcher. "We've just been there for eighteen years," he said, having been asked to explain the Conservatives' defeat. "It's twenty-three years since the Labour Party last won an election, and I think the mood that I found going round the country: people were saying 'Look, it's just time for a change.'" Parkinson was by no means the only Conservative to blame his party's defeat on the widespread feeling in the country that it was time for a change.

At one level, of course, this theory is true. In May 1997 large numbers of voters did undoubtedly feel it was time for a change; that was why they voted for change and why, because so many of them did so, a change actually occurred. It would be very odd to have a change of government when voters did not feel it was time for a change. But at this level the theory, while true, is utterly platitudinous. The question is not whether people thought it was time for a change but why.

At another level, however—the one suggested by Lord Parkinson —the theory, while it ceases to be platitudinous, becomes merely wrong. Parkinson's key sentence is "We've just been there for eighteen years." The clear implication is that, consciously or subconsciously, voters have a political clock in their minds, one that ticks away over the years. At some point the clock's alarm bell rings and tells the voters "Time's up. Time for a change." The implication is that after a certain period of years any government, irrespective of its record and irrespective of the nature of the Opposition, will be thrown out of office.

But there is no evidence at all to substantiate such a view and excellent grounds for rejecting it. For one thing, it is doubtful whether most voters—who are only marginally interested in politics, at best—have any very precise idea of how long a government that has been in for a long time has been in for. In the early 1960s the Labour Party abandoned one of its proposed campaign slogans, "13 wasted years," partly because few voters thought the previous few years had been wasted but partly also because it turned out that almost no one knew what the number "13" referred to. In other words, the political alarm clocks that are supposed to exist in voters' minds have, in the great majority of cases, never been set.

But even if they had been (and some people certainly do know roughly how long any given government has been in power), there is no reason to think that the mere passage of time, as such, causes any substantial numbers of voters to vote for a party they would not otherwise have voted for. Far more important is how the government and the Opposition parties have used the time available to them, however long that may be. Many voters felt it was time for a change in 1970 and again in 1979, even though the Labour governments thrown out then had only been in power for five or six years. Not enough voters felt it was time for a change in 1992, even though the Conservatives by then had been in power for twelve years. Of course, governments that have been in power for a very long time may, partly for that reason, become arrogant, complacent, tired, stale, and out of touch; that may be what Parkinson had in mind on election night. But that is not what he said.

Another theory that will not withstand a moment's scrutiny is the theory that Labour won the election, and the Conservatives blew it, during the few weeks of the formal campaign, following the prime minister's announcement that Parliament would be dissolved. At least one book has already been written on the 1997 campaign, and many academic papers are pending.[2] But all the evidence suggests that the campaign was largely irrelevant. As the data presented in chapter 2 suggest, Labour would probably have won an election at any time from the late summer of 1994 onwards; it would certainly have won one at any time in early 1997, even if there had been no campaign at all.

Indeed, one of the most striking features of the 1997 campaign was its curious split-level quality. The politicians, as they always do on these occasions, puffed, panted, and rushed about the country. They stretched every sinew and strained every nerve. They gave speeches, they gave interviews, they gave their all. No camera angle was neglected, no photo opportunity was missed. At times the politicians resembled those manic characters in the jerky, speeded-up film comedies of the 1920s. But nothing happened. The audience, for whose benefit all these entertainments were laid on, remained almost completely inert. Scarcely a cough or a sneeze could be heard from the pit.

The opinion polls during the weeks before the campaign put Labour at roughly 51–54 percent.[3] During the six weeks of the campaign this figure gradually subsided to about 47–51 percent. And on polling day itself Labour won an even smaller proportion of the Great Britain vote, 44.4 percent. These changes look quite substantial until it is noticed that the Liberal Democrats were meanwhile gradually edging up from roughly 12–14 percent before and during the campaign to 17.2 percent on the day. Not all this shift from Labour to the Liberal Democrats will have been caused by voters switching from one party to the other on purely tactical grounds; but a lot of it will and, in that sense, much of the apparent decline in Labour's support should not be regarded as "real."

But what is most striking about the opinion poll findings—and is the true measure of the electorate's inertia—is the virtually complete failure of the Tory share of the vote to shift in any direction. Roughly 28–29 percent of voters told the polls before the campaign began that they intended to vote Conservative. The figures during the campaign were roughly 32–33 percent. The final figure was 31.5 percent. In other words, although the Tories did manage a slight overall recovery, most of what little net movement occurred in the course of the six-week campaign took the form of the various Opposition parties trading support with one another. The details changed a certain amount. The big picture remained substantially the same.

To be sure, the net movements recorded by the opinion polls conceal a much larger volume of gross movement among all the parties; a good deal of "churning"—switches between the parties that more or less cancel each other out—takes place at every general election. It is also true that the 1997 campaign might have made a difference if, for example, Labour's leaders had done something exceedingly foolish. But it never seemed likely that they would, and they did not. Largely as a result, the campaign was a nonevent. When it was all over, not even their fiercest critics could bring themselves to blame either John Major or the Conservative chairman, Brian Mawhinney, for the way they conducted the campaign.

The third theory that can be dismissed out of hand is less a theory than a speculation: John Major and the Conservatives would have done significantly better if they had campaigned on a more straightforwardly Eurosceptical platform and, in particular, had come out unequivocally against British participation in a single European currency. Certainly many of the Eurosceptics believed that such a line would not only be right in itself but could succeed as nothing else could in rallying support to the Conservative cause.

This view is without substance, a product of Eurosceptics talking to other Eurosceptics and persuading themselves that the heart of the nation beat in their bosoms alone. Although the polls did find substantial numbers of voters opposed to a single currency, they found even larger numbers broadly in favour of the government's "wait and decide" policy. Many voters, probably most, had mixed feelings about Europe (in so far as they had feelings at all): on the one hand, they were inclined to resent Brussels interference in Britain's internal affairs; but, on the other, they feared the prospect of Britain being sidelined in Europe. On top of all that, very few voters put Europe anywhere near the top of their personal political agendas—and those who did, and who held Eurosceptical opinions, were almost all Conservative supporters already.[4] There was no mileage for the Tories on the issue of Europe (quite apart from the fact that a more robustly Eurosceptical line would have further exposed the divisions in their own ranks).

If the mere lapse of time cannot explain Labour's victory, and neither can the 1997 campaign or the Conservatives' failure to adopt a harder line on Europe, where is an adequate explanation to be found? Large events do not always have large causes, but, as we shall see, this one certainly had.

Part of the Explanation: The Conservatives

To understand the scale of the Conservatives' 1997 defeat one needs to begin by understanding that, although the Conservative Party dominated the politics of the 1980s and most of the 1990s, its support in the electorate was much less solidly based than is often supposed. Conservative command of the House of Commons was never matched by any comparable command of the electorate. In that sense, the Conservative ascendancy of the Thatcher and Major years constituted something of an optical illusion. A voter revolt against the Conservatives—possibly on a massive scale—was always an event waiting to happen.

Consider the following data from the 1979–97 period bearing on the Conservatives' underlying electoral weakness:

• Although they won each of the four general elections between 1979 and 1992, the Conservatives never managed to secure as much as 45 percent, let alone 50 percent, of the United Kingdom vote. They won 43.9 percent in 1979, 42.4 percent in 1983, 43.4 percent in 1987, and 42.3 percent in 1992. None of those figures begins to constitute a sweeping electoral mandate. By the same token, substantial majorities at each election voted against the Tories: 56.1 percent in 1979, 57.6 percent in 1983, 56.6 percent in 1987, and 57.7 percent in 1992. However dominant their parliamentary position, the Thatcher and Major governments were always minority governments in electoral terms.[5]

• Conservative support virtually collapsed in by-elections throughout the period, not just after 1992. The average share of the vote cast for Conservative candidates in by-elections during the 1979 Parliament was 27 percent; during the 1983 Parliament it was 29 percent, during the 1987 Parliament 19 percent, and during the 1992 Parliament a derisory 17 percent.[6] Between 1979 and 1997 the Conservatives fought a total of 71 by-elections and their share of the vote fell in all but one of them. They gained only a single seat during the whole of this period (in unusual circumstances soon after the Falklands War) and lost no fewer than 23 of the 34 seats they were defending.[7] They won no by-elections at all from February 1989 onwards. Given a chance to vent their spleen against an incumbent Conservative government, the voters almost invariably took it.

• The Conservatives' poor performance in parliamentary by-elections extended to elections to the European Parliament. Four rounds of Euroelections were held between 1979 and 1997. The Tories did well in the first, held only a month after their return to power in 1979, when they won 48.4 percent of the United Kingdom vote. But after that their performance was uniformly dismal. They won 39.9 percent in 1984, 33.5 percent in 1989, and a mere 26.9 percent—the Tories' lowest-ever share of the vote in any national election—in 1994.[8]

• Despite the fact that they succeeded in being reelected, the

TABLE 7.1

PUBLIC APPROVAL RATINGS OF THE GOVERNMENT AND
OF THATCHER AND MAJOR, 1979–97

| Year | Approval, in mean percentages, of the | |
	government	prime minister
	Conservative	Thatcher
1979	35	43
1980	32	39
1981	25	31
1982	37	42
1983	42	49
1984	38	44
1985	30	36
1986	29	32
1987	39	44
1988	40	44
1989	32	37
1990	27	29[a]
		Major
1991	33	52[b]
1992	26	42
1993	14	23
1994	12	21
1995	13	23
1996	15	26
1997	25	34

SOURCE: Calculated from Gallup Political Barometers.

a. January–November 1990.   b. December 1990–December 1991.

Thatcher and Major governments' approval ratings were consistently poor. The Gallup poll asks approximately 9,000 British electors each month: "Do you approve or disapprove of the government's record to date?" As can be inferred from table 7.1 (p. 182), large majorities of voters did not think much of either the Thatcher or the Major government's record. Over the whole 1979–97 period the average proportion of Gallup's respondents approving of the government's record to date was only 29 percent—the lowest approval rating for any governing party since the war. In only two years did the government's approval rating reach or exceed 40 percent; in as many as nine, it fell below 30 percent. Although the worst years came after the 1992 election, the standing of the Thatcher and Major governments even before then was not high.

• Thatcher and Major as individual political leaders were also not held in high esteem. As in the case of the whole government, Gallup asks a large sample of voters every month: "Are you satisfied or dissatisfied with - - - - - as prime minister?" Many politicians and political commentators in Britain—and in other countries, notably the United States—imagined during the 1980s that Thatcher not only was the dominant figure in British politics but also was tremendously popular with the British public. As table 7.2 shows, they were in error: she was not. On the contrary, she was nearly the most ill-regarded prime minister since the war, with an average satisfaction rating lower than that of any other prime minister since 1945 except Edward Heath and her own successor, John Major.

TABLE 7.2

PUBLIC APPROVAL RATINGS OF GOVERNING PARTY

AND PRIME MINISTER, 1945–97

Governing party	Approval (mean %)	Prime minister	Approval (mean %)
Labour, 1945–51	40	Attlee, 1945–51	47
Conservative, 1951–64	43	Churchill, 1951–55	52
		Eden, 1955–57	57
		Macmillan, 1957–63	53
		Home, 1963–64	44
Labour, 1964–70	34	Wilson, 1964–70	45
Conservative, 1970–74	35	Heath, 1970–74	37
Labour, 1974–79	33	Wilson, 1974–76	46
		Callaghan, 1976–79	46
Conservative, 1979–97	29	Thatcher, 1979–90	39
		Major, 1990–97	31

SOURCE: Calculated from Gallup Political Barometers.

The Conservatives were thus always vulnerable. They remained in power for eighteen years not because they were generally liked and admired but despite the fact that they were not. They were given credit for regaining the Falklands from Argentina, for requiring local authorities to sell council houses to their tenants, and for curbing trade-union power, but they were associated in voters' minds with high levels of unemployment and cuts in public services, and their economic policies were widely regarded as having led to a more mean-spirited and divided society. Substantial majorities of voters disapproved of the Conservative policy of selling off state-owned firms to the private sector.[9]

Indeed one of the most striking features of the politics of the Thatcher-Major years was the Conservative Party's failure to win public opinion around to the major tenets of its public philosophy. After the party's third successive election victory in 1987, Ivor Crewe asked, "Has the electorate become Thatcherite?" and confidently answered, "No." He wrote:

> A distinctive feature of Thatcherism is its pedagogic impulse. It has been at pains to educate the electorate about economic realities.... Not since Gladstone has Britain been led by such an opinionated and evangelical Prime Minister as Mrs. Thatcher. But there is precious little evidence that she has succeeded. Her missionary preaching has fallen on deaf ears.... The public has not been converted to economic Thatcherism—not to its priorities, nor to its economic reasoning, nor to its social values.[10]

In a survey conducted in 1989, on the tenth anniversary of Thatcher's accession to power, the Gallup poll found that the proportion of voters agreeing with the Thatcherite view that "the important job for the government is to make certain that there are good opportunies for each person to get ahead on his own" had actually fallen since the time of Clement Attlee and the postwar Labour government (from 40 to 32 percent) while the proportion agreeing with the more statist or socialist doctrine that "the important job for the government is to guarantee every person a steady job and a decent standard of living" had actually risen (from 55 to 64 percent).[11] As schoolmistress to the nation, Thatcher was not a success—and her successor was, if anything, even less successful.

The Conservatives were able to win reelection in the 1980s and again in 1992 because, despite these ideological handicaps, a sufficient number of voters believed that the Conservatives in practice would be more likely than the Labour Party to govern sensibly and, in particular, to manage the economy well. Wavering voters' judgements of the Conservatives were largely pragmatic. The Conservatives won simply because enough waverers thought that at the end of the day the Tories, more than Labour, would "deliver."

One of the most important things that happened after the 1992 election was that that collective judgment began to be heavily revised. The revision took two main forms. One has already featured prominently in the pages of this book, indeed has been one of its themes. The other has tended, in most accounts of the election, to be slighted or ignored.

THE CONSERVATIVES' LOSS OF REPUTATION

The Conservative Party throughout most of its history, especially during the present century, has had a reputation for solid competence. The party might be dull and uninspired, it might be out of touch with the needs of ordinary people, its values might not be desperately attractive; but at least the Conservatives knew how to run things. They, far more than their opposite numbers in the Labour Party, were experienced men of affairs—landowners, industrialists, stockbrokers, bankers, barristers, and diplomats. Unlike people in the Labour Party, they understood the great world, knew who to talk to, had been taught which levers to pull. Like the Republicans in early twentieth-century America, Britain's Conservatives stood for sobriety, efficiency, and sound finance. Labour in power was liable to screw up; the Tories, whatever else one thought of them, would at least stay out of trouble—and keep the country out of trouble.

The history of Britain's financial crises in the twentieth century fed the Tories' reputation. Between 1900 and 1992 there were four full-blown financial crises involving the British government, and Labour administrations were implicated in all of them. In 1931 a so-called "National" government finally took Britain off the gold standard, but it was a Labour administration under Ramsay MacDonald that had failed during the previous weeks to deal adequately with the consequences for Britain of the international financial collapse (and MacDonald himself was still in office when Britain finally went off gold). In 1949 Labour under Clement Attlee devalued sterling, and in 1967 Labour devalued again under Harold Wilson. In 1976, faced with a plummeting pound, it was yet again a Labour administration, this time under James Callaghan, that was forced to call in the International Monetary Fund to oversee the conduct of Britain's financial affairs until such time as massive foreign loans could be repaid. Small wonder that millions of British voters, educated by events over more than six decades, got the idea that Labour governments, however desirable they might be in the abstract, were nevertheless apt to lead to trouble. They were accident-prone and unreliable. Under Labour no one could be sure what might happen next. The Conservatives represented safety; Labour represented risk. The two parties' contrasting reputations alone gave the Conservatives a substantial in-built electoral advantage, one that, by itself, was probably enough to carry them to victory in 1992.

What happened on 16 September 1992—Black Wednesday—was that a Conservative government threw all that away. In a matter of a few hours, Major, Lamont, and their ministerial colleagues managed to de-stroy a reputation for reliability and competence that had been built up over generations, possibly even centuries. At a stroke they reduced the Conservatives to Labour's level. Once upon a time, only one party had been thought liable to screw up. Now both were. The Conservatives' for-mer built-in advantage at once disappeared.

The effect of Black Wednesday was undoubtedly reinforced by the economic circumstances surrounding it and by the steps taken by the government to counteract its effects. The recession continued (despite the Tories' claims during the 1992 campaign that it would end almost imme-diately if they won). Job insecurity spread to the middle classes. Taxes rose to meet the government's rapidly growing budget deficit. Continuing high interest rates and the collapse of the housing market left thousands of home-buyers confronting "negative equity" (with their mortgage debt greater than the capital value of their homes). All these would have taken their toll without Black Wednesday, but it was Black Wednesday that turned what would in any case have been a period of considerable politi-cal difficulty into a crisis of confidence in the whole Tory party—a crisis that is not yet over.

Two bodies of survey evidence strongly support this view. One has already been referred to by Philip Norton in chapter 4: the effect of Black Wednesday on the two major parties' standing on the crucial issue of "economic competence."

Shortly before the 1964 general election the Gallup poll asked one of its monthly samples: "If Britain ran into economic difficulties, which party do you think could handle the problem best—the Conservatives under Sir Alec Douglas-Home [the then Tory leader] or Labour under Mr. Wilson?" At that time, even though Labour went on to win the elec-tion, the Conservatives were ahead on the issue by 11 points. Forty-five percent of voters thought the Conservatives would handle the economy best; only 34 percent thought Labour would.[12] The same question was asked only intermittently between 1964 and 1989 (with the names of any new Tory and Labour leaders substituted), but in 1989 the Gallup poll revived it on a more regular basis with a slightly altered wording: "With Britain in economic difficulties, which party do you think could handle the problem best—the Conservatives under - - - - - or Labour under - - - - -?"

One measure of the Conservatives' built-in advantage on economic competence before the autumn of 1992 is that, even when Labour was well ahead of the Conservatives in the Gallup poll in terms of voting intention, the Conservatives were almost invariably in the lead on the economy. In October 1989, for example, Labour enjoyed a 10-point lead over the Conservatives on voting intention but the Tories enjoyed a 10-point lead over Labour on the economy.[13] The strength of the Conservatives' relative position on the economy—at a time when economic issues were at the forefront of people's minds—was one of the clues during the 1992 campaign that Labour might not be doing quite as well as the voting-intention figures appeared to suggest.

Against that background, figure 7.1 tells the story of a dramatic transformation in the two parties' standings. Before the autumn of 1992 there was only a single month—March 1990, when the first poll tax bills thudded down on people's doormats—in which the Labour Party led the Conservatives on economic competence. After the autumn of 1992, as the figure shows, there was no month in which Labour did not lead the Conservatives on economic competence.[14] At times, especially during 1994 and 1995, the Labour leads were enormous. The Conservatives pulled back in early 1997, but by then it was too late and Labour was still comfortably ahead on the day. The events of Black Wednesday were not, of course, the whole explanation; but they were a crucial part of it.

The other body of evidence pointing to Black Wednesday's importance in sealing the Conservatives' fate is presented in figure 7.2. This figure sets out, for the months immediately before and after September 1992, the proportions of voters who approved of the government's record to date, who said they would vote Conservative at an early election and who believed the Tories would do a better job than Labour of managing the economy. As can be seen, public confidence in the government and the Tory party were already tending to diminish before Black Wednesday; but at that point they dropped like a stone. A person who knew nothing about British politics but merely looked at the three lines on the graph would realise that something terrible must have happened during September of that year.

The loss of the Conservatives' reputation for economic competence probably contributed more than any other single factor to their defeat in 1997. It explains, in a way that nothing else can, the failure of the party's fortunes to recover significantly between 1992 and 1997 despite the substantial improvement in Britain's economic fortunes. The Conservatives had counted on their boats being lifted by an incoming economic tide. The tide duly came in—interest rates and inflation both fell, employment and the rate of growth both rose—but the Tory boats remained grounded.

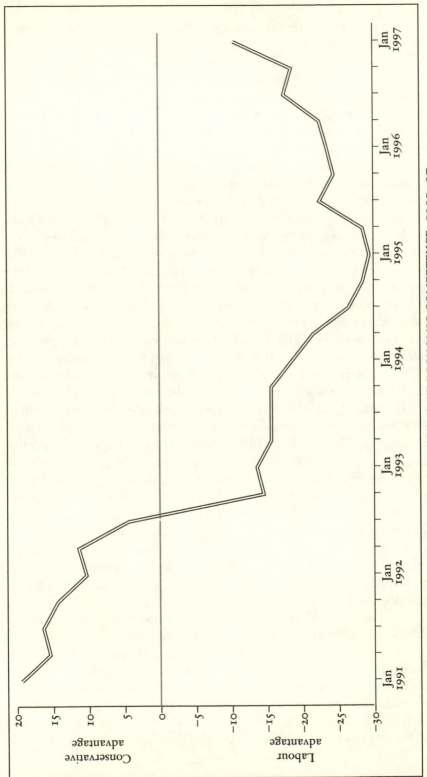

FIGURE 7.1. PUBLIC EVALUATIONS OF ECONOMIC COMPETENCE, 1991–97

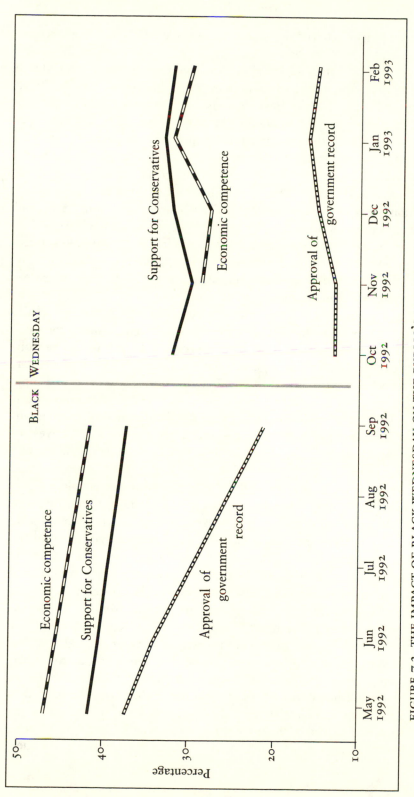

FIGURE 7.2. THE IMPACT OF BLACK WEDNESDAY ON THE PUBLIC'S PERCEPTION OF THE CONSERVATIVES

NOTE: The economic competence question was not asked by Gallup in June, July, August, or October 1992.

Voters no longer believed the economic improvement was a Conservative achievement.[15]

The Conservatives lost their reputation for economic competence between 1992 and 1997, and that was probably crucial; but, as David Denver and Philip Norton have demonstrated in earlier chapters of this book, they also lost their reputations for strong leadership, for unity, and for probity. Voters thought that John Major was weak and ineffectual (especially as compared with Tony Blair), that the Tory party was hopelessly divided, and that it, or at least many of its individual members, were "sleazy and disreputable."[16] It is doubtful whether any of these factors alone was decisive in defeating the Conservatives—once they had lost their reputation for economic competence, even a united, sleaze-free party under as strong a leader as Margaret Thatcher would almost certainly have gone down to defeat in 1997—but, taken together, they undoubtedly contributed to the government's air of bumbling incompetence, thereby helping to turn a defeat into a rout.

Probably more important in determining the final outcome was the widespread sense among the electorate that voters had returned the Conservatives to office in 1992 only, within weeks, to be betrayed. The Conservatives promised prosperity and low taxes, but they delivered neither. The recession was supposed to end but did not. Thousands of people who had voted Conservative lost their jobs, their houses, their businesses. The tax burden on the average family, far from lessening, increased substantially. Not only, it seemed, were the Conservatives incompetent: they were no longer to be trusted. They were cheats, con men, bent pennies.

David Denver in chapter 2 cites the large number of people, 76 percent, who told Gallup following the 1993 budget that they felt they and others had been "misled" by the Conservatives on the tax issue during the 1992 campaign; the feeling that the Conservatives had not told the truth on taxation persisted throughout the Parliament. But the feeling went much wider than that. By the time of the election, large numbers of voters doubted whether the Conservatives could be trusted to keep any of their promises. Table 7.3 makes gruesome reading from the Conservatives' point of view. The figures speak for themselves. Questioned by Gallup in March 1996, a minuscule 15 percent of voters thought the Tories had kept their election promises; more than four times that number, 69 percent, thought they had not. Only 28 percent thought the Tories would be at all likely to keep their promises if they won the next election; 65 percent thought they would not. A year later, on the eve of the election, Gallup asked in the same vein: "Do you think the Conservative government over the past few years has been basically an honest

TABLE 7.3

PUBLIC PERCEPTIONS OF THE CONSERVATIVE GOVERNMENT'S
"BROKEN PROMISES," MARCH 1996 (IN PERCENTAGES)

"On the whole, do you think that the Conservatives have or have not kept their election promises?"

Have	15
Have not	69
Don't know	14

"If the Conservatives win the next election, how likely do you think they will be to keep the promises they make then?"

Very / fairly likely	28
Not very / not at all likely	65
Don't know	7

SOURCE: *Gallup Political and Economic Index,* Report No. 428, April 1996, 5.

or basically a dishonest government?" Only 29 percent—the great majority of them Conservative supporters—thought the government had been "basically honest." More than twice as many, 67 percent, thought it had been "basically dishonest."[17]

Not surprisingly under the circumstances, the Conservatives came to suffer from a credibility gap that was probably even wider than that suffered by Lyndon Johnson during the Vietnam War. Even when the Conservatives were speaking the truth, and could prove that they were, they were not believed. Towards the end of their time in office, members of the government were naturally proud of their success in turning round the economy, and Michael Heseltine, the deputy prime minister, repeatedly boasted that under the Tories, mortgage interest rates were at their lowest for thirty years, that the basic income tax rate was the lowest for fifty years, and that unemployment was falling more rapidly in Britain than in any other European country. He was speaking the simple truth—but few believed him. Only 32 percent thought mortgate rates were that low, only 24 percent thought the basic tax rate was that low, and only 29 percent thought unemployment was falling in Britain more than elsewhere.[18] In the early weeks of 1997, a speaker at a private Conservative dinner told his audience bluntly that the Tories' credibility gap was so wide that, if the government announced that the sun would rise in the east the next day, most Britons would probably get out of bed and instinctively face west. By the end, it was that bad.

In Act 2 of *Othello* Cassio complains to Iago: "Reputation, reputation, reputation! O, I have lost my reputation! I have lost the immortal part of myself, and what remains is bestial." To which Iago replies: "Reputation is a most idle and false imposition; oft got without merit and lost without deserving." Iago's cynicism may have been, and may still be, justified; but Cassio's lament is more to the point. A reputation for competence and trustworthiness, once lost, is not easily regained. That is one problem facing the Conservatives in the election's aftermath.

But, however serious it was, the Tories' loss of reputation was not the only handicap under which they laboured in fighting the 1997 election: they also suffered from the near-universal belief among the electorate that, under the Tories, the basic public services—things like health, education, and public transport—had suffered, were suffering, and would continue to suffer. At one level, to assert this is to assert the obvious: just about everyone in Britain knows that in 1997 the Tories were damaged by their perceived neglect of the public services. But, at another level, the sheer scale of the damage does not appear to have been taken on board by most politicians and commentators. There is a sense in which the 1997 election was a referendum on the future of the welfare state and the public services—and the Conservatives lost it.

THE STATE OF PUBLIC SERVICES

The British people are overwhelmingly dependent on the public services, i.e., the services provided, directly or indirectly, by the government. The vast majority rely solely on the National Health Service for their health care; 87 percent of Britons do not have private health insurance, and even most of those who do have it still receive most of their care—especially in accidents and emergencies—from NHS doctors and hospitals. The vast majority likewise rely on the state for their children's education; despite the fame of Britain's "public" (i.e. fee-paying) schools, more than 98 percent of all school-aged children in Britain are enrolled in state schools. A large majority, especially in London and other large cities, rely on public transport. Millions depend on other state or state-subsidised services such as day nurseries for young children, social housing for those who cannot afford their own homes, and home helps, chiropody, and "meals on wheels" for the elderly.

In some countries government-provided services like these are provided mainly for the poor. In Britain they are provided for almost everybody. Every study ever undertaken of public expenditure in Britain has shown that, if anything, the middle classes and the well-off benefit even more from the public services than the working classes and the poor.[19] People on above-average earnings take more advantage of the NHS than the poor, their children stay on longer at school and university, they make more journeys by public transport (including commuting to work), and they are certainly more likely to attend a state-subsidised theatre, concert hall, or opera house.

One of the most significant political developments of the 1980s and early 1990s was the growing sense that the quality of all these services was declining and that the Conservatives—because of their determination to cut taxes and public spending and their generalised hostility towards the state sector—were to blame. As time went on, moreover, the public's discontent began to extend beyond complaints about specific services (grumbles about long waits in hospital casualty departments, poor standards in schools, and overcrowded public transport), though those were serious enough, to a wider sense that what might be called the whole "public domain" was under threat. The British pride themselves on their public-spiritedness. Increasingly their own government seemed to lack public spirit. Concerns about the public services and the quality of life easily merged into wider concerns about law and order and social cohesion.

Concerns like these were among the factors that had all along alienated voters from the Conservative Party and helped depress the Tory vote, but for reasons that are not entirely clear they came increasingly to the fore after 1992 and contributed to depressing support for the Tories still further. By 1997 they appear to have been of enormous significance in most voters' minds.

Table 7.4 tells part of the story. The Gallup poll each month asks voters an open-ended question in which they are invited to name the two "most urgent problems facing the country at the present time." The table shows how the proportions naming the health service and education rose, seemingly inexorably, between 1992 and 1997. The proportion mentioning the health service more than doubled; the proportion mentioning schools and education nearly trebled. By 1997 the health service had overtaken unemployment as an issue in people's minds, and education was catching up rapidly. The importance attached to law and order also increased markedly during these years.

The trouble for the Conservatives was that they found themselves, or had managed to place themselves, on the wrong side of all these issues. They had been in power for the previous decade and a half and were therefore inevitably blamed for whatever shortcomings existed in the public services. Their individualistic, anti-state rhetoric suggested that, at best, they had ideological doubts about these services and, at worst, were actively opposed to them. The Labour Party for its part was already associated in most voters' minds with the NHS and the state education service. In the special case of law and order, New Labour, with its slogan "Tough on crime, tough on the causes of crime," managed to sug-

TABLE 7.4
THE CHANGING AGENDA: THE ELECTORATE'S
"MOST URGENT PROBLEMS," 1992–97

Year	Health	Education	Law and order	Unemploy-ment	Cost of living
1992 (May–Dec)	18	11	5	66	25
1993	22	8	13	72	19
1994	26	11	18	65	16
1995	33	15	15	55	14
1996	32	22	16	48	10
1997 (Jan–Apr)	41	29	14	36	4
Net change, 1997 less 1992	+23	+18	+9	–30	–21

SOURCE: *Gallup Political and Economic Index.*

NOTE: Figures relate to the annual percentage average of respondents identifying what they believe to be the two "most urgent problems" facing the country.

gest both that Conservative social policies had been largely responsible for the increases in crime and also that Labour, whatever its past record, would, if elected, not be soft on crime. By the time of the election, Labour led the Conservatives on all these issues (as well as most others).

In some ways more impressive, however, than the simple tallies of which party was in the lead on which issues were the responses to survey questions in which voters were given the opportunity to identify the concerns that were uppermost in their own minds. The responses to such questions invariably suggested that millions of voters were deeply worried about the future of the welfare state and the public services generally and that these worries cut across all regions, all age groups, and all social classes.

For example, when Gallup in March 1995 asked respondents whether they agreed or disagreed with the proposition that "this government understands the problems that people like me face in our daily lives," a massive 85 percent disagreed, and when the same respondents were asked whether they agreed or disagreed that "public services like health and education will improve under the Conservatives," almost the same proportion, 83 percent, also disagreed.[20] It is harder to come nearer unanimity than that in the real world. Similarly, when those in the survey cited earlier who said they thought the government had not kept its promises were asked "What things have you in mind?" 35 percent volunteered taxation, but almost as many, 34 percent, cited the NHS, and the third largest group, 23 percent, cited education.[21]

A year later Gallup conducted a survey that was deliberately confined to voters who said they had voted Conservative in 1992 but were now inclined to support one of the other parties or else did not know what they would do. These "lost Tories"—people whom the Conservatives still hoped to win back—were given a list of "reasons people give for no longer supporting the Conservatives" and asked how important each item on the list was in influencing their own thinking. Table 7.5 sets out the proportions replying "very important" to each item. As the figures in the table make clear, concerns about the health service and the

TABLE 7.5

"THE LOST TORIES": REASONS GIVEN

FOR NO LONGER SUPPORTING THE CONSERVATIVES

Reason for no longer supporting the Conservatives	*Percentage of respondents citing the reason as "very important"*
Conservatives continuing to undermine the NHS	66
Public services—not just the NHS—continue to decline under the Conservatives	55
Conservatives have broken their promises too often, they can no longer be trusted	47
Conservatives said they would keep taxes down but instead they've increased them	44
It's time for a change	43
Conservatives said they would take us out of recession but I don't think they have	38
Conservatives are a shambles	36
Conservatives are making a mess of the economy	34
Labour is more electable now	33
John Major is not a good prime minister	26
There is more and more crime under the Conservatives	23
Neil Kinnock probably wouldn't have made a good prime minister but Tony Blair has the look of a good leader	21
Budget deficit and government borrowing are too large	20
Liberal Democrats and Paddy Ashdown look very impressive	13

SOURCE: *Gallup Political and Economic Index,* Report No. 428, April 1996, 8–9.

NOTE: The question asked former Conservative supporters to identify whether any of the reasons provided for no longer supporting the Tories were "very important in influencing [their] own thinking, fairly important, not very important or not at all important."

public services in general were uppermost in these Tory defectors' minds, even ahead of taxation.

But perhaps the most striking testimony to voters' concerns—and indeed fears—about the future of the welfare state comes from a series of surveys that Gallup conducted prior to the election under the generic heading "The Fear Factor." Each of the two major parties at the time was trying to play on voters' fears of the other, so Gallup compiled a list of "concerns that many people have about what might happen if a Conservative government were reelected under John Major" and a separate list of concerns that people had about a possible Labour government. Respondents were asked: "Could you tell me for each whether this is something you are concerned about or not?" Table 7.6 (pp. 198–99) reports the responses in one such survey to the items relating to the Conservative Party. The survey happens to be the one conducted closest to the election—the fieldwork was concluded only a week before polling day—but the pattern of responses actually varied only a little from month to month.

The table repays careful study. It shows, among other things, just how widespread the various concerns listed by the Gallup poll were; no item was cited by fewer than 58 percent of respondents. It also shows that majorities of the Tories' own supporters shared most of the general public's worries about what might be in store if the Conservatives were reelected. Most important for our present purposes, it shows that large numbers of voters were deeply concerned about what might happen under the Conservatives to the public services, the welfare state, and the nation's social fabric. More than 80 percent, for example, said they were concerned that "under the Conservatives the National Health Service might no longer be a good service freely available to all" and that "there might be a growing 'underclass'—people, many of them living in inner-city areas, who have no jobs and no skills and seem destined to spend the rest of their lives largely cut off from the rest of society." More than 70 percent feared that "the Conservatives' social policies might lead to continuing high levels of crime and lawlessness." The figures in the table suggest a mixture of personal concerns and concerns about the wider society—and of personal concerns arising out of concerns about the wider society.

Moreover, although the extent of people's actual willingness to pay higher taxes in order to fund improved public services remains a highly contentious issue, there is a good deal of evidence that by 1997 the trade-off in most voters' minds between improved services and tax increases had tilted, at least to some degree, in favour of tax increases. The most popular single manifesto pledge made by any party was the Liberal Democrats' pledge to put a penny on the standard rate of income tax to fund educational improvements. Fully 85 percent of voters said they would approve of such an increase.[22] The figures reported in table 7.7 (p. 200) also suggest an increasing tilt towards public approval of tax increases. As the table shows, when the Conservatives first came to power in 1979, the proportion of voters believing that "taxes should be cut, even if it means some reduction in government services, such as health, education and welfare" was the same as the proportion believing "government services such as health, education and welfare should be extended, even if it means some increases in taxes." But, as the figures in the table indicate, by 1997 service-extenders had come to outnumber tax-cutters by more than 10 to 1.

From whatever angle the evidence is examined, it is evident that the Conservatives lost so heavily in 1997 not only because of their economic mismanagement, especially early in the Parliament, and their "broken promises," but also because voters no longer trusted them to maintain Britain's social fabric, both physical and moral. Despite the fact that under their stewardship the country was increasingly prosperous, the Conservatives by 1997 had become associated in millions of voters' minds with social decay. They paid a heavy price for that association at the polls.

The Other Part of the Explanation: Labour

It would be wrong, however, to give the impression that the outcome of the election can be explained solely in terms of the Conservatives' errors and misfortunes. Needless to say, the Labour Party was also part-author of its own success. Old Labour might well have won in 1997—given the scale of the Tories' problems, it probably would—but New Labour's victory was on an altogether more prodigious scale. Patrick Seyd has described the emergence of New Labour in chapter 3. Here we look at Tony Blair and New Labour's impact on the electorate.

It is scarcely too strong to say that in 1992 the Labour Party had reached a dead end. It had fought an election against an unpopular government and an unpopular party in the midst of a deep recession; it had lost. Not only had it lost, but it had secured only 35.2 percent of the popular vote, scarcely more than it had secured five years before. Moreover, it had lost for the fourth time in a row despite having conducted a thorough overhaul of its policies and despite having fought a campaign that most observers at the time adjudged well organised, imaginative, and professional. In the immediate aftermath of Labour's 1992 defeat, one commentator wrote:

TABLE 7.6

PUBLIC CONCERN ABOUT A FUTURE CONSERVATIVE GOVERNMENT (BY SOCIAL GROUPS)

Percentage concerned

	Voting intention			Age					Class				Total
	Con.	Lab.	Lib. Dem.	18–24	25–34	35–44	45–64	65+	AB	C1	C2	DE	
Old people might no longer be able to rely on the state to look after them if they became ill	74	93	95	86	89	90	91	83	86	88	89	86	87
Even if taxes were cut, people and their families might have to pay more of the costs of things like health care, pensions	73	92	91	83	86	88	88	79	82	87	86	86	86
Under the Conservatives the NHS might no longer be a good service freely available to all	66	95	90	86	89	90	86	76	84	87	88	84	85
There might be a growing "underclass"	65	92	87	80	83	82	86	81	83	84	82	83	83
Under the Conservatives income tax might be cut but other taxes such as VAT would just be put up	64	86	79	75	77	81	80	72	75	77	82	77	78

A culture of despair and disillusionment might develop	57	88	85	72	78	78	75	77	77	78	76	77
The number of unemployed might remain very high for a long period of time	56	88	79	79	75	78	76	75	74	78	81	77
The quality of services on things like the trains and buses might deteriorate and prices might go up	54	85	80	73	76	77	73	70	74	74	78	74
The Conservatives' social policies might lead to continuing high levels of crime	49	85	77	79	75	71	67	68	67	76	75	72
People might become less public-spirited	54	80	78	55	71	78	72	66	70	73	76	71
The cost of people's mortgage might increase	49	69	60	66	62	58	58	52	57	73	65	62
Britain might become isolated and lose influence in Europe	43	68	61	56	59	59	58	57	59	56	59	58

SOURCE: *Gallup Political and Economic Index*, Report No. 441, May 1997, 24. Additional data supplied by Gallup.

NOTE: For each item, respondents were asked "whether this is something that you are concerned about or not."

Classification categories: AB = professional, managerial, and executive; C1 = routine white-collar; C2 = skilled manual; DE = unskilled manual.

TABLE 7.7

PUBLIC VIEWS ON TAXATION VS. GOVERNMENT
SPENDING, 1979–97 (IN PERCENTAGES)

	1979	1983	1987	1992	1997
Taxes should be cut, even if it means some reduction in government services, such as health, education, and welfare	34	22	12	10	7
Things should be left as they are	25	22	21	20	18
Government services such as health, education, and welfare should be extended, even if it means some increases in taxes	34	49	61	66	72
Don't know	7	6	5	4	3

SOURCE: *Gallup Political and Economic Index,* Report No. 441, May 1997, 30.

> The obstacles to be overcome [by the Labour Party] are formidable, consisting as they do of the party's narrowing social base, of its ties to the declining and now largely discredited trade union movement, of an ideology and set of social attitudes that seem firmly anchored in the past, and, perhaps above all, of voters' accumulated suspicion of a party associated in their minds, fairly or unfairly, with high taxation, high inflation, numerous strikes, the endless disruption of public services and hopelessly incompetent economic management.[23]

It was that image of the Labour Party—and indeed that Labour Party —that the "modernisers" were determined to change.

What Labour needed after 1992, and had probably needed for more than a decade, was, so to speak, a "symbolic moment"—a defining moment when it said to the world, in effect, "We have changed. We are new. We are no longer the party we were. You can put your trust in us again." The German Social Democratic Party had engineered such a symbolic moment at its Bad Godesberg conference in 1959, when it had publicly repudiated its former commitments to Marxism and the destruction of capitalism. The British Labour Party did not, in the event, engineer such a moment; but such a moment nevertheless occurred, with John Smith's death in 1994 and the election of Tony Blair.

Tony Blair was the perfect leader for the Labour Party in the 1990s. He might almost have been a product of computer-aided design. He was young. He was classless. He was squeaky clean. He had no ties to the trade union movement.[24] He carried virtually no ideological baggage. Above all, he was persuaded, in a way that John Smith had never been, that change in the Labour Party had to be root-and-branch. His success in winning large majorities in all three sections of Labour's electoral college gave him a secure base from which to launch his campaign for change. His own political daring, together with the Labour Party's by-now desperate desire for victory, did the rest. In scarcely more than a year, Labour was a party transformed. It had even abandoned its old Clause 4.

The evidence is overwhelming that the electorate saw what was happening and, with very few exceptions, approved of what it saw. As David Denver argues in chapter 2, there was a genuine "Blair effect." In September 1994, only two months after Blair took over, a MORI survey found 65 percent of the adult population agreeing with the proposition that "Labour has changed for the better in recent years."[25] Over the summer of 1994 Labour's lead over the Conservatives in all the opinion polls increased by about 10 points.

Moreover, as David Denver points out, the improvement in Labour's position was sustained. A good measure of Tony Blair's personal contribution to Labour's success from 1994 onwards is provided by comparing the last two years of Neil Kinnock's period as leader, the roughly two years of John Smith's leadership, and the nearly three years of Tony Blair's leadership between 1994 and the election. All three men led the party at a time when the Conservatives were deeply unpopular, but, as table 7.8 shows, the party under Blair—and Blair himself—forged far further ahead in the later period. More people said they would vote for the Labour Party; more thought Labour was united; more thought Labour's standing in the country was high; more thought Blair was proving a good leader of the Labour Party and that he would make the best prime minister. Given that Kinnock had generally been accounted, fairly or unfairly, a poor leader of the party, the contrast between Blair and Smith is particularly striking. If Smith did well as leader, Blair did brilliantly.

The improvement in Labour's fortunes under Blair was not only long-lasting; it was clearly predicated on profound changes in the way people thought about the party. For example, in July 1991, during Kinnock's leadership, the Gallup poll asked respondents whether they agreed or disagreed with a number of statements, some favourable, some unfavourable, about the Labour Party. The same question was repeated

TABLE 7.8

PUBLIC ATTITUDES TOWARDS THE LABOUR PARTY
UNDER KINNOCK, SMITH, AND BLAIR, 1990–97

	Mean percentage		
	Kinnock (Apr 90– Mar 92)	*Smith (Aug 92– Apr 94)*	*Blair (Aug 94– Apr 97)*
Labour support (voting intention)	41	47	56
Labour Party unity	43	44	51
Labour's "party popularity"	45[a]	39	64
Best prime minister	28	32	41
Good leader of the Labour Party	37	46	59

SOURCE: *Gallup Political and Economic Index.*

a. Gallup's "party popularity" question asks respondents if they think that most people in the country are "holding a favourable opinion of the - - - - - party," leaving aside their own views. For Kinnock, the question was asked in only two months (July and October 1991) of the twenty-four months covered.

in July 1996. Table 7.9 charts the improvement in Labour's image over the five years, showing a large increase in the number of people agreeing that "Labour has a strong team of new young leaders" and a sharp drop in the number agreeing that "the economy would be in a worse state under Labour." Views of Labour in 1991 were ambivalent; in 1996 they were much more uniformly favourable.

The same message is conveyed in a different form by table 7.10 (p. 204), which also compares Labour's image under Kinnock with its image under Blair. In this case respondents were offered a list of "reasons people give for not wanting to vote Labour at the next election" and asked which of them they personally had the most sympathy with. As the figures in the table show, there were a number of issues on which the change of leadership made little difference, but the top row and bottom row are the most interesting. Before the 1992 election there had been widespread doubts about Kinnock as a potential prime minister; in 1996 few voters seemed to have similar reservations about Blair. At least as significant is the fact that, whereas in 1992 only 20 percent of the survey's respondents rejected all the items on the list (replying "none of these" or "don't know"), in 1996 nearly twice as many, 37 percent, did so. Not the least of Tony Blair's achievements was to make Labour "available" as an option to wavering voters in a way it had never been under Kinnock (and had only doubtfully been even under Smith).

This last point is important. Labour won, and won big, in 1997, but

TABLE 7.9

THE PUBLIC'S PERCEPTIONS OF THE LABOUR PARTY,
1991 AND 1996 (IN PERCENTAGES)

	July 1991	*July 1996*
Labour has become too extreme		
Agree	31	20
Disagree	61	68
Don't know	9	13
Labour is the only party that can turn out the present government		
Agree	69	78
Disagree	26	16
Don't know	6	7
Labour party leadership is poor now		
Agree	47	22
Disagree	44	66
Don't know	9	12
Labour is too split and divided		
Agree	42	32
Disagree	50	56
Don't know	8	12
The economy would be in a worse state under Labour		
Agree	41	26
Disagree	47	58
Don't know	13	15
Labour has a strong team of new young leaders		
Agree	42	57
Disagree	36	22
Don't know	23	21

SOURCE: *Gallup Political and Economic Index,* Report No. 431, July 1996, 6.

there is no reason to think that the prospect of a New Labour victory aroused much positive enthusiasm among ordinary voters (as distinct from Labour Party members and sympathisers). There was probably more positive enthusiasm in 1945 and again in 1964, when large numbers of voters—so far as one can tell—believed the election of a Labour government would mean real change. The truth about 1997 is almost certainly that a large majority of voters simply wanted the Tories out and found in Blair's New Labour a suitable instrument for achieving their purpose. Blair and the modernisers did not so much give voters reasons for voting Labour as remove their former reasons for *not* wanting to

TABLE 7.10

REASONS FOR NOT WANTING TO VOTE LABOUR,

1992 AND 1996 (IN PERCENTAGES)

	Feb 1992	Oct 1996
Kinnock/Blair would not make a good prime minister	26	7
Labour is in the pockets of the trade unions	12	13
A Labour government would not do a good job of managing the country's economy	8	12
If there were a Labour government, the rest of the world would lose confidence in Britain	8	6
A Labour government would not provide a strong enough national defence	7	5
I would pay a lot more taxes under Labour without there being anything much to show for them	13	11
Prices would rise even faster under a Labour government	6	9
None of these / don't know	20	37

SOURCE: *Gallup Political and Economic Index*, Report No. 434, October 1996, 6.

vote Labour. It is probably significant that, when asked shortly before the election how they would feel if a Labour government under Blair were formed, only 29 percent of voters said they "would be delighted." Far more, 49 percent, merely said they "wouldn't mind."[26]

That said, no one should minimise the extent, if not the depth, of Labour's victory. It is true that Labour won only 43.1 percent of the United Kingdom vote (44.4 percent in Great Britain alone), lower than in 1964 or 1966. But these totals are a little misleading. To them should be added the large numbers of people who voted Liberal Democrat but who would have voted Labour if the Labour candidate in their constituency had had any chance of winning. In addition, two other pieces of evidence support the idea that, whatever the precise voting figures on the day, a large majority of voters wanted the Tories out and did not mind if Labour came in.

One comes from a Gallup survey conducted shortly before the election, which asked: "If you had to choose, which would you prefer to see after the election, a Conservative government led by Mr. Major or a Labour government led by Mr. Blair?" The results, excluding the small proportions of those who replied "neither" or "don't know," were unequivocal: Labour, 64 percent; Conservative, 35 percent.[27] Then, during the 48 hours immediately after the election, Gallup asked people to say how they had voted on 1 May. Forty-nine percent were already claiming they had voted Labour, even though the actual figure was nearer 44 percent.[28] The psychology of misrecollections such as this would make a fascinating study, but the central point from our point of view is that many voters were clearly eager to be associated with Labour's victory, even if they had not actually contributed to it. Labour's victory may not have been greeted with jubilation by any huge number of voters, but it was greeted with equanimity bordering on contentment by a considerable majority. Whatever the precise numbers, New Labour undoubtedly had a mandate to govern.

Conclusion

There is an old saying in British politics: "Oppositions don't win elections. Governments lose them." Like so many old sayings, this one needs to be rephrased. It should read: "Governments are capable of losing elections—but only if there is an Opposition party available that people are willing to vote for."

The Conservatives undoubtedly lost the 1997 election. They forfeited their reputation for economic competence—and their reputations for almost everything else besides—and they also managed to give the impression that they did not desperately care about, or were actively opposed to, the great public services on which the great majority of the British people depend. (They also managed, in passing, to appear weak, hopelessly disunited, sleazy, and disreputable.) But Labour under Tony Blair also won the election. There is no way in which Labour could have won such a large majority—and won Broxtowe, Harrow West, and Sittingbourne and Sheppey—without Tony Blair and the Labour Party having persuaded millions of voters that the party had indeed changed and changed fundamentally. If the Conservatives deserved their defeat, New Labour certainly deserved its victory.

Notes

1. Anthony King, "The Implications of One-Party Government," in *Britain at the Polls, 1992,* edited by Anthony King (Chatham, N.J.: Chatham House, 1992), 224, 246.
2. The book is Nicholas Jones, *Campaign 1997: How the General Election Was Won and Lost* (London: Indigo, 1997).
3. For the detail, see Ivor Crewe, "The Opinion Polls: Confidence Restored?" *Parliamentary Affairs* 50 (1997): 569–85.
4. According to the Gallup poll, and contrary to Eurosceptics' belief, the months preceding the election witnessed a swing in public opinion away

from outright opposition to Britain joining a single currency (30 percent agreement in March 1997, down 7 percent from the previous September) and towards the government's preferred "wait and decide" policy (55 percent agreement, up 18 percent). Moreover, while the Eurosceptics would have us believe that the British public's fears over Europe focussed almost completely on the prospect of unwanted interference from Brussels, the Gallup evidence showed that the public was also concerned that "Britain might become isolated and lose influence in Europe" under a future Tory administration (60 percent agreement). Finally, the issue of Europe was not considered by the British public to be a particularly "urgent problem" facing the country. Throughout the period from April 1992 to December 1996 the quarterly average of the proportion of respondents who regarded "Europe" as the country's "most urgent problem" was never, according to Gallup, more than 7 percent. By the first quarter of 1997 this figure had risen, but only to 13 percent, and by the time of the election it had fallen back to 9 percent. These data are taken from the *Gallup Political and Economic Index*.

5. Details of British election results can be found in David Butler and Gareth Butler, *British Political Facts 1900-1994* (Basingstoke, Hants.: Macmillan, 1994), 218-19.
6. Calculated from F.W.S. Craig, *Chronology of British Parliamentary By-Elections, 1833–1987* (Chichester: Parliamentary Research Services, 1987); David Butler and Dennis Kavanagh, *The British General Election of 1992* (Basingstoke, Hants.: Macmillan, 1992); and *The Times Guide to the House of Commons*, May 1997 (London: Times Books, 1997).
7. Ibid.
8. Butler and Butler, *British Political Facts*, 220–21.
9. For evidence bearing on these points, see Anthony King, "Voters Give 'Thatcher's Britain' a Cool Reception" and "Thatcher: The Tide Turns," *Sunday Telegraph*, 30 April 1989, 1, 25.
10. Ivor Crewe, "Has the Electorate Become Thatcherite?" in *Thatcherism*, edited by Robert Skidelsky (London: Chatto and Windus, 1988).
11. See note 9.
12. *The Gallup International Public Opinion Polls: Great Britain 1937-75*, vol. 1, *1937–1964* (New York: Random House, 1976), 763.
13. *Gallup Political Index*, Report No. 351, November 1989, 7.
14. Unfortunately the standard economic-competence question was not asked at all frequently or regularly before 1989, and it is therefore impossible to know whether there were earlier periods when Labour was ahead. Even if there were, however, it seems doubtful whether, before 1992, Labour was ever ahead on the issue for more than a few months at a time.
15. Between 1979 and 1992 there was a very strong aggregate-level correlation between support for the Conservatives and voters' economic expectations. As economic confidence rose in advance of the 1983, 1987, and 1992 general elections, so did support for the governing party: voters wished to preserve the political status quo that had created their economic optimism. This relationship broke down in September 1992. It had depended on the

Conservatives' superior reputation—compared with Labour's—for competent economic management. The loss of this reputation prevented the Conservatives from converting the subsequent rise in economic confidence into a substantial electoral recovery. See David Sanders, "Economic Performance, Management Competence and the Outcome of the Next General Election," *Political Studies,* 44 (1996):203–31.

16. See above, pp. 23–36, 40–41, and 80–103.
17. *Gallup Political and Economic Index, Report No.* 440, April 1997, 9.
18. *Gallup Political and Economic Index,* Report No. 426, February 1996, 17.
19. See, among others, Julian Le Grand, *The Strategy of Equality: Redistribution and the Social Services* (London: Unwin Hyman, 1982).
20. *Gallup Political and Economic Index,* Report No. 415, March 1995, 8.
21. *Gallup Political and Economic Index,* Report No. 428, April 1996, 5.
22. *Gallup Political and Economic Index,* Report No. 441, May 1997, 28.
23. King, "Implications of One-Party Government," 245–46.
24. He was sponsored in his Sedgefield constituency by the Transport and General Workers' Union, but his connection with the union was nominal.
25. *British Public Opinion* 17 (October 1994): 6.
26. *Gallup Political and Economic Index,* Report No. 441, May 1997, 26.
27. *Gallup Political and Economic Index,* Report No. 440, April 1997, 5.
28. Data supplied by the Gallup Organisation.

8

The New Electoral Battleground

David Sanders

As we saw in chapter 1, the 1997 general election was remarkable for the many records it broke. This chapter considers the implications of this decisive result for the character and future of British politics. It first examines the relevance of the historical parallels that can be drawn between Labour's 1997 victory and the elections of 1945, 1906, and 1964. It also assesses the value of comparing Tony Blair's problems and achievements in 1997 with those of Bill Clinton in 1992. The chapter then focuses on what the outcome of the general election tells us about the character of contemporary British politics. It considers the impact of the continued decline in class-based voting that was clearly evident and assesses the importance of the unprecedented increase in electoral volatility that took place between 1992 and 1997. Finally, it examines the election's likely implications for the interparty battles of the present Parliament. It argues that much will depend on how the Conservative Party comes to terms with its humiliating defeat.

Historical Parallels

Whenever an election produces as decisive an outcome as that in Britain in May 1997, it is tempting to search the historical record for comparable circumstances that could offer insights into the sort of government and pattern of politics that might result. One obvious point of comparison, given the size of their respective majorities, is between Blair's administration and Clement Attlee's reforming Labour government of 1945–50. Attlee used his House of Commons majority of 146 to carry through a reform programme that transformed the way in which the British state operated. His government took the major industries of the day—coal, gas, electricity, road and rail transport, civil aviation, and steel—into public ownership. It also instituted Britain's modern welfare state, the comprehensive system of social insurance that was intended to (and to a degree still does) protect all citizens against ill health, impoverishment, unemployment, and industrial injury.[1]

There are certainly important similarities between the Attlee and Blair governments' initial positions. Both were elected on huge swings and with enormous Commons majorities. Yet there were also important differences, not least in the ambition and the clarity of the two governments' mandates. Attlee was elected on a manifesto that was unambiguously committed to radical reform. The massive extension of the welfare state and the large-scale nationalisation programme that followed simply involved the government's delivering on its election promises. Blair's New Labour Party, in contrast, has been deliberately modest in the promises it has made. Although it places a heavy rhetorical emphasis on the importance of education,[2] it has also made it "absolutely clear"—in one of Blair's favourite phrases—that a New Labour government will maintain tight control of public spending. Any changes in social and economic policy will be effected without increasing expenditure. As the 1997 manifesto declared,

> The myth that the solution to every problem is increased spending has been comprehensively dispelled.... New Labour will be wise spenders not big spenders.... Save to invest is our approach, *not tax and spend*.... New Labour will establish a new trust on tax with the British people. The promises we make we will keep.... New Labour is not about high taxes on ordinary families.... *There will be no return to the penal tax rates that existed under both Labour and Conservative governments in the 1970s.*[3]

This self-imposed constraint—thought necessary to win the support of middle-class voters who were unprepared to vote for higher taxes—stands in stark contrast to the position Labour had previously adopted, especially in 1945. The only mandate Blair's government can claim in the fields of economic and social policy is the authority to run the status quo more efficiently and more sympathetically than its Conservative predecessor did. Indeed, Blair's government possesses a mandate for radical change in only one area: the devolution of constitutional powers to national assemblies. Although Blair has a majority that appears to give him the authority to pursue as radical a political agenda as he wishes, his limited electoral mandate severely proscribes his freedom of manœuvre. A further constraint, moreover, is his government's current conviction that any burst of social or economic radicalism that adds substantially to the tax burden on voters could lead to a serious loss of electoral support. Opinion polls since the mid-1980s have consistently suggested that voters are prepared to pay higher taxes in order to fund better public services.[4]

Labour's strategists recall, however, that these sentiments were clearly evident in 1992 but failed to translate into support for their party, even though it had explicitly promised to raise taxes in order to improve public service provision. These electoral considerations suggest that, in his first term at least, Blair is unlikely to match the sort of fundamental transformation achieved by Attlee in the years after 1945.

It should be stressed, however, that in British politics reforming governments do not necessarily have to possess the legitimating mandate of a prior manifesto commitment. Although the comparison is now almost a century old, there are perhaps some lessons about the art of the possible to be learned from the Liberal government elected in January 1906.[5] The 1906 election shares two obvious similarities with 1997: the outgoing government was hopelessly divided on a major policy issue,[6] and the new government was elected with an enormous majority.[7] In 1906, however, the Liberals were elected without having made any formal manifesto commitments whatsoever. The only official statement of Liberal intent was made by the then Opposition leader, Sir Henry Campbell-Bannerman, in a speech at the Albert Hall in December 1905, when he reasserted the party's determination to preserve free trade.[8]

Notwithstanding this lack of prior commitment, the 1906 Liberal government turned out to be one of the most radical in British history. If Labour after 1945 created the modern welfare state, it was able to do so only because of the foundations that had been laid by the Liberals before the First World War. Asquith's 1908 budget established a state-sponsored, noncontributory old age pension scheme. In 1909 Lloyd George's "people's budget" significantly raised income tax and introduced new taxes on land transactions.[9] The increased public revenues thus obtained were subsequently used to create labour exchanges for unemployed workers and to fund the unemployment benefits that eventually formed part of the 1911 National Insurance Act.[10] These were extremely radical developments for their time, all the more remarkable for their being introduced without any real electoral mandate.

Even Asquith's government, however, was unable to enact unmandated constitutional change. The House of Lords, which had always had a large Conservative majority, consistently sought to obstruct the Liberals' reforming programme. In response, Asquith fought two general elections—in January and December 1910—primarily on the platform of House of Lords reform.[11] The Liberals' victories in those two elections provided them with sufficient political momentum to secure the passage of the 1911 Parliament Act, which radically circumscribed the powers of the House of Lords, allowing "money bills" to become law without requiring House of Lords consent, and restricting its ability even to delay

House of Commons legislation by more than a year.[12] The 1906 Liberal government's inability to effect constitutional change without a mandate, then, did not in any serious way impair its efforts to introduce serious social and economic reform.

By contrast, the Blair government already possesses a clear mandate for both House of Lords reform and devolution. Like his Liberal counterparts in 1906, however, Blair has no mandate for profound changes in social and economic policy. Between 1906 and 1909 the Liberals simply used the opportunity that a large House of Commons majority presented to them. They judged reform to be both necessary and popular and acted accordingly. It is possible that Blair, after some contemplation, may decide to do something equally radical. Politicians, after all, are capable of changing voters' minds. There can be no question but that Blair's leadership transformed Labour's image in the eyes of many British voters. Given his success in this regard, the Labour leadership may come to the conclusion that it *can* persuade the voters of middle Britain that higher taxes are *not* inimical to their interests if they are combined with improved public services and falling crime and unemployment. In these circumstances, the possibilities for a reinvigoration of state activity aimed at reducing poverty and giving disadvantaged groups more opportunity are very considerable. If Blair is prepared to seize the political agenda, notwithstanding his lack of a formal mandate, his government could prove radical indeed.

A third comparison that can be drawn is between the Blair government and Harold Wilson's Labour government of 1964. Again there are obvious similarities. Both Blair and Wilson were elected after an extended period of Conservative rule (thirteen years in 1964, eighteen in 1997) that had latterly been punctuated by scandal. Both governments were notable for the inexperience of their frontbench teams. In Wilson's government, only the prime minister and his foreign secretary, Patrick Gordon Walker, had previously been in the cabinet.[13] Blair himself has no prior experience of office, and not a single member of his government has held a cabinet post. Only five—Margaret Beckett, Gavin Strang, Jack Cunningham, Michael Meacher, and Lord Richard (Ivor Richard)—have even been junior ministers.[14]

The most obvious difference between 1964 and 1997, however, relates to the size and character of the two governments' stated ambitions. Harold Wilson contrived to give the impression in 1964 that he possessed a panacea for Britain's long-running economic ills. Wilson was much taken with the achievements of indicative planning in France and with the apparent success of directive planning in the Soviet Union.[15] His panacea was a thoroughgoing National Plan for investment, scientific development, and technical innovation. A new ministry, the Department of Economic Affairs, was established under the control of the deputy prime minister, George Brown. The DEA was charged with implementing policies that would achieve an economic growth target of 25 percent over the 1964–70 period. In the event, the planning experiment foundered in the face of a series of economic crises, and the planning targets were abandoned. Tony Blair's government is not encumbered by the delusion that it has the answer to Britain's economic ills. To be sure, it stresses, as Wilson's government did, that education—investment in human capital—is crucial to any country's long-term economic success. Unlike Wilson, however, Blair has deliberately sought to suppress expectations about what educational reform can achieve, given that few additional public funds for education will be available in the medium term. Blair, moreover, promises no simple, or new, route to economic prosperity. His government broadly accepts the monetary and fiscal strategies adopted by the previous Conservative governments. It even embraces the privatisation of state-owned enterprises, a principle that Labour in the 1980s opposed vehemently. Unlike the Labour government of 1964, which sought, through planning, to extend the state's role in economic activity, New Labour actively embraces the reduced economic role of the state that has resulted from eighteen years of the Conservatives' market-oriented reforms. In this sense, the Blair government's economic agenda is fundamentally different from (and more limited than) that of its 1964 counterpart.

There is another important sense in which Tony Blair's government differs from its predecessors in 1945 and 1964: the condition of the domestic economy. Both Attlee and Wilson were afflicted by an overvalued currency and by serious balance-of-payments deficits that continually required remedial (and politically unpopular) action to curtail domestic demand. In both cases, moreover, devaluation eventually proved unavoidable in the face of these unremitting balance-of-payments problems. Attlee's government devalued in 1949. Wilson's, having failed to devalue early (which might have given its planning strategy a chance of success), devalued in 1967. In contrast, Blair and his chancellor of the exchequer, Gordon Brown, have inherited an economy in reasonably good condition. To be sure, Labour is confronted with a currency that is perhaps marginally overvalued; public borrowing is almost certainly too high and will have to be reduced. Nevertheless, inflation and interest rates are at their lowest sustainable levels for a generation; the unemployment rate is almost half that experienced by other major EU countries and falling; and productivity and international competitiveness have been growing strongly. In these circumstances, the 1997 Blair government appears far less vulnerable than its counterparts in 1945 and 1964 to punishment by disillusioned "economic" voters resentful of the government's inability to generate sufficient material prosperity. Indeed, in 1997 the prospects for a Labour government that will serve at least two full parliamentary terms look better than on any previous occasion when Labour has won a general election.

A fourth comparison that has been drawn is between Tony Blair and Bill Clinton in the United States.[16] The similarities between the two men are more than superficial. Both took over as leader of a left-of-centre party that had failed to win an important election since the mid-1970s. Both based their election strategies on a wide, nonideological appeal that moved their respective parties towards the political centre. Both jettisoned many of the redistributive, pro-labour, pro-welfare policy stances that their parties had previously espoused. Both drew increased support from groups that their parties had previously found hard to attract: from the business community (in Clinton's case, especially from small and medium-sized businesses), from blue-collar workers "won over" during the 1980s by a right-wing populist leader, and from middle-class voters disillusioned with the broken tax pledges of the previous administration.[17] Both were elected, moreover, with just over 43 percent of the popular vote. On top of all that, once in office, both found their policy options heavily constrained by their commitment to fiscal and monetary rectitude on the one hand and their promise not to resort to traditional leftist "tax and spend" policy solutions on the other. Any reforms would have to be implemented within extremely tight budgetary limits.

But if there are similarities between Clinton and Blair there are also two significant differences. First, the constitutional position of the president in a system based on checks and balances is always far more constrained than that of a British prime minister. Clinton after 1994 was confronted by a Republican Congress that could (and did) reject his budget, his legislation, and even his cabinet nominees. The compromises that followed inevitably undermined his specific policies and his administration's overall strategy. In Britain a government with even a modest majority may be regarded, in Quintin Hogg's famous phrase, as an "elective dictatorship"; a prime minister with a majority of 179 is virtually unassailable. Prime Minister Blair, in contrast to President Clinton, was from the outset free to pursue whatever legislative strategy he wanted. His only real constraint was the electoral feasibility of the course he decided to pursue—and the next national election was five years away.

A second difference between Clinton and Blair relates to temperament and character. Both men are obviously good communicators who find it easy to interact with people in all kinds of social situations. This similarity, however, masks a significant difference between the two. Blair is a strategic thinker who can be both ruthless and deliberately confrontational in pursuit of what he considers to be important. His first major act as party leader was to seek to rescind Clause 4 of Labour's constitution. This was a public declaration of war against what remained of the Labour left. Blair's success established his complete dominance of the party, a position he retained throughout his period as Opposition leader. In office, Blair was equally prepared to offend members of his own party in pursuit of some greater goal. Prior to his first EU summit, in Amsterdam in June 1997, he met privately with former prime minister Margaret Thatcher, widely hated in the Labour Party, to solicit her advice on possible bargaining strategies for the negotiations. Blair, in short, is prepared to define his goals clearly and to pursue them ruthlessly without worrying too much about whom he antagonises in the process. Clinton, in contrast, has been characterised as a leader who is unable even to define his administration's core goals, let alone to follow them through with conviction. As Colin Campbell observes,

> At several important turning points in the administration, observers have noted that the president has failed to devise fundamental strategies, revealed a tendency to store up ideas and let them gush out without any thematic coherence, and put his team through a seemingly endless succession of relaunches. Asked to comment on yet another downturn in his approval levels, Clinton himself acknowledged his lack of a core strategy: "I think in a way it may be my fault. I keep, I go [*sic*] from one thing to another."[18]

Tony Blair's period as prime minister, in essence, is likely to be characterised by far more decisive and determined leadership than anything experienced under Bill Clinton.

That said, Clinton's success in maintaining his 1992 electoral coalition in the 1996 presidential election was of enormous interest to Labour's campaign strategists. It suggested that a formerly left-of-centre party could continue to appeal to enough voters if it managed the economy effectively, avoided foreign policy disasters, and kept most of its promises on taxation. Here is an achievement that Blair's team certainly hopes to emulate. The basis for a new Labour electoral coalition was laid in 1997. Blair's task in the coming Parliament is to consolidate that coalition in order to make Labour the "natural party of government" in the twenty-first century.

What, then, do these four comparisons tell us? The performance of the Attlee government indicates what can be achieved in policy terms even in the face of severe economic difficulties, given propitious organisational circumstances (in this case, *dirigiste* wartime patterns of production and distribution) and the presence of a huge majority in the House of Commons. Asquith's reforms indicate what can be done in the sphere of social and economic policy even in the absence of an electoral mandate for reform. Harold Wilson's experience illustrates the medium-term electoral danger of a government failing to come to grips early enough with the key macroeconomic problem it faces—in this case, an overvalued currency. Finally, Clinton's success in 1996 shows that an electoral coalition built on a wider cross-class appeal than that typically associated with left-of-centre parties can be maintained across more than one election. If these are somewhat limited "lessons of history," so be it. This is perhaps the most that historical and international comparison can deliver. If we wish to achieve a deeper understanding of the implications of the 1997 election, we need to consider its specific features and to relate them to the specific political and economic conditions that preceded it.

What Does the Election Outcome Tell Us about the Character of Contemporary British Politics?

DOWNSIAN RATIONALITY THRIVES IN BRITAIN

In his seminal study of political rationality, *An Economic Theory of Democracy*, Anthony Downs made a number of claims about the behaviour of voters and political parties under conditions of rationality.[19] Central to his analysis of party activity was the idea that rational, office-seeking parties will adjust their policy positions to correspond to the policy preferences held by the majority (or by a winning minority) of voters. In a two-dimensional, left-to-right policy space, this kind of adjustment is likely to produce movement towards the centre where, given a normal distribution of voter preferences, the largest number of voters is concentrated. In Downs's view, rational voters in turn will support the party that advocates policy positions that correspond most closely to their own preferences. The principles underlying this analysis are well illustrated by Labour's self-transformation and its subsequent electoral success. In the 1983 general election, under its most radical leadership since the early 1920s, Labour suffered its worst defeat since 1931. It took a long time for the message thus delivered by the electorate to sink in. The party certainly moved back towards the centre ground under Neil Kinnock in the 1980s, particularly with its 1989 policy review. As late as April 1992,

however, Labour remained committed to the sort of "tax and spend"
—"socialist"—solutions to social and economic problems that continued
to alienate middle-class, middle-income voters. Labour's response after
its fourth successive general election defeat in 1992 was, quite simply, to
cease to be a socialist party. Labour's residual commitment to socialism
had been a major factor preventing an electoral breakthrough. In these
circumstances, socialism and any belief in challenging the interests of the
capitalist class had to be comprehensively abandoned, and the new (i.e.,
old) principles of sound money, private enterprise, and tightly controlled
state spending had to be warmly embraced. The transformation of socialist old Labour into social democratic New Labour under Tony Blair
was not lost on large swathes of the British electorate. The voters
showed by the way they cast their votes in May 1997 that they were indeed convinced that Labour had undergone a fundamental change. In
true Downsian fashion, Labour moved towards them. In equally Downsian fashion, they responded.

The "one-party system" that appeared to be emerging after the 1992
election collapsed under the weight of its own contradictions. After the
1992 general election, in the wake of four successive Conservative victories, a number of commentators wondered whether Britain might not be
moving in the direction of a one-party state.[20] They were not implying
that Britain was becoming totalitarian but that it might be becoming a
country in which the electorate continually votes the same party into office over a protracted period—as occurred in Sweden between 1930 and
1985 and in Japan between 1948 and 1993. The outcome in 1997 laid to
rest such fears (or hopes). Three characteristics of the incipient one-party
system contributed to the Conservatives' downfall—evidence, perhaps,
that in a mature democracy self-correcting mechanisms are likely to ensure the maintenance of party competition over time.

One feature of the emergent one-party system was that the Opposition's arguments were increasingly ignored by a government that seemed
to view itself as having a monopoly of truth and a unique ability to identify and defend British interests. It became common practice for Conservative party spokespeople, both in public and in private, to dismiss Labour as both unelectable and absurd. Conservative ministers increasingly
gave the impression that it was some years since they had last talked to a
living human being. More and more they enveloped harsh realities in
clouds of official statistics. Asked about the length of hospital waiting
lists, they recited meaningless statistics about the total numbers of people
being treated by the NHS. Asked about falling educational standards,
they cited statistics, which might or might not mean anything, about the
numbers of pupils passing A-levels each year. The government's numbers

were clearly meant to impress, but all they did was persuade more and more voters that Tory ministers were either incorrigibly evasive or never set foot outside their offices. There can be no doubt that this "arrogance of power" caused considerable resentment among voters in Scotland and Wales, who had voted in very small numbers for the Conservatives in 1987 and 1992 and felt increasingly marginalised by the policies emanating from Westminster. By the same token, voters throughout the country, who feared that the NHS and state schools were being systematically weakened by Conservative policies, believed their concerns were being ignored—no matter what messages they sent to the government via local elections, by-elections, and opinion polls. It was hardly a surprise in the end that the Tories lost all their seats in Scotland and Wales and the votes of almost everyone who put education and the NHS at the top of their list of personal concerns.

The second feature of the one-party system after 1992 was that, with Labour and the Liberal Democrats seemingly in permanent opposition, lobby groups increasingly used contacts with Conservative backbenchers as a means of influencing government decisions. There was little point in lobbying Opposition parties since their views were invariably discounted by the government, and there appeared to be little prospect of their achieving power. This pattern of lobbying led in turn to the development of a virtual "market" in backbench influence, with Conservative MPs, among other things, accepting cash for asking parliamentary questions. The activities of the lobbyist Ian Greer, and his association with MPs such as Tim Smith and Neil Hamilton, led to allegations of widespread sleaze in Conservative ranks and eventually to the establishment of the Nolan Committee. Neil Hamilton's determination to resist pressures on him to give up his Tatton seat, in the face of a considerable amount of published and unpublished evidence against him, ensured that "sleaze" remained high on the political agenda through the election campaign. As we saw in chapter 7, sleaze in the end may not have been crucial in bringing about the Conservatives' defeat. To the extent that it did play a role, however, the abuse of office and other forms of malpractice in the Tories' ranks had undoubtedly been fostered by the Conservatives' mounting conviction, developed over much of the previous decade, that they were electorally invulnerable, that they did not merely control the institutions of government but actually owned them.

The third feature was that, however long the Conservatives remained in power, regardless of the diminishing size of their Commons majority, the main opposition was the government's own backbenchers. Conservative ministers learned anew, if they had ever forgotten, that their *opponents* sat on the opposite side of the House of Commons; their *enemies* sat on their own. After 1992 this phenomenon increasingly produced what Anthony King called "over the shoulder" politics, with ministers apparently more concerned to debate policy points with their own backbenchers than with the Opposition.[21] The ironic twist to this development was that it was constant backbench Conservative sniping over Britain's relations with the EU that fatally weakened Conservative unity. And this damage to what had hitherto been one of the Conservatives' greatest electoral assets also figured significantly in the Conservatives' defeat. In short—and in an almost dialectical fashion—the nascent one-party system that had appeared to be emerging in 1992 was swept away under the weight of its own contradictions. The result was probably good for British politics. Heaven knows what might have happened if Labour, following its dramatic move to the centre and the Conservatives' massive display of inner turmoil, had failed to win.

It is worth noting, in addition, that Britain's newly revived competitive party system is just that: a competitive *party* system. Notwithstanding the increased prominence of single-issue groups such as the anti-abortion lobby, the animal rights movement, and the direct-action anti-roads activists, groups of this kind have not yet usurped the traditional political role of parties as the articulators and aggregators of the many and diverse groups in British society. The Labour Party in the early 1990s, like the Conservative Party in the late 1990s, may have had fewer members and less income than the environmental group Greenpeace.[22] But it was Labour that decisively won the 1997 general election while Greenpeace remained what it had always been: a peripherally influential lobby group. Left-to-right ideology may have declined as a focus for interparty politics since the end of the Cold War and may yet decline still further. But, as and when new lines of political cleavage emerge, it is likely that political parties will still remain the focus for groups intent on effecting major changes in British society and the British economy.

"Electoral tribalism" has continued to decline and "consumer voting" has continued to grow. One of the trends evident in British politics over the past thirty years has been the decline of class-based voting. In the 1960s, British voters tended to support the party that they thought best represented their class interests.[23] The Conservatives' stance as the party of property and enterprise resonated with the middle class and the rich, while Labour's broadly redistributive position attracted disproportionate support from working-class voters and the less-well-off. In 1964 roughly three-quarters of middle-class voters supported the Conservative Party, while two-thirds of the working-class voted Labour.[24] These proportions declined gradually during the 1970s and 1980s, leading to the conclusion that a process of long-term "class realignment" was taking place.[25] This

process was presumed to be the consequence of changes in patterns of employment and lifestyle that had eroded traditional class communities and identities. In addition, the Wilson and Callaghan governments had both fought difficult battles with the trade unions, in the process undercutting their own distinctive appeal to working-class voters.

The pattern of voting in the 1997 general election put paid to any lingering doubts that class-based voting played anything like the role in the late 1990s that it had in previous decades. Table 8.1 compares the class-vote relationship in 1964 and 1997. The results are summarised in the changes in the two indices shown in the lower half of the table.[26] As these indices show, the class-vote relationship—whether measured in "absolute" or "relative" terms—progressively weakened from the 1960s to the 1990s. Indeed, the marked reductions in both indices between 1992 and 1997 suggest that the process may even be accelerating as Britain approaches the millennium.

The counterpart to the decline of class-based voting has been a decline in partisan identification. It has long been known that the proportion of British voters who "strongly identify" with either of the two

TABLE 8.1

OCCUPATIONAL CLASS AND VOTE, 1964–97

| | 1964 | | 1997 | |
	Nonmanual (%)	Manual (%)	Nonmanual (%)	Manual (%)
Conservative	62(a)	28(c)	38	29
Labour	22(b)	64(d)	40	58
Liberal Democrat	18	8	18	12

	Absolute class voting index^a	Relative class voting index^b
1964	76	6.4
1966	78	6.4
1970	64	4.5
1974 (Feb)	64	5.7
1974 (Oct)	59	4.8
1979	52	3.7
1983	45	3.9
1987	44	3.5
1992	47	3.3
1997	29	1.9

a. (a − b) + (d − c)
b. (a / b) / (c / d)

main parties declined from roughly three-quarters of the electorate in the mid-1960s to just over half in the late 1980s.[27] Recent evidence suggests that this figure has since fallen below 40 percent.[28] The proportion of the electorate that "*very* strongly" identifies with the main parties has shown a similar pattern of decline. In 1964, 20 percent of voters were very strong Conservative identifiers and 22 percent very strongly identified with Labour. By 1987 the corresponding figures had fallen to 10 and 9 percent respectively, and they have remained at similar levels since.[29]

But if the traditional influences on British voting preferences have largely lost their potency in recent years, what, if anything, has replaced them? One obvious candidate, though it is notoriously difficult to measure, is the growth of alternative sources of identity—apart from class —that have no obvious attachment to the established political parties. The sort of anecdotal evidence favoured by exponents of postmodernism suggests that ethnicity, region, gender, sexual preference, and even lifestyle are increasingly important for some people as ways of defining themselves. How far this is really the case is difficult to assess. One thing seems certain, however: important changes *are* taking place in the way in which voters think about party politics. These changes have significant implications for explanations of voting that focus on social cleavages as the main basis of partisan support. In terms of the Michigan school's "funnel of causality," it would appear that variables "closer" to the vote may now have a greater impact on party preferences than the sort of deep-seated factors such as class and party identification that lie further back in the causal sequence.[30] On this account, voters are becoming more and more like discriminating consumers who evaluate competing products.[31] As a result, voting decisions are now more heavily influenced by voters' assessments of the main parties' relative managerial competence, by their issue preferences, and by their evaluations of the rival frontbench teams' leadership abilities.

Political commentators sometimes speak of particular elections as involving a major "realignment" of the electorate. A realigning election is one in which a party attracts disproportionate support from "new" groups of voters and then retains them, or most of them, in subsequent elections. Recent examples of realigning elections include Ronald Reagan's successful appeal, in 1980, to blue-collar workers and southern Democrats (who remained loyal to the Republicans in 1984 and 1988) and Margaret Thatcher's appeal to the manual working class (many of whom remained loyal to the Conservatives in 1983 and 1987). The idea of voters as consumers, however, suggests that "alignment" and "realignment" may be the wrong way of thinking about the sources of party support. It is entirely possible that in modern party politics there are no permanent or even semipermanent electoral coalitions. Freed from the constraints of their previous class and partisan identities, voters increasingly shift their allegiances towards whichever party is able to offer the most attractive policy or managerial package. If such a pattern is indeed emerging, it contains an important warning to New Labour. What was won so comprehensively in 1997 could be just as easily lost in 2001 or 2002 if Labour fails to please the huge numbers of floating voters who now exist.

There is certainly evidence to suggest that the British electorate has become more volatile in recent years. The so-called Pederson index of electoral volatility is constructed by summing the change in each party's percentage share of the vote between pairs of elections and then dividing by two.[32] Table 8.2 shows how Britain's volatility pattern compares with that of other European party systems over the postwar period. As the table shows, with the exception of a brief interlude in the 1970s (when support for the Liberals and Scottish Nationalists surged simultaneously), Britain's volatility score for much of the postwar period was well below the European average. Indeed, apart from the 1970s, British volatility remained both low and fairly constant from 1945 onwards: the 1990–94 score, for example, was not substantially different from those of the 1950s and 1960s.

TABLE 8.2

PEDERSON INDEX OF ELECTORAL VOLATILITY, AVERAGE
FOR 13 EUROPEAN PARTY SYSTEMS, 1948–94, AND
FOR BRITAIN, 1948–97 (IN PERCENTAGES)

	1948–59	1960–69	1970–79	1980–89	1990–94	1997
European average	7.8	7.3	8.2	8.5	13.8	
UK	4.4	5.2	8.3	3.4	5.1	13.0

SOURCE: Jan-Erik Lane, David McKay, and Kenneth Newton, *European Political Data Handbook,* 2d ed. (Oxford: Oxford University Press, 1997).

NOTES:
    The index is constructed by summing the change in each party's percentage share of the vote between elections and then dividing by 2.
    The reported figures for 1948–59, 1960–69, and so on, give the average volatility figures for election-on-election change during the specified period. The UK figure for 1980–89, for example, covers a period in which two elections occurred (in 1983 and 1987). The volatility score is calculated in this instance by adding the average change in each party's percentage share of the vote between 1979 and 1983 to the average change between 1983 and 1987, then dividing by 2. The figure for 1997 represents the average change that occurred between 1992 and 1997.

In 1997, however, a marked change occurred. British volatility more than doubled, to approach the European average (an average that had it-self increased since the 1980s), but without large changes in the vote shares of the Liberal Democrats and the SNP. Part of the explanation for this dramatic increase probably lies in the general impact on West Euro-pean party systems of the end of the Cold War. With the collapse of So-viet-style communism, the right lost its rallying external threat and the left its prime example of socialist "success." These developments, in turn, reduced the potency of ideological brand imaging for parties right across the political spectrum. Amid the multiplicity of new appeals that parties were consequently obliged to make, voter volatility increased throughout Europe (though it remains to be seen whether the increased volatility of the immediate post–Cold War period represents a long-term step-shift, the beginning of new upward trend, or a temporary adjust-ment to an external shock). As table 8.2 shows, however, the increase in volatility in Britain in 1997 was even greater than that experienced else-where in Europe. It seems likely that this extra volatility represents the additional effects of the longer-term processes of class and partisan de-alignment just described.

The credibility of the opinion polls has been restored. On the face of it, this topic might seem somewhat tangential to a subject of such impor-tance as "the character of British politics." Yet, in a curious way, the fail-ure of the opinion polls accurately to predict the outcome of the 1992 election had a significant effect on the course of party politics during the following five years. Given the Conservatives' strong showing in 1992, despite the pollsters' predictions of a hung Parliament or even a Labour victory, Conservative strategists were subsequently disinclined to believe the evidence of intense public disapproval revealed in poll after poll. It was firmly believed in Conservative circles, at least until the spring of 1997, that voters' opinion poll responses largely reflected the exigencies of "political correctness" (it was unfashionable to admit publicly to sup-porting the Tories) rather than any deep-seated resentment towards them, that all would come right in "the only poll that mattered," that on election day. The idea that the Conservatives' policies and their leader-ship's failure to demonstrate any managerial competence were seriously prejudicing the Conservatives' chances of reelection was not seriously en-tertained. As a result, instead of either shifting its policy ground or tak-ing radical action to restore its damaged leadership reputation, the party simply blundered on, offering more of the same to a wholly disillusioned electorate. That the 1997 outcome was broadly in line with opinion poll predictions came as a considerable relief both to the pollsters and to aca-demics who base their research on sample survey evidence. It also provided an important warning to any future government that might be tempted to disregard such evidence. For all their real and imagined failings, opinion polls remain the least unsatisfactory way of gauging the state of public opinion, on both specific policy issues and the parties' overall images. One important aspect of the democratic process is that governments endeavour to respond to the wishes of the electorate. The restoration of the pollsters' credibility in 1997 meant that any evidence they provided about voters' views and preferences would have more attention paid to it—by both government and Opposition—than had been the case, on the government side at least, after 1992.

Economic voting was transmuted during the 1992 Parliament but did not disappear. The elections of 1992 and 1997 appeared to demonstrate the irrelevance of claims that "it's the economy, stupid" that determines election outcomes. The Conservatives won the 1992 election in the teeth of the longest recession since the 1930s. They lost in 1997 when inflation, unemployment, and interest rates were at historically low levels and were predicted to remain so by most informed observers. QED: the economy does not matter. Such an account, however, fails to acknowledge the importance of voters' economic perceptions (as opposed to official economic statistics) as sources of their electoral preferences. In April 1992, notwithstanding objective economic conditions, most voters did not hold the Major government responsible for the length and depth of the recession, and many believed that their own economic circumstances were most likely to improve if the Conservatives continued in office. Within a matter of months, however, as we have seen in previous chapters, these perceptions had been reversed. The ERM crisis of September 1992 produced a sea change in voters' perceptions of the Conservatives as competent economic managers. In the wake of the crisis, the Conservatives lost an electoral resource that they subsequently proved unable to recover. The loss of their reputation for competence, combined with the rival and newly moderated attractions of Blair's New Labour, meant that the Conservatives failed to convert the increased economic optimism of 1996–97 into greater electoral support. Pre-election moods of economic optimism undoubtedly helped the Conservatives to achieve their election victories in 1983, 1987, and 1992. The connection then between optimism and Conservative support, however, was predicated on the Conservatives' superior reputation for economic management. With that reputation destroyed by the ERM crisis, the recovery in expectations of 1996–97 failed to translate into a Conservative political recovery.[33] Economic perceptions still mattered in 1997, but those perceptions focused on the managerial competencies of the major parties rather than on the "feel-good factor" that had so ably assisted the Conservatives over the previous decade.[34]

What Does the Result of the 1997 Election Imply for the Future of British Politics?

In order to anticipate the likely battleground of British politics over the next few years, we need first to consider the ways in which the major parties have so far interpreted their fortunes in May 1997: the lessons that political parties draw from their own performance and that of others profoundly affects the strategies they adopt.

LABOUR'S ANALYSIS OF ITS VICTORY

Tony Blair's core team of advisers were from the outset very clear about what had *not* led to their election victory. Labour had not won because it had promised any of the following: socialist, "tax and spend" solutions to the nation's social and economic ills; a serious redistribution of income or wealth towards the poor and away from the estimated 40 percent of the population that enjoyed secure and relatively well-paid employment;[35] the repeal of the Conservatives' 1980s anti-trade union legislation; or the reversal of the supply-side economic reforms that, under Thatcher and Major, had significantly increased British labour market flexibility and corporate profitability.

In the view of Labour's key strategists, the party *had* won for three main reasons, each of which had fairly obvious implications for Labour's behaviour in government if it wished to maximise its chances of reelection in 2001 or 2002.

First, Labour had been able to present itself as a modernised, moderate, social democratic party that had rid itself of the damaging ideological baggage of its socialist past. New Labour's positive image under Tony Blair had contained three key elements: (1) demonstrated political and managerial competence (witness Blair's successful assault on Clause 4: anyone who could run the Labour Party so effectively could certainly run the government); (2) fiscal and monetary rectitude (there would be no ballooning public deficit or inflationary surge under New Labour); and (3) an independent attitude towards "special interests" (the trade unions, in particular, could expect no favours from Blair). In order to maintain this image in the eyes of the electorate, Labour's course of action was clear. If it was not to frighten off the middle-class voters it had so assiduously courted since 1994, it must behave in office with the same prudence and moderation it had displayed in opposition. As Blair commented on election night, "We have been elected as New Labour. We will govern as New Labour."

The second main factor underpinning Labour's electoral success had been the extent to which its main policy stances resonated with the mood of the British public. In each of the policy areas that voters considered important, Labour had positioned itself carefully. It would pursue policies that (1) would not require any general increase in taxation, (2) were not radically different from the Conservatives', but (3) were sufficiently distinctive for voters to recognise that Labour would introduce *some* changes. On the NHS, Labour promised to end the internal market in health-care provision, thus reducing bureaucracy and freeing up resources for more patient care. On education, it undertook to reduce class sizes in primary schools (to be paid for by phasing out the "assisted places scheme" that allowed selected children to attend private schools at the taxpayer's expense) and to raise standards by more effective monitoring procedures. On unemployment, a "windfall" tax on the profits of the privatised utilities was to be earmarked for schemes to move 250,000 young and long-term unemployed back into permanent employment. On Europe, Labour promised a more conciliatory approach, its preparedness to compromise being symbolised by its determination that Britain should sign up to the employment protection provisions of the Social Chapter. On devolution—one of the few areas where Labour *was* radically different from the Conservatives—Labour was firmly committed to holding referendums on whether Scottish and Welsh assemblies should be created. Finally, to appease radicals concerned about Labour's shift to the right on the economy, the leadership promised a Freedom of Information Act, the incorporation of the European Convention on Human Rights into United Kingdom law, and the ending of hereditary peers' voting rights in the House of Lords. As with the preservation of Labour's moderate image, the implications of these various pledges for the New Labour government were straightforward. Labour must deliver what it had promised if voter disillusionment was to be avoided. The Queen's Speech, which formally opened the new Parliament in May 1997, showed Labour's clear intention to deliver on all these promises.

The third component in Labour's victory had been Tony Blair's leadership qualities, combined with the organisational and presentational skills of his advisory team. There was not much Labour strategists could do about Blair's qualities of leadership as prime minister other than to ensure that he was not overwhelmed by too much work. Their hope was that he would prove as astute as prime minister in his judgments about the British electorate's aspirations as he had been as Opposition leader. On the organisational and presentational side, however, decisive action could be taken. Within days of the election, it was clear that the top men in Labour's campaign team (and they were all men) had taken up positions of great authority in and around 10 Downing Street. Peter Mandelson, the mastermind of Labour's campaign, became minister without portfolio with a seat on every key cabinet committee. Jonathan Powell became Blair's chief of staff at Number 10. Alastair Campbell was appointed chief press officer. Both Powell and Campbell, though essentially political appointees, were given direct authority over civil servants. These three, along with David Miliband, chief of policy in the Number 10 Policy Unit, and Charles Whelan, special adviser to the chancellor, Gordon Brown, were to have daily meetings to discuss the formulation, presentation, and implementation of policy across every department.[36] All important decisions taken at departmental level were to be vetted by Blair and his team. Fearful that the civil service, contrary to its own vehement protestations, might be resistant to a change in direction after eighteen years of Conservative government, Blair's team also appointed a series of political "special advisers" in key ministries (some paid as civil servants, others as party workers). The purpose underlying these arrangements was simple. Labour's frontbench team—inevitably, after eighteen years in opposition—was extremely inexperienced. The party's efforts to implement even a modest reform programme must not be hampered or delayed either by ministerial incompetence or by inconsistencies in policy resulting from conflicting initiatives produced by different departments.

THE CONSERVATIVES' ANALYSIS OF THEIR DEFEAT

As we have already noted, the Conservatives had been in a virtual state of denial in the run-up to the election. In the final months, some Conservative MPs had been prepared to admit in private that an electoral defeat was likely. Nevertheless, few, if any, foresaw the scale of their actual rejection. It was small wonder in these circumstances that the Conservative Party should be so traumatised. The obvious danger was that the party might leap to false conclusions about the causes of the disaster and, as a result, arrive at equally mistaken remedies. It was a reflection of the Conservative Party's maturity—of its ability to respond to electoral realities—that in the contest that followed John Major's resignation as party leader the two leading candidates, Kenneth Clarke and William Hague, were respectively of the centre-left and centre-right. The election of the Eurosceptic but otherwise moderate Hague as leader was a clear indication that the party had, at least to some extent, come to terms with the scale of its defeat, if not necessarily its character.

Contrary to the claims of the party's hard right, the Conservatives had *not* lost the 1997 election because the party had been insufficiently Eurosceptic: Europe had simply not interested enough voters to make it a serious rallying issue,[37] and some of the biggest swings against the Conservatives had been in seats held by virulently Eurosceptic MPs.[38] The party had *not* lost because it had been insufficiently radical in pushing forward the privatising supply-side reforms of the 1980s: the Major government had privatised and deregulated with vigour, though without any obvious political reward. It had *not* lost because the chancellor had failed to deliver the sort of preelection miniboom that had worked to the Conservatives' electoral advantage in 1983, 1987, and 1992; on the contrary, voters' economic expectations rose progressively in the eighteen months prior to the election.[39] Finally, the Conservatives had *not* lost because they had failed to cut taxes. During 1996 Clarke, as chancellor, had cut taxes on a scale that, if the experiences of the 1980s and early 1990s had been anything to go by, should have produced clear electoral benefits. No such benefits were forthcoming.[40]

With the hard right's explanations for the defeat discredited, the views of the centre-right dominated. Their analysis focused on three factors. The first, and probably most important, was the Conservatives' loss of their reputation for economic competence. The restoration of this reputation must accordingly be a top priority, though all the party could do from a practical point of view was to continue to commit itself to a balanced budget and to reestablish its image as the party that instinctively understood, because of its long-standing links with business, how to maximise prosperity.

The second factor they recognised was the failure of political leadership—specifically John Major's leadership—that had permitted sleaze and disunity over Europe to flourish throughout the 1992 Parliament. The response here was self-evident. Any hint of sleaze must be dealt with swiftly and mercilessly. On the question of disunity, it was imperative that all party members back the position adopted by the newly elected leader. As William Hague announced soon after his election: "The days of disunity, factions and groups within groups and parties within parties must come to an end. . . . I am going to involve everyone and all parts of the party in my leadership."[41] The leadership could only hope that the frustrations of being in opposition would provide sufficient incentive for dissidents to suppress any disloyal sentiments they might otherwise be tempted to express.

A third factor contributing, in however small a way, to the Tories' defeat was their atrophied grassroots organisation. The number of party members had declined alarmingly between 1979 and 1997. Their average age in the mid 1990s was no less than 64.[42] Given the increasing volume of evidence in Britain that grassroots activism can make a real difference to a party's electoral performance,[43] the Conservatives clearly needed to develop strategies for widening their membership and, in particular, for making Tory activism more attractive to the young.

There was a fourth factor underlying the Conservatives' defeat that was perceived by only a minority, generally on the left, of the party. As Anthony King argues in the previous chapter, in their search for tax cuts and expenditure savings the Conservatives had simply gone too far in cutting back on public services. Notwithstanding the Conservatives' continuing ideological preference for private rather than public provision, the policy implications for the Conservatives were clear. If they wished to maximise their future electoral chances, they needed to move back towards the centre ground on the "taxes *versus* services" issue. They would have to acknowledge that a case could be made for modest tax increases to fund essential health and education services, particularly if those services made a significant contribution to the preservation of social stability and the minimisation of crime. At the time of writing, the Conservative leadership showed few signs of having learned this particular lesson. They must learn it, however, if they are to have a hope of defeating Labour next time.

THE LIBERAL DEMOCRATS' ANALYSIS
OF THEIR INCREASED SHARE OF COMMONS SEATS

Although the Liberal Democrats failed to increase their share of the popular vote in 1997, they more than doubled their representation in the House of Commons. Somewhat surprisingly, Liberal Democrat leaders have not been very forthcoming in providing explanations of their success. The points made here, therefore, reflect my own understanding of the kind of analysis that I suspect the Liberal Democrat leadership is making privately.

The first factor accounting for the Liberal Democrats' success was undoubtedly the quality of their leader, Paddy Ashdown. His tireless campaigning and faultless television appearances were crucial in galvanising support in the final weeks of the campaign. There is every reason to suppose that Ashdown will remain as leader—though if he does not, a popular and able successor, Charles Kennedy, is waiting in the wings. Second, the party was skillful in taking advantage of Labour's moves towards fiscal orthodoxy. Labour's commitment not to exceed the Conservatives' planned spending targets allowed the Liberal Democrats to position themselves as the party that *was* prepared to raise taxes in order to pay for improved public services. This pledge undoubtedly appealed to some former Labour supporters disenchanted with New Labour's timidity on public spending. If Labour's timidity persisted in office, the Liberal Democrats would undoubtedly seek to strengthen their arguments for increased public spending in order to garner yet further support from the disillusioned left. A third reason for the Liberal Democrats' success was the excellence of their strategy for targeting their campaigning efforts on winnable seats. This strategy had been built on the party's long record of success in local government elections (in June 1997 it held 4,756 local council seats, in comparison with only 4,449 held by the Tories). Strenuous efforts would undoubtedly be made in the coming years to persuade voters who were prepared to support the Liberal Democrats locally to support them nationally as well.

All three of these factors—sound leadership, a strong and reasoned commitment to increased public spending, and intelligent campaign targeting—can undoubtedly be deployed to the Liberal Democrats' electoral advantage in the future. The same cannot be said, however, of the fourth factor that underpinned their success: tactical voting against the incumbent Conservatives. Although the full extent of tactical voting will not be known until the publication of the 1997 British Election Study, it seems likely that tactical voting played at least as great a role in 1997 as it did in 1992.[44] The crucial feature of tactical voting in a three-party situation is that would-be tactical voters who wish to vote against one party have to be fairly indifferent as between the other two. With the Conservative government hugely unpopular in 1997, many tactical voters were genuinely indifferent about the choice between Labour and the Liberal Democrats: what mattered was that the Conservatives were ousted. It was relatively easy in these circumstances for anti-Conservative voters to support whichever of the two Opposition parties appeared to have the best chance of defeating the Tory in their constituency. The position in 2001 or 2002 is unlikely to be so straightforward. As discussed below, the Conservatives and the Liberal Democrats are likely to take very different stances on a number of important issues, such as devolution, Europe, and taxation. In these circumstances, it seems unlikely that many tactical voters will be sufficiently indifferent between them to permit much anti-government (i.e. anti-Labour) tactical voting to take place.

If they are unable to rely on tactical voting as a means of boosting their parliamentary representation, the Liberal Democrats will need to devise new strategies for maximising their electoral support. The party has a critical choice to make. On the one hand, it could distance itself as much as possible from Labour in order to avoid being contaminated by any future Labour unpopularity. On the other hand, the Liberal Democrats could seek to cooperate as fully as possible with Labour in the hope that such an approach would offer the best chance of persuading the government to adopt proportional representation; in that case, tactical voting would not be much of an issue one way or the other. It is unclear at the time of writing which broad approach, if either, the Liberal Democrats will adopt. They may simply wish to wait on events. The case for deciding sooner rather than later is that party "brand imaging"—like any other form of brand imaging—takes time to imprint itself on people's minds. If the Liberal Democrats delay too long, they risk leaving themselves with insufficient time to be able to present a clear alternative to the voters.

THE ELECTORAL BATTLEGROUND
OF THE 1997 PARLIAMENT

Where does this discussion leave us? Table 8.3 (pp. 232–37) outlines the topography of the likely electoral battleground over the next few years. Columns 2–4 of the table describe the positions that the parties are likely to adopt on the issues listed in column 1. Column 5 identifies the parties whose positions are likely to converge on each issue, column 6 those whose positions are likely to diverge. The rows of the table fall into three broad categories. The first refers to the strategies that the parties seem set to deploy in their efforts to define distinctive brand images that will prove attractive to voters in 2001 or 2002. The second summarises the positions the parties are likely to adopt on each major policy issue. The third identifies the groups of voters that each party is likely to target.

Many of the entries in table 8.3 are self-explanatory. Several points, however, require clarification. The most obvious relates to "ideology." An ideology is a more or less integrated set of beliefs that guides an individual's (or a group's) political actions and acts as a filter for interpreting new information. These beliefs can be arrayed along a series of dimensions. From a theoretical perspective, four major dimensions underlie most ideological positions:[45]

1. Rewards need to be distributed across society. What are the preferred *goals* of distribution? Does the individual or party favour a broadly even or an uneven distribution of rewards across society?

2. What are the preferred *mechanisms* of distribution? To what extent does the individual or party support state intervention to achieve the above goals? To what extent should goals be achieved by allowing market forces to operate freely?

3. What are the preferred instruments for ensuring social, economic, and political order? To what extent does the individual or party prefer an *authoritarian* as opposed to a *liberal* approach to problem solving?

4. To what extent should state-level decision making be subject to democratic control? To what degree does the individual or party favour *democratic* as opposed to *oligarchic* forms of governance?

The use of a single, left-to-right ideological model presupposes that these four dimensions can be superimposed on one another. Indeed, the

(Continued on p. 236)

TABLE

THE ELECTORAL BATTLEGROUND OF

Issue	Conservatives	Labour
		1. Party strategy
Ideology	Retains basic antagonism to the state; state should act as an enabler, not provider. Accepts inequality as essential for wealth creation, which benefits all. Favours market mechanisms and authoritarian solutions.	Retains belief that state should take a creative role in economic management. State should act as regulator and provider of social insurance. Favours equality in principle but redistributive policies limited to symbolic attacks on fat cats. Favours market mechanisms for private sector and authoritarian solutions.
Europe	Two positions: 1. Con1 (Leadership): agnostic on EMU; broadly pro-EU as it is currently constituted, as an association of sovereign nation-states. 2. Con2 (Backbenchers): anti EMU; wish to see EU powers reduced.	Agnostic on EMU; broadly pro-EU as it is currently constituted, as an association of sovereign nation-states.
Managerial efficiency	Promote image of managerial efficiency and competence in all main policy areas: NHS, education, unemployment, and taxation.	Maintain image of managerial efficiency through pursuit of effective policies.
Identity	National UK identity the priority. Downgrade regional identities because of disintegrative potential of devolution. Downgrade EU identity because of supranational threat to national sovereignty.	Encourage sense of multiple political identities at subnational, national, and supranational levels. Devolution necessary to preserve integrity of UK; without it, pressures for independence will grow.

8.3

BRITISH POLITICS IN THE 1997 PARLIAMENT

Liberal Democrats	*Convergence*	*Divergence*
for "brand imaging"		
Similar to Labour but favours liberal rather than authoritarian solutions to social and economic problems.	Con-Lab Lab-Lib	Con-Lib
Pro-EMU; pro-EU on principle. Would accept strengthening of powers of central EU institutions.	Con1-Lab	Con1-Lib Lab-Lib Con2-Lab Con2-Lib
As for Conservatives, though not a priority.	Con-Lab Lab-Lib Con-Lib	
Similar to Labour.	Lab-Lib	Con-Lab Con-Lib

Continued ...

TABLE 8.3

Issue	Conservatives	Labour
		2. Positions on the major issues
NHS	Firm commitment to maintaining. Favour mixture of public and private provision. No extra funding.	Firm commitment to maintaining but abolish "internal market." No extra funding.
Education	Emphasis on parental choice and selection; no extra funding.	Permit selection where it is the clear parental choice; no funds to subsidize private education. No extra funding.
Unemployment	Key to reduction is flexible labour market. Favours welfare-to-work schemes. Opposes "windfall tax" to fund unemployment reduction schemes.	Key to reduction is flexible labour market. Favours welfare-to-work scheme, funded by "windfall tax" on privatized utilties.
Taxation	Keep direct taxation low in order to maximize labour market incentives.	Keep direct taxation low in order to maximize labour market incentives and to retain support of ABC1s who are unprepared to pay higher direct taxes.
Law and order	Tough on crime and criminals.	Tough on crime but complementary rhetorical commitment to (1) being tough on the causes of crime and (2) individual rights, e.g., through incorporation of European Convention on Human Rights into UK law.
Defence	NATO as core of policy plus maintenance of independent nuclear deterrent.	NATO as core of policy plus maintenance of independent nuclear deterrent.

— Continued.

Liberal Democrats	Convergence	Divergence
identified as important by voters ▬▬▬		
Firm commitment to maintaining, but spend more on it, funded from increased taxation.	Con-Lab	Con-Lib Lab-Lib
Increase spending through higher taxation.	Con-Lab	Con-Lib Lab-Lib
Uncertain.	Con-Lab	
Increase direct and indirect taxation to fund essential welfare state spending.	Con-Lab	Con-Lib Lab-Lib
Similar to Labour.	Lab-Lib Partial Con-Lab	
NATO as core of policy but position on deterrent unclear.	Con-Lab	Con-Lib Lab-Lib

Continued . . .

TABLE 8.3

Conservatives	Labour
	3. Target
Centre-ground, cross-class appeal. Priority is to win back *ABC1s* and homeowners lost in 1997. Hope for Eurosceptic recruits from Labour and Liberal Democrats.	Centre-ground, cross-class appeal. Retain support of *ABC1s* and homeowners recruited in 1997.

(Continued from p. 231)
left-to-right model assumes that to know an individual's position on one dimension is, for the most part, to know his or her position on the others. If someone is broadly in favour of greater equality, then he or she is also likely to be "left-wing" on the remaining dimensions—to be in favour of relatively extensive state intervention in society and economy, liberal solutions to social and political problems, and as much democratic control of government decisions as possible. In contrast, someone who opposes greater equality—perhaps on the grounds that it weakens incentives—is also likely to be "right-wing"—to be in favour of free markets, authoritarian solutions, and limitations on democratic control.

Until the late 1980s, the positions of the three major parties could be analysed quite straightforwardly using the simple left–right continuum. Labour derived most of it support from those on the left, the Conservatives from those on the right, and the Liberal Democrats from those somewhere in between.[46] The repositioning of Labour under Tony Blair —in response to the Conservatives' continuing electoral success—has involved Labour's shifting its ground dramatically on three of the four underlying dimensions just described. Labour is still committed to the principle of equality, but it has explicitly denied itself the freedom to do anything much about it by promising not to use the most obvious device available: more progressive and higher income tax rates. In terms of the balance between state intervention and market forces, Labour has fully embraced the principle of privatisation. Although Labour objects to the operation of artificial market mechanisms in public service provision, it now explicitly recognises that most productive economic activity is best undertaken within the private sector. Finally, with regard to the liberal versus authoritarian balance, the new home secretary, Jack Straw, has

— *Continued.*

Liberal Democrats	*Convergence*	*Divergence*
voters		
Retain cross-class appeal (always a feature of LD support). Supplement by increased support from (1) radicals let down by lack of real change under Labour; (2) voters in the regions disillusioned with Westminster-driven politics.	Con-Lab	Con-Lib Lab-Lib

advocated strong measures against crime in language that would have been given a rapturous reception at any Conservative conference. Straw's sentiments dominated Labour's manifesto commitments on law and order:

> Youth crime and disorder have risen sharply, but few young offenders end up in court, and when they do half are let off with another warning.... Far too often young criminals offend again and again while waiting months for a court hearing.... We will replace widespread repeat cautions with a single final warning.... New parental responsibility orders will make parents face up to their responsibility for their children's misbehaviour.... We will implement an effective sentencing system to ensure ... stricter punishment for serious repeat offenders.... The attorney general's power to appeal unduly lenient sentences will be extended.... We will tackle the unacceptable level of anti-social behaviour and crime on our streets. Our "zero tolerance" approach will ensure that petty criminality among young offenders is seriously addressed.[47]

The only dimension on which Labour has not visibly moved onto Conservative ground concerns the question of democratic control. Here its promises to end the voting rights of hereditary peers and to devolve power to Scotland and Wales to continue to differentiate it from the Tories. Given Labour's clear shifts on the first three dimensions, however, it is easy to see why "ideology" offers Labour and the Conservatives far less scope for brand imaging in the late 1990s than it once did. In fact the main brand imaging beneficiaries of Labour's rightward shift are, for reasons already given, the Liberal Democrats.

Table 8.3 also specifies "Europe" as a possible area for future party differentiation. William Hague's victory in the Conservative leadership contest has important implications for the way in which the European issue develops. Although the leaderships of both major parties are broadly sympathetic to the principle of a European Union of sovereign nations, Hague is much more resistant than Blair to any further erosion by the EU of national sovereignty. Blair is essentially a pragmatist on the question of European Monetary Union (EMU): if the single European currency can be shown to work, he is in favour of Britain joining; if it cannot, then sterling must be preserved. Hague, however, has made it clear that he is opposed to EMU on principle. His hope, of course, is that, while positioning the Conservative Party close to the centre ground on most policy issues, he can simultaneously contrive a distinctively sceptical position on Europe and convince enough voters that Britain's position in Europe is a key electoral issue.

His difficulty in this connection is twofold. First, British voters seem stubbornly unprepared to regard Europe as a major issue compared with taxation, unemployment, the health service, and education. Second, even if Hague could convince voters of Europe's importance, he would still be confronted with a situation in which he would find it difficult to make electoral capital. On the one hand, if Labour did not join EMU by 2002, Blair would have demonstrated his resolve to reject membership absent the right conditions; he would also be able to argue that he had retained an option to join if it looked as though, at some future date, membership would be in Britain's interests. On the other hand, if Blair's government did join EMU before 2002, it would be far too early to tell whether such a move was bad for Britain or not. Any Conservative threat to withdraw if it won the next election would cause intense anxiety on the financial markets. The Conservatives would be inviting a barrage of criticism: withdrawal would generate dangerous uncertainty; it would inflict damaging transactions costs on exporters; sterling would risk being a weaker currency than the euro, and long-term British interest rates would have to rise accordingly, with negative consequences for mortgage holders and manufacturing investment. In these circumstances, a vote for the Conservatives would carry a high risk. The innate conservatism of the British electorate would probably dispose it to stick with Labour. In short, in advocating a strongly Eurosceptical position, the Conservatives would be on weak electoral ground whether or not Blair joined the single currency. Tory Euroscepticism would be no more likely to yield an electoral dividend in 2002 than it had in 1997.

"Identity" is a third feature of table 8.3 that requires explanation. The history and traditions of the Conservative Party are intimately bound up with the notion of national sovereignty. Since the nineteenth century, the party has seen itself as the champion of the United Kingdom's territorial integrity.[48] It is perhaps not surprising in these circumstances that the party's mainstream vehemently opposes Scottish and Welsh devolution. Tories regard any such devolving of power as the start of a process that can only result in the Union's breaking up. In the same way that European supranationalism represents an assault on national sovereignty from above, so subnational devolution represents an assault from below. The irony of the Conservative position, of course, is that, while the Conservatives see themselves as the defenders of the Union, their electoral support in Scotland and Wales has declined to such an extent that the party now has no Scottish or Welsh representation: while protesting their singular ability to appreciate and represent the true interests of the Union, the Conservatives in Parliament are, for the time being, an exclusively English party.

Notwithstanding this irony, the Conservatives strongly reject Labour's devolution proposals. (After eighteen years of Thatcherite and post-Thatcherite radicalism, the opportunity to pose as a genuinely conservative party must be rather comforting.) The Conservatives' intention is to go on stressing the importance of Britain's national identity and to emphasise the dangers inherent in devolving power simply as a concession to the strength of Celtic identities. A Scottish Parliament and a Welsh assembly will act as foci for ever more insistent Scottish (and perhaps Welsh) demands for greater autonomy. As the Conservative manifesto put it,

> the development of new assemblies in Scotland and Wales would create a new layer of government which would be hungry for power. It would risk rivalry and conflict between these … assemblies and … Westminster. And it would raise serious questions about whether the representation of Scottish and Welsh MPs at Westminster—and their role in matters affecting English affairs—could remain unchanged.[49]

In short, devolution threatens to open a constitutional Pandora's box that, in the long term, will create far more problems than it solves.

The Conservatives' antidevolutionist stance contrasts sharply with the position taken by Labour and the Liberal Democrats. In their view, devolution now is the only way of preventing an escalation in voter dissatisfaction in Scotland that, if left unchecked, might develop into mass support for full independence. To preserve the Union, therefore, it is necessary to meet the legitimate demands of Scottish (and perhaps Welsh) voters that decision making be brought closer to the point where policies are implemented. As we have seen, Labour and the Liberal Democrats are pragmatic about the implications of greater European integration. They reason that, if a particular supranational development is in British interests, decision makers should not allow sentiments about the preservation of national autonomy to prevent Britain from embracing it. By the same token, the two are equally pragmatic with regard to subnational pressures for greater autonomy. If the pressures are legitimate, and if the failure to respond to them would create even more serious difficulties, then emotive debates about the possible loss of so elusive a legal concept as "national sovereignty" are an irrelevance. Both parties hope, of course, that voters across the United Kingdom will take a similar view. The Conservatives, in seeking to make devolution a major issue during the coming Parliament, are confident that they will not. The available evidence suggests that the Tories may be seriously misreading the electorate's mood in this regard. A Gallup poll conducted in March 1997—at a time when the Conservatives were striving to make the Union a major election issue—indicated that 64 percent of British voters favoured the creation of a Scottish Parliament.[50] Most voters, quite simply, do not share the Conservatives' analysis of the devolution issue. And ultimately it is their verdict that will determine whether or not devolution proceeds.

A fourth feature of table 8.3 is its identification of the various issue positions the parties seem set to adopt. Identifying the stances of Labour and the Liberal Democrats in this context is relatively easy as there is no reason to suppose, given the continuity in their respective leaderships, that their policies during the 1997 Parliament will differ substantially from those advocated during the election campaign. For the Conservatives, however, the situation is trickier. William Hague is something of a blank sheet. Although he is a committed Eurosceptic and is believed by the Thatcherite right wing to be "one of us,"[51] he undoubtedly wishes to develop a broad policy strategy that will appeal both to all shades of party opinion and, crucially, to the voters. In these circumstances, Hague's thinking is likely to be driven primarily by Downsian calculation. Put simply, after what happened on 1 May 1997 the Conservatives will have to reestablish a strong position in the centre ground if they are to attract sufficient voters to mount a serious comeback. Hague—who is, if nothing else, an astute politician—is likely to see the force of this logic and to act accordingly by adopting centrist stances (Europe excepted) on most of the major issues. As table 8.3 indicates, this produces far more policy convergence between Labour and the Conservatives than between either of them and the Liberal Democrats.

Table 8.3 also identifies the target voters that each party will probably concentrate attention on over the next few years. Given the decline in class-based voting in Britain, it is evident that all three major parties will be making a cross-class appeal. The key battleground, however, will almost certainly be among nonmanual, ABC1 voters and homeowners. These were the groups that swung disproportionately to Labour in 1997 and that the Conservatives must win back if they are to stand any chance of reelection in the short or medium term. In addition, the Conservatives will seek to capitalise on the apparent Euroscepticism of large swathes of the British electorate.[52] As noted earlier, however, they will find it difficult to convince enough voters that the European issue matters sufficiently to them to affect the way they vote. The Liberal Democrats, for their part, will seek to boost their support by appealing to radicals who feel Labour's moves to the political centre prevent it from properly addressing the issues of inequality and poverty. The Liberal Democrats will also seek to extend the strategy they have successfully pursued in the southwest of England—of increasing their support among voters in the regions who feel their interests are not adequately protected by the Westminster-centred approaches of the two major parties.

One final point needs to be made about the contents of table 8.3. Apart from its brief reference to devolution, the table says nothing of constitutional reform. The long-term effects of Labour's planned constitutional changes on the character of British politics, however, could be considerable. As noted earlier, in addition to devolution, Labour intends to reform the House of Lords by terminating the voting rights of hereditary peers, to introduce a Freedom of Information Act, and to incorporate the European Convention on Human Rights into British law, in effect giving British citizens a "bill of rights" for the first time. Labour also intends to adopt a form of proportional representation for elections to the European Parliament and to encourage debate about the possible establishment of devolved assemblies in the English regions.[53] Although these developments will doubtless be accompanied by intense political jockeying among the major parties, they are unlikely to provide much of an electoral rallying point for any of them. Scottish devolution excepted, British voters are not particularly interested in constitutional issues.[54] And for the most part, they are extremely sanguine about Labour's plans for reform.[55] By the time of the next election, it will be far too early to tell if Labour's putative reforms have inflicted serious damage on anyone or anything. In these circumstances, British voters are unlikely to find their passions being roused by constitutional questions, no matter how important the issues involved may appear to disinterested observers. In short, although major changes in the British constitution are likely to occur in the coming years, they are unlikely to act as a focus for the immediate electoral battles ahead.

Summary and Conclusions

One of the key messages of the 1997 election was what it revealed about
the earlier contest in 1992. The Conservatives' victory in 1992 had put
them 8 percentage points ahead of Labour—an apparently decisive margin. Yet the size of Labour's victory in 1997—12 percent ahead of the
Conservatives—points to the fundamental fragility of the earlier result.
Such a decisive change in preferences during the lifetime of a single Parliament could not have occurred unless many voters in 1992 had only
just passed the critical threshold that led them to vote Conservative.
What happened in 1997 strongly suggests that in 1992 hundreds of
thousands of voters had only just managed to persuade themselves to
vote Tory. As Anthony King suggests in chapter 7, they had done so with
heavy hearts and holding their noses. Precisely for that reason, those
same voters found it remarkably easy to desert the Conservatives after
1992, when the Major government's incompetence and broken promises,
and the emergence of New Labour, gave them solid grounds for switching. Labour's huge success in 1997 partly reflected the fact that it had
only just failed in 1992. The key question for the future of British electoral politics is whether Tony Blair can convert the pro-Labour sentiments of 1997 into a permanent feature of the political landscape.

There are good reasons for supposing that Blair will find it hard to
make permanent the electoral coalition he assembled in 1997. The main
difficulty he confronts is the increased volatility of the electorate. Not
only does Blair have to contend with long-term trends in class and partisan realignment and the concomitant rise of "consumer voting." His
party's position is also vulnerable to the increased volatility that has
characterised all European electorates since the end of the Cold War.
The dramatic reversal suffered by the right-wing government in France in
June 1997—after its stunning victory only three years earlier—should
give even the most optimistic Labour strategist pause for concern.

Yet there is also reason to suppose that Labour could consolidate its
electoral position over the next few years. In the first place, Labour has
inherited an economy in better shape than anything enjoyed by a previous incoming Labour government. Second, Blair can also draw some inspiration from the fact that, by remaining on the centre ground where he
secured his initial victory, Bill Clinton in the United States was able to retain much of his 1992 Democratic electoral support four years later.
Third, Labour may well be assisted by the Conservatives' failure to come
to terms with the electorate's mood over Europe. With William Hague as
leader, the Tories are committed to an unequivocally rejectionist stance

on EMU. In adopting a hardline posture on this single issue, the party runs the considerable risk of negating the benefits it should derive from moving to the centre on other issues. By taking up an uncompromising stance on EMU the Conservatives could forfeit a golden opportunity to capitalise on the new high levels of electoral volatility. In so doing, they could present Labour with a better chance than it would otherwise have to convert its recent recruits into longer-term sympathisers.

The decline of class-based voting and of partisan attachments has undoubtedly made British politics more fluid in recent years. Yet many voters, although they are now more discriminating electoral consumers, do not want to invest a large amount of time and effort investigating all the pros and cons of voting for this or that party; they have better things to do and think about. In the past, most British voters used their class positions and the party identifications they inherited from their parents to simplify their voting decisions. It seems likely that the new electoral consumers also simplify their voting decisions—but that now they do so primarily on the basis of their perceptions of the overall competence of the main parties.[56]

As a result, images of competence or incompetence are crucial to the parties' electoral fortunes. During the 1980s and early 1990s, the British brand leader in the competence stakes was without doubt the Conservative Party; it accordingly retained the loyalty of some voters even though they were disposed, on other grounds, to withhold their support. In an era of electoral volatility, brand leadership can never be as powerful a mechanism for retaining the loyalty of voters as class and party identification were in the past. Nevertheless, brand leadership and the concomitant brand loyalty that accompanies it confer a head start in any electoral race. The opportunity for Labour is that it is now well positioned to assume a brand leader role in British politics. Tony Blair's firm leadership, together with an assured touch by Gordon Brown at the Treasury and by Robin Cook at the Foreign Office, could reinforce the widespread belief among voters—clearly evident at the time of the 1997 election—that Labour is now the party of managerial competence. If it does, the Conservatives are in trouble.

Acknowledgements

The author is indebted to Anthony King for his enormously helpful comments on an earlier draft of this chapter.

Notes

1. Kenneth Harris, *Attlee* (London: Weidenfeld and Nicolson, 1982), 320–21.
2. Page 6 of Labour's manifesto was headed "We will make education our number one priority." See Labour Party, *New Labour Because Britain Deserves Better* (London: Labour Party, 1997).
3. Ibid., 11–12; emphasis added.
4. For details over the 1979–97 period, see *Gallup Political and Economic Index,* May 1997.
5. The government was initially headed by Sir Henry Campbell–Bannerman, who died in April 1908 and was succeeded by Herbert Asquith. Asquith served as prime minister until 1916, when he was replaced by David Lloyd George. The expression "politics is the art of the possible" is attributed to Bismarck. For a brief comparison between 1906 and 1997 from a Conservative perspective, see John Charmley, "The Consolation of Tory History," *Sunday Telegraph,* 4 May 1997.
6. In 1906 the crucial division within the Conservative and Unionist movement was over free trade: whether it should be retained, as advocated by prime minister Arthur Balfour, or replaced by protectionism and imperial preference, as advocated by Joseph Chamberlain. It has been estimated that in the aftermath of the election there were 109 "Chamberlainites," 32 "Balfourians," and 11 "Unionist Free Fooders" on the Conservative side of the House of Commons. See R.C.K. Ensor, *England 1870–1914* (Oxford: Clarendon Press, 1949), 386. In 1997, of course, the issue dividing the Conservatives was Britain's relations with the European Union.
7. The Liberals had an overall majority of 84. They obtained 377 seats compared with 132 for the Conservatives, Liberal Unionists 25, Irish Nationalists 83, and Labour 53.
8. A.K. Russell, *Liberal Landslide: The General Election of 1906* (Newton Abbot: David and Charles, 1973), 101–3. Campbell–Bannerman also promised that the Liberals would end the system of indentured "Chinese labour" in the Transvaal, which they duly did. See Ensor, *England 1870–1914,* 390.
9. Ensor, *England 1870–1914,* 414.
10. Ibid., 516.
11. Ibid., 430.
12. Ibid., 424–25.
13. Wilson had been president of the Board of Trade under Attlee; Gordon Walker had briefly been commonwealth secretary in 1950.
14. Beckett is president of the Board of Trade; Cunningham is agriculture minister; Strang is minister for transport; Meacher is minister for the environment; and Richard is Lord Privy Seal.
15. Ben Pimlott, *Harold Wilson* (London: HarperCollins, 1992), 275–79.
16. See, for example, Matthew d'Ancona, "Are They by Any Chance Related?" *Sunday Telegraph,* 1 September 1996.
17. Theodore Lowi and Benjamin Ginsberg, *Democrats Return to Power: Politics and Policy in the Clinton Era* (New York: Norton, 1994), 5–10.

18. Colin Campbell, "Management in a Sandbox: Why the Clinton White House Failed to Cope with Gridlock," in *The Clinton Presidency: First Appraisals,* edited by Colin Campbell and Bert A. Rockman (Chatham, N.J.: Chatham House, 1996), 64.

19. Anthony Downs, *An Economic Theory of Democracy* (New York: Harper & Row, 1957).

20. Anthony King, "The Implications of One–Party Government," in *Britain at the Polls, 1992,* edited by Anthony King (Chatham, N.J.: Chatham House, 1992), 223–48.

21. Ibid, 228–31.

22. This somewhat disparaging comparison (for Labour) was drawn by Andrew Marr in his *Ruling Britannia: The Failure and Future of British Democracy* (London: Michael Joseph, 1995), 42.

23. David Butler and Donald E. Stokes, *Political Change in Britain: The Evolution of Political Choice,* 2d ed. (London: Macmillan, 1974).

24. See table 8.1.

25. Bo Särlvik and Ivor Crewe, *Decade of Dealignment* (Cambridge: Cambridge University Press, 1983).

26. The two separate indices are provided to reflect the different interpretations of the class-vote relationship advocated by Crewe, on the one hand, and by Heath et al., on the other. Crewe favours the use of the absolute index on grounds of its simplicity and clarity. It shows that class location has become much less important as a determinant of vote since the 1960s and reflects the fact that the decision calculus of the typical voter has changed. Heath et al., in contrast, argue that changes in the political landscape, such as the increasing role played by the Liberal (Democrat) and nationalist parties and the disastrous performance of Labour in 1983 and 1987, have obfuscated rather than eroded the class–vote relationship; they suggest that the use of a relative index takes more account of these changing circumstances. Heath et al.'s conclusion is that the "social psychology" of voting, as reflected in the class-vote relationship, has remained broadly constant over the last 35 years. Crewe's response is that the Heath et al.'s analysis confuses cause and effect. Crewe contends that the emergence of the Liberals in the 1970s and Labour's failure in the 1980s were results of class dealignment, not factors that need to be controlled for when a suitable measure of class voting is being devised. See Ivor Crewe, "On the Death and Resurrection of Class Voting: Some Comments on *How Britain Votes*," *Political Studies* 35 (1986): 620–38; Ivor Crewe, "Changing Votes and Unchanging Voters," *Electoral Studies* 11 (1992): 335–45; Anthony Heath et al., *How Britain Votes* (London: Pergamon, 1985); Anthony Heath et al., *Understanding Political Change* (London: Pergamon, 1991).

27. Ivor Crewe, Neil Day, and Anthony Fox, *The British Electorate, 1963–1987* (Cambridge: Cambridge University Press, 1991), 47.

28. Malcolm Brynin and David Sanders, "Party Identification, Political Preferences and Material Conditions: Evidence from the British Household Panel Survey, 1991–92," *Party Politics* 3 (1997): 53–77.

29. Ivor Crewe et al., *The British Electorate, 1963–1987; Gallup Political and*

Economic Index.

30. Angus Campbell et al., *The American Voter* (New York: Wiley, 1960).

31. This notion was first advanced in the British context in Hilde T. Himmelweit et al., *How Voters Decide: A Longitudinal Study of Political Attitudes and Voting Extending over Fifteen Years* (London: Academic Press, 1981).

32. Mogens N. Pederson, "The Dynamic of European Party Systems: Changing Patterns of Electoral Volatility," *European Journal of Political Research* 7 (1979):1–26.

33. David Sanders, "Economic Performance, Management Competence and the Outcome of the Next General Election," *Political Studies* 44 (1996): 203–31.

34. David Sanders, "Why the Conservatives Won—Again," in King, *Britain at the Polls 1992,* 171–222.

35. Hutton distinguishes those in families with secure, well-paid jobs (which he estimates to constitute around 40 percent of the population) from two other groups: those without employment or adequate social security support (30 percent) and those in insecure and typically lowly paid employment (30 percent). See Will Hutton, *The State We're In* (London: Vintage, 1996).

36. Ewen MacAskill, "Civil Service Makes Way for Blair Elite," Guardian, 3 June 1997.

37 Gallup asks a regular monthly question on the "most urgent problem facing the country." It is rare for more than 10 percent of respondents to specify "Britain's relations with Europe." Even in February 1997, the most recent month before the election for which data are available, the figure was only 15 percent. See *Gallup Political and Economic Index,* February 1997.

38. Three of the most prominent MPs thus affected were Sir Teddy Taylor, Teresa Gorman, and Michael Portillo.

39 See David Sanders, "Economic Performance, Management Competence and the Outcome of the Next General Election."

40. David Sanders, "Economic Perceptions and the Outcome of the Next General Election." Paper presented to the Political Studies Association specialist conference on Elections, Public Opinion and Parties, University of Sheffield, 13–15 September 1996.

41. Speech to Conservative MPs and peers at Conservative Central Office, Smith Square, 19 June 1997.

42. Seyd et al., *True Blues: The Politics of Conservative Party Membership* (Oxford: Clarendon Press, 1994).

43. Seyd et al., *True Blues;* David Denver and Gordon Hands, *Modern Constituency Electioneering: Local Campaigning in the 1992 General Election* (London: Frank Cass, 1997); Ron Johnston and Charles Pattie, "The Impact of Constituency Spending on the Result of the 1987 British General Election," *Party Politics* 1 (1995):261–73.

44. The constituency-level results of the 1997 election suggest that Labour and the Liberal Democrats together benefited from tactical voting by at least 30 seats. This figure represents the difference between the share of the seats

that the Conservatives would have been expected to get on the basis of uniform swings to Labour and the Liberal Democrats (which would have given the Conservatives around 195 seats in the House of Commons) and the actual outcome (which gave the Tories 165 seats).

45. These distinctions are based on those initially made in Jean Blondel, *An Introduction to Comparative Government* (London: Weidenfeld and Nicolson, 1968).

46. Butler and Stokes found that, although voters' first party preferences were strongly related to ideology, their second preferences were sometimes inconsistent with it; for example, some voters had Labour as their first preference, the Conservatives second, and the Liberals third. Butler and Stokes explained this pattern by reference to variations in voters' perceptions of the parties' general competence to govern. See Butler and Stokes, *Political Change in Britain,* 323–37.

47. *New Labour Because Britain Deserves Better,* 22–23.

48. Robert Blake, *The Decline of Power, 1915–1964* (London: Granada, 1985).

49. The Conservative Party, *You Can Only Be Sure with the Conservatives: The Conservative Manifesto, 1997* (London: Conservative Central Office, 1997), 50–51.

50. In March 1997, Gallup asked 1,000 respondents across Great Britain:
"There is talk at the moment of the Scottish people being given their own parliament to manage their own affairs. Do you think they should be given such a parliament or not?"
The responses were:
Yes, should, 64 percent
No, shouldn't, 31 percent
Don't know, 5 percent

51. This belief was both symbolised and reinforced by Hague's appointment of the arch-Thatcherite Cecil Parkinson as party chairman.

52. A Gallup poll conducted in December 1996 found that 45 percent of respondents either favoured complete withdrawal from the EU or a significant reduction in Brussels' powers. The question asked was:
"People hold different views about how they would like to see the European Union develop. Which of these alternatives comes closest to your own view?"
• A fully integrated Europe with all major decisions taken by a European government (this response was chosen by 10 percent of respondents).
• No European government but a more integrated Europe than now, with a single currency and no frontier controls (17 percent).
• The situation more or less as it is now (18 percent).
• A less integrated Europe than now, with the European Union amounting to little more than a free-trade area (22 percent).
• Complete withdrawal from the European Union (23 percent).
• Don't know (11 percent).
See *Gallup Political and Economic Index,* January 1997.

53. *New Labour Because Britain Deserves Better,* 32–35.

54. Each month since the late 1950s, Gallup has asked British voters an open-ended question about what they think the two most important problems facing the country are. Constitutional issues have hardly ever featured in voters' responses. During the 1992 Parliament, they did not figure at all.

55. In January 1997, Gallup put the following question to sample of 978 respondents:

"As you may have heard, Labour and the Liberal Democrats are currently discussing constitutional changes such as the Freedom of Information Act, a bill of rights, reform of the House of Lords and possible changes in the way in which MPs are elected; and the discussions between the two parties have been described as 'positively dangerous.' From what you know, do you regard the discussions between the two parties and what they might lead to as 'positively dangerous' or not?"

The responses were:

    Yes, 28 percent
    No, 63 percent
    Don't know, 8 percent

56. Downs refers to this sort of simplification as the "standing vote": "Some rational ... [actors] ... habitually vote for the same party in every election. In several preceding elections they have carefully informed themselves about all the competing parties and the issues of the moment; yet always came to the same decision about how to vote. Therefore they have resolved to repeat this decision automatically without becoming well informed, unless some catastrophe makes them realise that it no longer expresses their best interests. Like all habits, this one saves resources, since it keeps voters ... [from investing] ... in information that would not alter their behaviour. It is thus a rational habit." Anthony Downs, *An Economic Theory of Democracy*, 85.

APPENDIX

RESULTS OF BRITISH GENERAL ELECTIONS, 1945–97

	Percentage of popular vote						Seats in House of Commons					
	Turnout	Con.	Lab.	Lib.[a]	Nat.[b]	Other	Swing[c]	Con.	Lab.	Lib.	Nat.	Other	Government majority
1945	72.7	39.8	48.3	9.1	0.2	2.5	-12.2	213	393	12	0	22	146
1950	84.0	43.5	46.1	9.1	0.1	1.2	+3.0	299	315	9	0	2	5
1951	82.5	48.0	48.8	2.5	0.1	0.6	+0.9	321	295	6	0	3	17
1955	76.7	49.7	46.4	2.7	0.2	0.9	+2.1	345	277	6	0	2	60
1959	78.8	49.4	43.8	5.9	0.4	0.6	+1.2	365	258	6	0	1	100
1964	77.1	43.4	44.1	11.2	0.5	0.8	-3.2	304	317	9	0	0	4
1966	75.8	41.9	47.9	8.5	0.7	0.9	-2.7	253	363	12	0	2	95
1970	72.0	46.4	43.0	7.5	1.3	1.8	+4.7	330	288	6	1	5	30
Feb 1974	78.7	37.8	37.1	19.3	2.6	3.2	-1.4	297	301	14	9	14	-34[d]
Oct 1974	72.8	35.8	39.2	18.3	3.5	3.2	-2.1	277	319	13	14	12	3
1979	76.0	43.9	37.0	13.8	2.0	3.3	+5.2	339	269	11	4	12	43
1983	72.7	42.4	27.6	25.4	1.5	3.1	+4.0	397	209	23	4	17	144
1987	75.3	42.3	30.8	22.6	1.7	2.6	-1.7	376	229	22	6	17	102
1992	77.7	41.9	34.4	17.8	2.3	3.5	-2.0	336	271	20	7	17	21
1997	71.4	30.7	43.2	16.8	2.6	6.7	-10.0	165	419	46	10	18	179

a. Liberal Party 1945–79; Liberal/Social Democrat Alliance 1983–87; Liberal Democrat Party 1992–97.

b. Combined vote of Scottish National Party (SNP) and Welsh National Party (Plaid Cymru).

c. "Swing" compares the results of each election with the results of the previous election. It is calculated as the average of the winning major party's percentage point increase in its share of the vote and the losing major party's decrease in its percentage point share of the vote. In the table, a positive sign denotes a swing to the Conservatives, a negative sign a swing to Labour.

d. Following the February 1974 election, the Labour party was 34 seats short of having an overall majority. It formed a minority government until it obtained a majority in the October 1974 election.

Index

The Contributors

David Denver is reader in politics at Lancaster University and author of *Elections and Voting Behaviour in Britain* and *Modern Constituency Electioneering*.

Anthony King is professor of government at the University of Essex and author of *SDP: The Birth, Life and Death of the Social Democratic Party* and *Running Scared: Why America's Politicians Campaign Too Much and Govern Too Little*.

Iain McLean is professor of politics at Oxford University and a student of British politics, Scottish politics, and electoral systems.

Pippa Norris is associate director of the Joan Shorenstein Center on the Press, Politics, and Public Policy at Harvard University and author and editor of books on the media, British politics, and gender issues.

Philip Norton is professor of government at the University of Hull, director of Hull's Center for Legislative Studies, and author of books on Parliament, the Conservative Party, and the British constitution.

David Sanders is professor of government at the University of Essex, a constructor of econometric models of British electoral data, and author of *Losing an Empire, Finding a Role: British Foreign Policy since 1945*.

Patrick Seyd is professor of government at the University of Sheffield and coauthor of survey-based studies of Conservative and Labour Party members, *True Blues*, and *Labour's Grassroots*.